Praise for *Caged Eyes*

"Compelling, horrifying and yet moving, *Caged Eyes* gives us a true account of what happens to so many women in the US military, where they are outnumbered, disrespected, and all too often preyed upon. Lynn Hall's memoir focuses on one of the most elite institutions in the armed forces, the Air Force Academy, but her tale reflects that of as many as one in three military women throughout the United States. It is a story of misogyny, injustice, and brutality, yet thanks to Hall's integrity and resilience, it is also the story of how women have and will fight back."

—Helen Benedict, author of
The Lonely Soldier and *Sand Queen*

"Lynn Hall is a powerful writer who tells an epic story. She vividly captures what it means to be raped by a fellow cadet—someone she considered family. She brings to life, in a deeply personal way, the double betrayal. First she was assaulted by a friend, and then she was silenced by an institution she loved, one that proved sadly incapable of enacting true justice. Hall is an incredibly resilient human being and this is a spectacular book about finding one's voice and speaking out about injustice."

—Helen Thorpe, author of *Soldier Girls:
The Battles of Three Women at Home and at War*

"Brave, direct, and unflinching, Hall portrays, with compelling detail, the battle that women fight against sexual violence. Her story is heartbreaking but also honest and inspiring. Her powerful voice makes this an absolutely necessary book, addressing a critically important issue."

—Sue William Silverman, author of *Because I
Remember Terror, Father, I Remember You*

"*Caged Eyes* is an incredible story of a young woman's odyssey. As Lynn Hall seeks to fulfill her dream to fly, she confronts unspeakable familial and health roadblocks due to sexual abuse first at home and later while a student in the Air Force Academy. Hall's story confronts us with a modern-day pilgrim's progress through the sometimes torturous path of growing up female in a man's world. Due to her resilience and the love of friends, this is ultimately a tale of resurrection and hope for women struggling for sexual equality."

—Peggy Sanday, author of *Fraternity Gang Rape:*
Sex, Brotherhood, and Privilege on Campus

"As a vulnerable young woman, Lynn Hall encountered a succession of men, and then a prestigious institution, that not only abused her but tried to coerce her into silence. But they did not succeed. This beautiful and inspiring memoir represents the triumph of her voice—and by extension that of countless other victims and survivors—over the actions and inactions of perpetrators and bystanders who might have been able to inflict pain, but who could never hold a candle to her strength of character and moral integrity."

—Jackson Katz, PhD, cofounder of Mentors in Violence
Prevention, the first system-wide gender violence prevention
program in the US military, and author of *The Macho Paradox:*
Why Some Men Hurt Women and How All Men Can Help

CAGED EYES

Caged Eyes

An Air Force Cadet's Story
of Rape and Resilience

LYNN K. HALL

Beacon Press
BOSTON

Beacon Press
Boston, Massachusetts
www.beacon.org

Beacon Press books
are published under the auspices of
the Unitarian Universalist Association of Congregations.

20 19 18 17   8 7 6 5 4 3 2 1

This book is printed on acid-free paper that meets the uncoated paper
ANSI/NISO specifications for permanence as revised in 1992.

Text design and composition by Kim Arney

Many names and other identifying characteristics of people
mentioned in this work have been changed to protect their identities.
Some military terminology has been altered for readability.

Library of Congress Cataloging-in-Publication Data
Names: Hall, Lynn K., author.
Title: Caged eyes : an Air Force cadet's story of rape and resilience / Lynn K. Hall.
Other titles: Air Force cadet's story of rape and resilience
Description: Boston : Beacon Press, [2017]
Identifiers: LCCN 2016004391 (print) | LCCN 2016005069 (ebook) |
ISBN 978-0-8070-8933-0 (hardcover : alk. paper) | ISBN 978-0-8070-8934-7 (ebook)
Subjects: LCSH: Hall, Lynn K. | United States Air Force Academy—Biography. |
United States. Air Force—Women—Biography. | United States. Air
Force—Women—Crimes against. | Women military
cadets—Colorado—Biography. | Women military cadets—Crimes
against—Colorado. | Rape victims—United States—Biography. |
Rape—Colorado. | Sexual harassment in the military—Colorado. | United
States Air Force Academy—History—21st century. |
Meningitis—Patients—Biography.
Classification: LCC UG638.5.M1 H35 2016 (print) | LCC UG638.5.M1 (ebook) |
DDC 362.883092—dc23
LC record available at http://lccn.loc.gov/2016004391

For all survivors

CONTENTS

Author's Note   *xi*

Prologue   *xiii*

PART I: Space Odyssey

CHAPTER 1   3

CHAPTER 2   14

CHAPTER 3   23

CHAPTER 4   37

CHAPTER 5   52

CHAPTER 6   65

PART II: Broken

CHAPTER 7   81

CHAPTER 8   90

CHAPTER 9   98

CHAPTER 10   107

CHAPTER 11   113

PART III: Dark Ages

CHAPTER 12   125

CHAPTER 13   137

CHAPTER 14   149

CHAPTER 15   160

CHAPTER 16   168

PART IV: Warrior Spirit

    CHAPTER 17   181

    CHAPTER 18   190

    CHAPTER 19   202

PART V: Higher

    CHAPTER 20   215

    CHAPTER 21   223

    CHAPTER 22   231

Epilogue   240

*Select Recommendations for Resources
on Sexual Assault in the Military*   248

Acknowledgments   251

In order to allow readers unfamiliar with the military to read this memoir more easily, I have simplified some nonessential terminology and eliminated several acronyms. For instance, instead of referring to the officer who oversees a squadron as "air officer commanding" or "AOC," I have instead chosen to simply call him a commander. Another example is the simplification to call all working units of cadets "squadrons," though sometimes they are called "flights." The cumulative effect of these changes is a narrative that is slightly less reflective of cadet vernacular, but also one that is more accessible to the uninitiated.

As is true with any memoir, in order to tell a story spanning four years in a very limited number of pages, I have had to omit a great number of events. In making these choices and in recreating some dialogue, I have done my best to honor the factual and emotional truth of my experiences.

PROLOGUE
_____

*What could be more supportive of our fighting women and men than
exposing the forces that permit their mistreatment?*

—Dr. Mic Hunter, *Honor Betrayed:
Sexual Abuse in America's Military*

Mitchell Hall felt colossal to me, inspiring yet humbling, like much
of the Air Force Academy. It was not just a cafeteria or a chow hall,
but rather a dining facility fit for officer candidates of the world's
most dominant military. Like all of the buildings at the Academy,
Mitchell Hall's outer aluminum frame resembled an airplane's me-
tallic shell. Inside, two-story panoramic windows opened to the
snow-covered pine forests blanketing the Rocky Mountain foothills. Air Force–blue tablecloths adorned four hundred rectangular
tables arranged in a perfect grid.

We flooded through the doors of Mitchell Hall at the end of
the noon meal formation, when awed tourists watched us cadets
march to lunch. From the staff tower, a man's voice commanded,
"Wing, take seats," and all four thousand of us sat in unison. The
Air Force Academy bragged that we were the cream of the crop:
America's most driven, disciplined, bright, and honorable young
adults, destined for charmed careers, first as Air Force commanders,
fighter pilots, or intelligence officers, and later as aerospace engi-
neers, politicians, or generals. A few of us might even reach our
most coveted profession—astronaut. To prepare us for these future
lives, the Academy packed our schedule with academics, athletics,
and military training, which demanded no less than eighteen hours

of effort each day of our four-year tenure. We were allowed twenty minutes for the noon meal.

It was a Monday in late February 2003, and as an underclassman, I sat at the table's foot. Waitstaff rushed down the aisles, delivering hot dishes. Today's meal: Chicken à la King over pasta. I passed the platter to the head of the table so that the seniors could serve themselves first. I sat perfectly still on the front six inches of my chair, back straight, my hands flat in my lap. I focused my eyes on the black eagle at the top of my white, round plate; otherwise, upperclassmen would demand that I "cage my eyes." I had not yet earned the privilege of allowing my eyes to stray.

There was an excess of energy in the dining hall. Cadets talked loudly, but this buzz wasn't excitement; it was anger. "Liars," I heard repeatedly. "Bitches." Over the weekend, seven women had appeared on ABC's *20/20* telling their stories of having been raped, ostracized, and punished here at the Air Force Academy. Watching from their computers in their dorm rooms, the cadets in my hallway had erupted in immediate fury, slamming doors and yelling: "Those fucking liars!" "How dare they attack *our* Academy?" I had watched the seven women on a grainy feed on my laptop in horror. I was angry, too, although I knew each word they spoke was true. One of the women had been raped by the same man who had raped me. My anger at them came from fear. I had trusted those women on TV. Together we had formed a rape survivors' support group and had shared in painstaking detail what had happened to us. We connected our stories and their similarities and had realized—together—the pervasiveness of our traumas. Nearly simultaneously a handful of the women in our ever-expanding underground network of survivors were discharged from the Air Force. A few left by choice. Some were kicked out after they reported their rape, for offenses such as having sex in the dorms, even though they insisted it wasn't consensual. Then their collective outrage drove them to seek out the media.

But what did they think would happen to us women at the Academy when they went public? While I admired their courage, I felt betrayed—furious that they could be so inconsiderate to those of us left behind.

Too nauseated to eat, I held my body taut while the upperclassmen at the head of my table debated "what the fuck was wrong" with these women. All nine cadets I sat with happened to be men, supposedly my Air Force family. "Collaborate to graduate," cadets often chanted. Graduating from the Academy required tremendous teamwork. Academy administrators designed our training—the academic projects, athletics, inspections, field programs—to foster collaboration and solidarity. As an underclassman, even something as simple as walking to the bathroom was illegal unless a "wingman" came with me. Without a wingman, I'd have to pee in my dorm room sink. Cadet rules were so strictly enforced that the distinction between violating them and breaking actual Academy laws was blurred.

One of the seniors directed his attention to my end of the table and asked, "What do you think of those fucking whores who're tarnishing our Academy?" Fucking whores. I had felt that way about myself. That I was a whore. That's exactly how my perpetrators had made me feel. Perpetrators, plural. I had been raped by an upperclassman, but I had also been molested back home in the months before becoming a cadet. What kind of weak, helpless girl could be victimized by multiple men? I was smart—my high school's valedictorian. And I was tough—strong enough to finish the Academy's rigorous basic training. And yet I had been a victim, too, repeatedly. It wasn't until I had confessed to my survivors group that I had been assaulted more than once, and another woman had answered, "Me, too," that I questioned the self-recrimination that for months had kept me silent. Maybe I wasn't a fucking whore. Maybe there wasn't anything inherently wrong with me that had brought on the sexual assaults.

After the senior's question, I felt the eyes of the nine men around me monitoring my every twitch. The cadet across the table thrust his closed fist into the air between us, a standard way for a freshman to raise a hand. "Sir, may I make a statement?" The senior nodded to him. The freshman dropped his hand and looked directly at me, a stern, unblinking stare that confirmed my roommate had leaked my secret and that he knew of my own rape allegation. He said, "Sir, I think a woman who gets herself raped isn't strong enough to defend herself, let alone the country, and shouldn't be in the military."

PART I

Space Odyssey

CHAPTER I
_____

You can have anything you want if you want it badly enough.
You can be anything you want to be, do anything you set out to
accomplish, if you hold to that desire with singleness of purpose.
—Attributed to Abraham Lincoln

The Air Force Academy is perched high above the city of Colorado
Springs, its buildings clustered together at the base of the Rocky
Mountain foothills. On the June day I became a cadet, I looked out
the car window as the aluminum structures grew closer. The Cadet
Chapel's seventeen silver spires jutted high above the dorms, reflecting the morning sun. I twisted my head out the open passenger
window. The cloudless Colorado sky directly above seemed so blue
it was more of a dark purple, a reminder that I was already nearly a
mile and a half above sea level and climbing.

Climbing. Fulfilling my dreams. I was eighteen, and I couldn't
imagine I would ever want anything more than to be a cadet, a pilot,
an astronaut. Beyond fulfillment of my career ambitions, entering
the Academy meant I wouldn't have to cope with my devoted but
erratic mother or have occasion to miss my absent father. At the
Academy it wouldn't matter that my flight instructor in a paramili-
tary organization, a former Air Force officer whom I'd thought of as
a father figure, made me have sex with him. It wouldn't matter that
the first time he touched me, my mother saw and didn't stop him. It
wouldn't matter that I hadn't been tough enough to stop him, either.
Beyond the Academy gates, the people in my childhood who had
hurt me couldn't access me. In signing the paperwork pledging my
allegiance to my country, I would punch a life-sized reset button.

Donning an Air Force uniform and fulfilling Academy training would transform me into a stronger, braver person than I had been at home. I knew that to be true.

A guard wearing fatigues and a blue beret waved our car through security gates and then saluted Jeff, my driver, who saluted back. Jeff was the only other graduate from my rural Missouri high school to go to the Air Force Academy. Tall and broad shouldered, he had played football as a cadet and was now one of the Academy's many football coaches. Jeff and his wife had picked me up from the airport the night before and provided my last civilian dinner and last civilian bed.

We drove by the football stadium where white paint on the gray bleachers formed the words "Air Force." Creed's song "Higher" came on the radio. I smiled at the irony of listening to it as my last song before I lost the privilege of music. "I love this song," Jeff said, and cranked the volume louder. Most Christians, like Jeff, thought the song referred to heaven. But for me, it signified the Air Force Academy. Back at home, I had written a line inspired from the song on a notecard and hung it above my desk: I'm strong enough to make these dreams mine. My creed.

I was fourteen the day I decided I wanted to become an astronaut. Over breakfast during a Florida vacation with my mom and stepdad, I saw a newspaper article about a space shuttle launch scheduled for that afternoon. I begged them to go. As a math and science nerd, space dominated my life. I had named my pet lovebird after my favorite planet, Neptune. Posters of the moon and Mars hung on my bedroom walls next to David Duchovny from the *X-Files*. My favorite movie was *The Right Stuff*, Arthur C. Clarke's *2001: A Space Odyssey*, my favorite book. I had pleaded for a telescope for Christmas, and spent Friday nights with the astronomy club. I was always looking up at the contrails that crisscrossed the Missouri sky.

In the heart of Cape Canaveral, while my mom, stepdad, and I searched for a patch of grass to sit on among hundreds of people, my eyes gravitated toward the space shuttle launch site miles away. I imagined the astronauts, inside their clunky helmets and bulky orange space suits with American flags sewn to the shoulders. When the loudspeakers announced "T minus ninety seconds and counting," the crowd erupted in cheers. "Main engines start, three, two, one . . ." A puff of flames ignited under the shuttle. The explosion cackled like a massive firework. I could have sworn that I felt the heat on my cheeks. The shuttle shimmied into the air, the trail of clouds following it. "Lift off of space shuttle *Columbia!*"

The shuttle's progress was slower than I had imagined, making me afraid it would fall back to Earth, yet its speed remained fixed. It amazed me that scientists could calculate exactly how much fuel the shuttle needed to accelerate at the perfect velocity so that it could escape Earth's gravity just enough to send it into orbit and not get lost forever. Those figures were dependable, consistent, accounting for each and every variable like weight and wind. Unlike the state of my home life, mathematics always remained predictable. I tracked *Columbia* into the sky until the only trace of it was a trajectory of the smoke.

Watching the explosion propel the shuttle into space shaped my dreams. I would become a pilot first, I decided. The higher the plane flew, the better. Then I would become an astronaut, a dream no doubt shared by many kids. Those of us who didn't outgrow it turned to the Air Force and Naval Academies. Both institutions combined four-year undergraduate degrees with training to become commissioned military officers. The Air Force Academy's thriving Russian foreign-language program was proof of how many cadets secretly dreamed of going into space. The United States worked closely with Russian cosmonauts, so learning their language was just one small advantage cadets could give themselves. Historically a vast majority of Academy graduates went on to become pilots, but only few became astronauts. Thirty-eight Academy graduates, including one woman, had managed it. So why couldn't I? Unlike some of the girls in my high school who dreamed of weddings and babies, I looked to the stars. I believed my destiny was graduating high school and beginning my career in 2001, the beginning of my space odyssey.

Mom always made our education a priority, telling my oldest sister, Amy, that she'd be a lawyer, and my middle sister, Megan, she'd be a doctor. None of us would have kids, she said. She thought we would be too busy with careers for pedestrian desires such as marriage and children, and so we discussed colleges and careers, not makeup or boys.

Only 10 percent of applicants gained admission into the Academy, so I obsessed over my perfect GPA. I ran for and became president of our student council, played sports, earned my private pilot's license, and filled my summers with a NASA-sponsored internship and other programs.

I was lucky my mom and stepdad, who were middle class but hardly wealthy, were willing to spend so much money on all these activities. Service academies aren't an option for kids without those funds who have to enlist. Cadets usually came from some kind of privilege.

I was so hyperfocused on my future, I rarely saw my friends outside of school. I didn't date. My career mattered more than my social life.

As proud as I was to have earned a US Congressional nomination and an appointment to become a cadet, that victory was a small hurdle compared to the training ahead. Having read every published account of cadet life, I knew the ins and outs of all the challenges in front of me.

The Academy designed the six weeks of Basic Cadet Training to be the hardest of a cadet's life. Through physical, mental, and emotional stress, I would be stripped of my individual identity. I was willing, even eager, to do this because I trusted the Academy would build me into something greater: an officer candidate with self-confidence based on the attributes my training would instill in me—discipline, integrity, attention to detail, the ability to multi-task under extreme pressure, unwavering loyalty to classmates, and mental and physical strength. At the end of the summer and Basic Cadet Training, I would begin academic classes similar to those at a civilian university, though it wouldn't be until March, nearly at the end of the first year, when I would endure one last test: Recognition, a grueling three-day event. If I survived, a ceremony would mark me as a fully worthy cadet. Then it would still be three years until I graduated with a bachelor's degree and a commission as an Air Force officer.

Driving to the Academy for in-processing, I was about to forfeit my pink V-neck T-shirt and khakis for a camouflage battle dress uniform. My backpack contained the only personal possessions allowed: underwear, sports bras, tampons, and a Bible. I had packed the Bible not because it gave me inspiration, but because I was using it to smuggle in pictures. I had taped photos inside the covers from the last few weeks of civilian life: one of my mom, middle sister Megan, and me the night I graduated valedictorian from my high school; one of me sitting in a Cessna aircraft on the day I first soloed an airplane; and a bunch of pictures of my teenage friends. The photos, my own strength, and the classmates whom I hadn't yet met would be the only things that I would have to rely on to get through Basic Cadet Training. I repeated my mantra: I'm strong enough to make these dreams mine.

After Jeff dropped me off, I boarded a bus to take me to the cadet area. A chaplain wearing combat fatigues sewn with a small, fabric cross over his left pocket offered us a prayer. He bowed his head. "God please watch over these young people. Give them the strength to help them endure the next six weeks." Out of respect, I bowed my head, too. But I didn't think God would have anything to do with me finding the will to complete training. Only I could get myself through.

Everyone remained quiet. We all knew what was about to happen.

"Welcome to *my* Academy!" yelled an upper-class cadet at the front. My stomach twisted at the fierceness of his tone, even though I had been expecting it. I was used to yelling; on my mom's angry days, she often called me a brat and a bitch. I had learned to cordon off my reactions, to register less fully the anger and fear. But when my body did respond, I felt it in my stomach.

"You are not cadets yet!" The cadet who yelled strolled the aisle, passing where I sat near the window. On instinct my hands fell into my lap. The cadet's blue-brimmed hat cast darkness across his face. His square jawline and broad shoulders seemed unnatural, like he came from a *Terminator* movie. "You are nothing. You are worthless. Stop lounging in my seats. Sit up straight, front six inches of your chair." I straightened up immediately, as did all the other basics.

"Cage your eyes!" the other upper-class cadet yelled. "That means stop gazing. Your eyes should be straight forward. Don't look at me. Don't look at each other." My world became the short spiky brown hair in front of me. My left arm rested lightly against the sweaty arm of the guy next to me. He trembled. I reminded myself I would be yelled at frequently, but unlike when my mother yelled, it wasn't personal.

"If you think you are going to graduate, you are wrong! Most of you will not. I don't care how wonderful you thought you were in high school. That is over. You can forget about how special your mommy thinks you are. She is no longer here with you. Daddy isn't here with you. Your sweet girlfriend has already forgotten about you. She is already cheating on you. I will be surprised if any of you pathetic beings can hack it at *my* Academy." The bus had arrived at the cadet area. Hands in crisp, white gloves banged on the outside of all the windows. "If you choose to take the path of mediocrity, do not insult the long, blue line of Air Force Academy graduates by exiting this bus." The cadet yelled over the pounding on the windows. "However, if you choose to serve your nation and accept this country's greatest challenge, then prepare yourself for the hardest four years of your life."

Another cadet yelled, "Get the hell off my bus!" The hands banged harder, rattling the windows. "Get off my bus!" he shouted again and again. Those in front scrambled to their feet.

When it was my turn I stumbled down the stairs. Ten upper-class cadets surrounded me, all screaming. "Faster, faster! Stop gazing! Do you think this is summer camp? Cage your eyes!" I hurried to position myself on a pair of painted footprints on the ground among a large, solid white box, our guide for us to assemble into a perfect formation. Every generation of cadets before us had started their careers on these same footprints.

"Basic cadets, the position of attention," yelled the upperclassman in front of the formation. "Eyes caged straight ahead. Shoulders, up, back, and down. Arms pinned to sides. Hands cupped. Thumbs along your pants seam. Feet at a forty-five-degree angle. No extraneous movements." My body stiffened. "The seven phrases you are allowed to speak for the next year are as follows: 'yes, sir'; 'no, sir'; 'no excuse, sir'; 'sir, may I make a statement?'; 'sir, may I ask a question?'; 'sir, I do not understand'; 'sir, I do not know.' When appropriate, replace 'sir' with 'ma'am.' Do you understand me, basics?"

"Yes, sir," I yelled along with the others.

When the upperclassmen finished correcting us, we filed behind one another in a long line, through a wide, two-story box tunnel that led up a ramp, toward the cadet area. Silver block letters emblazoned the rock wall above the tunnel with the words "Bring Me Men," the opening line of a nineteenth-century poem, "The Coming American," by Sam Walter Foss.

The top of the ramp opened to the Terrazzo, a large quad that housed all the cadet buildings. Wide walkways of stone tile flanked the center, grassy area. I uncaged my eyes to look around. In the center of the quad old fighter planes were on display, one at each corner. Greasy whiffs from the dining hall mixed with the clean smell of pine trees. Walking across the Terrazzo for the first time was surreal. I had been dreaming about that moment for years. I was a cadet.

Orange arrows taped to the ground led us inside the academic building and through a maze of in-processing stations. At the medical station, I stood in front of piles of records and a flight surgeon who asked for my blood type. I responded, "B positive, sir."

He looked up at me and grinned. "Remember, you be positive, too." He laughed at his own joke. He told me to see the orthopedic surgeon to confirm I'd healed from the latest knee surgery, and to go to the optometrist to order glasses that fit my prescription. One of the reasons I had chosen the Air Force Academy over the Naval Academy was because the vision requirements to be an Air Force pilot were slightly less strict than the Navy's, which required a perfect twenty-twenty. I took my file and turned to follow the arrows down the hallway. I made a right and then didn't see the next arrow.

"Cage your eyes, basic," one of the upperclassmen yelled as I searched. Instinctively I looked at him rather than focusing my eyes straight ahead. I wasn't sure how I was supposed to look for the arrow while also keeping my eyes caged. "What's your name, SMACK?" I remembered that SMACK, a nickname for first-year cadets, stood for soldier minus ability, courage, and knowledge.

"Lynn Miller," I said.

"What am I, your kindergarten teacher?" He crossed the four feet between us, his face now inches from mine. My neck squeezed my head as far away from his face as possible. "The answer to that question is, 'Sir, the answer is Basic Cadet Miller.'" He stared at me, his eyes tunneling into mine, his breath hot on my face. "Say it!"

"Sir, the answer is Basic Cadet Miller." I tried to keep my voice steady.

"Basic Cadet Miller, get your shoulders, up, back, and down." I still wasn't sure what that meant. "Up," he said slowly as he stuck his pointer finger into the air. I pulled my shoulders up. "Back," he whispered toward my ear. "Down." Now, I stood straighter than I had ever in my entire life. "Stay that way for the next year, got it, SMACK?" Got it, I thought. I had survived my first correction. All I had to do was get through them one at a time. Feeling lost in this foreign world was part of the process, part of the tearing down of our egos, part of molding us into something greater. And I wanted to be molded.

While I waited in line to be immunized, I held a tiny "knowledge book" called *Wingtips* in front of my face and was told to memorize the six-paragraph "Code of Conduct" for members of the military verbatim by the end of the day. While I waited in lines, the book was to be positioned no more than four inches from my nose. Memorizing the quote, the "knowledge," seemed impossible. I couldn't concentrate on the little words so close to my eyes with so much bustling around me. "Stop spazzing," one of upperclassmen yelled when my eyes drifted from the page. He poked the book back toward my nose.

At the front of the immunization line, two medical techs simultaneously pushed needles into my arms. I stepped forward and received an additional needle in my left arm. I didn't have any idea what vaccinations they were giving me. As government property, it wasn't my business anymore and out of my control.

Haircuts followed blood samples. An officer directed us women either into the barber shop, or if our hair was already shorter than three inches, motioned us to continue to the next station. At the other end of the hall, the men's bathroom line was so long it wrapped around the next corner. But the women's line was nonexistent and I walked right into a stall. That's when I first fully realized I was entering a world in which I was the minority. I had known that only 18 percent of my classmates would be women, but I hadn't thought about the reality of that number and how it would translate into something as concrete as shorter bathroom lines.

In the stall next to me, a woman sobbed. I asked if she was okay. She said, "Yeah, it's just my hair." I would have shaved my head if that's what the Air Force asked of me, but still, I remembered the shock of seeing my long hair fall to the ground a few weeks earlier and understood her angst at being forced to cut it. We all resembled little boys now.

At the last group of stations, I stuffed my new wardrobe into huge green sacks. I had already broken in combat boots while at home. Now, I tried on shoes to accompany various uniforms and athletic clothing: New Balance tennis shoes, high-top athletic shoes, flip-flops, and black leather low quarters. I also picked up fatigues, USAFA T-shirts, USAFA athletic shorts, blues uniforms, black tees, belts, a silver baseball hat, flight caps, a swimsuit, a bathrobe, pajamas, bed linens, a comforter with silver trim, a silver blanket, a flashlight, shoe polish, a toiletry bag, a toothbrush, toothpaste, Finesse shampoo, a comb, and nail clippers. Every aspect of our lives—and each of our needs—had been planned and anticipated.

At the end of the in-processing obstacle course, upperclassmen escorted us to our respective squadrons. I struggled as I lugged the four bags across the Terrazzo and up two flights of stairs. A cadet dropped me off in front of my new flight commander, Cadet Garcia, a shortish Latino, slender but not overly skinny like many other cadets. He was the only nonwhite upperclassman I had seen all day. Here at a service academy, there were far fewer people of color than in enlisted ranks.

"Basic Cadet Miller, your room is this way." Cadet Garcia managed to say the words by only moving his lips a little. I wondered if he ever smiled. He waited for me to drag the bags over the hall's white and black linoleum tiles. Every few feet I passed an airplane's black silhouette stenciled onto the wall. Cadet Garcia stopped outside my room, empty except for two beds, two desks, and a vanity with a sink. I heaved my bags onto the mattress against the wall. "Your training manual will teach you how to put your things away," Cadet Garcia said.

I flipped through the pages of the spiral notebook, the knowledge book called *Wingtips* we had been holding to our noses earlier. It contained rules, protocols, and quotes we needed to memorize. The "Basic Cadet Bill of Rights" on the first page said, "As a basic cadet, you are protected from cadre touching you or making inappropriate requests." Further in the manual, instructions for meal procedures and room setups were five and nine pages, respectively.

I tried to make sense of the charts illustrating which uniform item went where in the closet, in a vain attempt to find the proper homes for my new belongings. Eventually a tall, tan blond dragged her bags into the room. "Guess we're roommates," I said.

"Guess so," she agreed. "I'm Jo. I'm from Miami."

"I'm Lynn. From Missouri. I was starting to think I wouldn't have a roommate."

She dropped her eyes. "I passed out after getting my blood taken."

To change the subject, I looked back down at *Wingtips* and said, "Well, I was just starting to make sense of where our uniforms go." Jo and I worked together to interpret the regulations and figured out one rule after another.

My relief at Jo's arrival wasn't about kinship between women. All through high school, I had been a member of Civil Air Patrol (CAP), a civilian auxiliary of the Air Force that helped teenagers prepare for the military. The organization had so many teenage boys, it trained me to not care about sometimes being the only girl. My relief with Jo was having a teammate who felt equally overwhelmed.

After everyone had finished in-processing, our squadron of thirty-six basics, including seven women, assembled on the Terrazzo to march to dinner. Dressed in fatigue pants, a white USAFA T-shirt with blue trim, and combat boots, my shoulders were back and down. Eyes caged. Cupped hands pinned to my sides. Like my classmates, I had fastened a blue nametag to my silver baseball hat's forehead. I kept my eyes locked on the shaved head in front of me.

That night I brushed my teeth in the vanity in our dorm room. After such a long day the toothbrush seemed heavy. Our door remained propped open, as required whenever it wasn't time to sleep. We wouldn't be allowed to climb into our beds until taps, a trumpet call that broadcasted over the dorm's loudspeakers. Since upperclassmen had taken my watch, I had no idea how late it was. From down the hall, I heard the unmistakable opening guitar chords of the Creed song I'd heard earlier that day. "Woo-hoo!" the upperclassmen cheered. Their hands slapped in high fives.

"Do you know what that song means, Basic Cadet Miller?" one of the seniors asked me, noticing me look out to the hall. "That's our class song. Every time you hear it, remember that we have less than one year remaining. You, Basic Cadet Miller, still have four." At eighteen, and after a single, exhausting day at the Air Force Academy, four years seemed like forever.

I imagined how blue the sky would be from the cockpit of my future plane, and what Earth would look like miles below. If being strong enough to make my dream a reality meant dealing with whatever the Academy dished out for four years, then that's exactly what I'd do.

CHAPTER 2

When you're eleven, you're also ten, and nine, and eight, and seven, and six, and five, and four, and three, and two, and one. . . . Because the way you grow old is kind of like an onion or like the rings inside a tree trunk or like my little wooden dolls that fit one inside the other, each year inside the next one.

—Sandra Cisneros, "Eleven"

On my first full day as a cadet, my classmates and I assembled on the Terrazzo to take the oath of office, a pledge of loyalty to the country. Twelve hundred new basics stood at attention in block formations by squadron. The junior and senior upperclassmen assigned to train us for the next six weeks, Cadet Garcia among them, were collectively called cadre. They formed up in a line at the front. Before marching us out onto the field where generals and parents waited for us, the cadre had given us two orders: not to drop our salute during the national anthem, otherwise we would bring shame to the uniform of our country, and not to lock our knees, otherwise we would pass out and bring shame to the uniform of our country.

While I waited for the ceremony to begin, I wiggled my toes against my combat boots' stiff sides. I kept the rest of my body rigid, at attention. With my cupped hands, my thumbs pressed against my camouflage BDU pants—short for battle dress uniform. Sweat dripped down my neck. Even though I was supposed to keep my eyes caged, they drifted to take in the beauty of the chapel and the mountains behind it. Hundreds of parents lined the chapel wall. I imagined my parents up there, too, fantasizing about what it would feel like to be comforted by their presence.

One day when I was five, I woke up to my mom stuffing clothes into black garbage bags. Dad had just left on a business trip, and my older sisters sat cross-legged on the kitchen counter looking out the front windows, just in case Dad had forgotten something and turned around. My mom packed us inside her van without discussion and drove us from our home in Colorado Springs, twenty minutes from the Academy, to her parents' house in Missouri. As I grew up, Mom gave a lot of reasons for leaving Dad. He was an alcoholic, drug dealer, and wife beater. He'd had sex with prostitutes, including men. On the day I was born, he dropped her off at the hospital and left. Mostly I believed her. I missed Colorado's mountains, and leaving my toys, friends, and softball games, but I didn't miss Dad.

I was twelve the last time I spent part of my summer with him. While flying to Colorado, I squished my face against the window to study the Rocky Mountains as they appeared on the horizon. Every time I visited Colorado, the shapes of the peaks became more familiar, and on that particular plane ride, they made me feel more at home than I had ever felt in Missouri. I belonged there in those mountains. And for once, I felt like I belonged with Dad, too. That trip marked the first time I'd visited him without my older sisters, who had both started college. It would be just me and Dad for two weeks, and I wanted the chance to get to know him. I had stopped believing Mom's lies about Dad, realizing she told them so we would like her better.

Dad picked me up outside of baggage claim in the black convertible he called the Firebird. Way cooler than Mom's station wagon. "Hey, Doozer," he said. My old nickname was given to me because I reminded my family of the little creatures, Doozers, on my favorite show, *Fraggle Rock*. I squeezed the black leather seat as Dad pulled onto the highway. Wind whipped my ponytail against my neck. Since it was too loud to talk, I put in my CD, Green Day. He smiled, his thin, blond hair flying in the wind, and let me turn up the volume.

I had a bedroom and bed to myself in Dad's house, which was located in an upscale neighborhood in the foothills. This was a vast improvement from that time I slept on a foldout lawn chair because Dad had been too depressed to replace the furniture Mom took in the divorce agreement. When Dad went to work in the morning, he gave me his computer password so that I could explore the Internet, which I had never heard of. With Dad gone all day, I hung out on the computer, loudly listened to music on his stereo, and ate whatever leftover food I could find. I enjoyed free reign in his house, which had vaulted ceilings, chandeliers, panoramic windows, oak trim, and hardwood floors. My simple house back in Missouri was about a third of the size. I started to understand why Mom had been afraid of me liking Dad better. At the end of the day, I swiveled in an armchair in front of the windows that faced Pikes Peak, waiting for Dad to come home. His dog, Bear Bear, a brown lab as big as me, slept at my feet while I ate bowlfuls of sugary cereal.

One night, while I was waiting for Dad to come home, I fell asleep on the couch watching *Mrs. Doubtfire*, a movie in which Robin Williams plays a newly divorced dad without custody who wants to see his kids so badly he cross-dresses and pretends to be a nanny. I had watched that movie every day since getting to Dad's, partly because it was one of the few videotapes he owned, and partly because I liked to pretend my dad wanted to see me that badly, too.

When I woke up the house was dark except for the patio light that illuminated short, leafy scrub oak. I felt sure my dad had to have come home already, but the house was empty. Finally I looked in the dining room. I hadn't checked there because Bear Bear peed on the carpet, and we never used it. I smelled urine as I rounded the corner from the kitchen, and there I saw him. Dad was passed out underneath the dining room table on the yellowed carpet. I realized, slowly, that he had drank too much. I remember everything about that moment except for Dad. I remember the pale, vertical blinds that were open to the back deck and the dark woods. The browned, crumpled leaves from the ficus tree scattered on the carpet. A pile of pink and white towels, all frayed at the edges, covered the scratched dining table. But I don't remember Dad. My twelve-year-old brain blotted out the memory of him, drunk and unconscious and lying in dog piss.

All of my memories of Dad were that way. I remember being eight and sitting at the top of a double black diamond, my skis twisted under my legs and the snow cold against my thick pants, as my big sisters took off down the steep slope. But I don't remember what my dad looked like following them, leaving me to ski down on my own. I remember the strappy, orange camisole Dad's Australian girlfriend wore sans bra the time we all went mountain biking one summer, but I have no recollection of him. Somehow, my brain redacted the images of Dad to ease his overwhelming absence from my life.

After finding my dad passed out under the table, I never asked to visit him again. He didn't call, either. It was my mother who suggested I see him the year I was fifteen when we visited the Air Force Academy, touring it to decide for sure that I wanted to become a cadet. Dad and I met for dinner at a Red Robin, just a mile from the Academy gates. Dad clenched his fingers around his glass of beer. "How's school, Doozer?" I told him about my favorite class, physics.

"Physics is in everything we do," I said. "It explains how cars stay on the road and how planes can fly and how the space shuttle is launched." Dad looked at me straight in the eyes and smiled.

"Physics is my favorite subject, too," he said. Dad knew a lot about science because he built computer chips. I looked at the big nose I had inherited, and realized I had gotten my love of science from him as well. I almost forgot about the dog piss. I felt badly for my dad, who had once returned from a business trip to find his wife and three daughters missing. It must have been hard to see us only a few times throughout our childhoods.

"Can we swap e-mails, Dad?" I asked.

"That would be great, Doozer," he said. I believed Dad when he told me he would e-mail. I scribbled my address on a white cocktail napkin and pushed it across the table. For a second both of our hands held onto the napkin before I let go and Dad folded it into his pocket. Dad never e-mailed.

As I waited to take the oath of office, I knew Dad wasn't there. He didn't even know I had become a cadet. My mom would have come, but I had wanted to say good-bye to her at the Saint Louis airport.

My relationship with my mom was complicated, because she was complicated. Mom worked at my high school, and the way we giggled and gossiped made my classmates envious. She spoiled me in all the ways a loving parent shouldn't but often does anyway: cooking two hot meals per day, folding my laundry, and never requiring chores. Yet, there was another side to her that people at school never saw.

On the good side, there wasn't anyone who supported me as much as Mom did. When I was in first grade I decided I wanted to become a pitcher, even though I was one of the smallest kids on the softball team. Despite being a single mom, and financially strapped, she found the money to pay for pitching lessons and practiced with me every night. Our yard was small and we had to stand against opposite sections of the chain-link fence so that there was enough room between us. She held an open glove in front of her knees, but my pitches rarely hit it. She chased the ball around our yard and sometimes the neighbor's, too. I tried again and again, until the lightning bugs flew around me and Mom called it a night. Slowly my aim became better and Mom didn't have to run after the ball anymore. But then she had a new problem: I figured out how to throw my body into the pitch so that it became fast. When I was in fourth grade she caught it at a weird angle one time and it broke her elbow. Even though she needed surgery, Mom didn't complain. I had become my team's star long before then.

I had learned such perseverance from watching Mom, who was almost deaf. She had been two when her own mother lost a newborn son. Depressed, Grandma neglected to take Mom to the doctor when she got measles. It wasn't until Mom was in eighth grade that her family found out she had lost most of her hearing. Mostly they had stopped speaking to her. Her Catholic school labeled her as dumb and beyond hope. The nuns told my grandparents she wouldn't graduate. But Mom taught herself to lip read. In high school she crammed for finals, staying up nights, even while her own parents told her it was useless. "Don't worry about school," my grandma told my mom. "You'll be married soon enough."

Mom did graduate from high school. She also married my dad young, and moved straight from her parents' house to her husband's.

She never had a career, so when she left my dad she had to work at McDonald's. I suspected she agreed to marry my stepfather after only knowing him for four months because it was too hard to support three little girls on her small paychecks. Maybe that was why Mom pushed us to be successful. She didn't want us to experience the limitations she had.

Mom went back to college and became a special education teacher the same year I graduated high school. I imagined her as a small child in the back of a Catholic schoolhouse, nearly completely deaf to the words of her teachers and the other kids. When she was an adult I witnessed her struggle to understand others and constantly fuss with her hearing aids. And when I spoke to Mom, I had to face her and carefully enunciate my words. Conversations in a car were nearly impossible. Despite these difficulties, she continued to advance in her new career. I admired her determination, and I emulated it. When I was in high school Mom drove me to and from student council meetings and softball and volleyball practices. Over dinner she asked about my tests and papers. She even found the Civil Air Patrol program, a civilian branch of the Air Force through which I could earn my pilot's license.

But there was a price to pay for Mom's attentiveness. Her otherwise unending support evaporated on her angry days. On those days Mom would shout that she shouldn't have had kids. My sisters were sluts and bitches, and I was a selfish brat. Even when she wasn't yelling at me, I could hear her cries from the other side of our tiny house. She'd threaten to kill us by driving off the road. To put me to bed early, she'd give me NyQuil. Sometimes a single dose, sometimes three. She called three cups of the green, mint-flavored liquid Goodnight Irene. When I was little I sucked my thumb, and Angry Mom used to yank it out of my mouth. Mom said the torn ligament in my thumb was the result of a fall from my tricycle when I was two, but I wondered. I also wondered about the arm I broke when I was one. She said I fell from my high chair.

Mom's anger never lasted. When it subsided the tears began. "I'm sorry, I'm sorry," she'd plead. Then she'd call herself fat, ugly, stupid, and a terrible mom.

"No, you aren't. We love you, Mommy," I'd invariably say. I knew that after she worked through her tears, Devoted Mom would return.

My mom remarried when I was nine, and the yelling in the house only worsened because then my stepdad, Pat, was screaming, too. I thought of him as the Hobbit because he was so short and hairy. His eyes bulged behind his thick, plastic glasses. Within a few years, my mom and stepdad kicked both my sisters out of the house. Mom banished sixteen-year-old Amy first; their fights were so violent that Amy tried to run Mom over with the car. Mom ousted seventeen-year-old Megan because she was dating a man who was half-Thai, a man the Hobbit referred to as a "chink." I also had three stepsiblings, but my parents didn't speak with a single one of them. Not even on Christmas or when my sisters got married. Watching Mom and Pat sever their connections with their children, I understood that my relationship with them was a delicate thread that could be sliced by the most insignificant wrongdoings.

Still, when Mom felt sad, she turned to me. I was a senior in high school when she filed for her second divorce. Her depression worsened. One morning she sat at the kitchen table, sobbing, as I got ready for school. "I can't handle it anymore," she said. A pile of Kleenex grew on the table. "I just want to kill myself. What else am I supposed to do, Lynn?" I looked at her short curly black hair, her olive skin, and her glasses with the flimsy, wire-rim frames. She waited for an answer I couldn't give. Over the years, Mom's suicide threats shocked me less and less. Usually I would tell her that she was strong and that she would move through whatever bad feelings she was having. But I couldn't that day. My compassion for her had worn thin.

"I have to go to school, Mom," I said before turning my back, effectively ending our conversation given her hearing loss. She cried more loudly.

"How can you leave me like this? You are such a spoiled brat." I knew I was selfish, just like I knew I was a hard worker. She had told me those things about myself for as long as I could remember. But there was no way I could stay home from school because she was suicidal again. Besides, I had spent too many weekends and holidays, even my own birthdays, entangled in her depression, though she was the adult, not me.

Mom kept crying as she drove me to school, and she didn't stop in front of the building as I anticipated. "You're going to stay home with me," she insisted again. I opened the door while the car was still moving and nearly jumped out before she slammed on the brakes. "Fine, Lynn, you win," she said.

I glanced at mom as I walked away. She sat behind the driver's wheel, forehead in hands. Her shoulders heaved in sobs. A better daughter would go back and apologize. Instead I faced away and crossed into the school.

Both parts of Mom were true: she instilled in me a drive to aim for the stars, literally, while also trying to pull me into her own turmoil. I admired her and felt gratitude for Devoted Mom while trying to ignore Angry Mom. Despite the bad days, she taught me that if she could deal with her hearing loss, I didn't have an excuse for not living up to my potential. Not even the dream of becoming an astronaut was too daring. Yet I knew that whatever I accomplished, it would be on my own. I couldn't rely on Mom. She might kill herself, or she might decide to go years without speaking to me, just as she didn't speak to my sisters. Besides, I never turned to her for comfort. She was my cheerleader, my coach, my ally, but we never hugged or shared deep conversations. Mom used to say, "When you were a baby and you cried, all you wanted was to be put down in your crib to be left alone." She would laugh, as if her admission that she never comforted me was funny.

One morning when I was nine years old, during a particularly rough fight between one of my sisters, the Hobbit, and my mother, I hid in my closet under my sweaters. I sought refuge there so often that I permanently kept a flashlight and a few of my favorite Roald Dahl books in the corner. Sometimes even the sound of the garage door and my anxiety about who would walk through the door—Devoted Mom or Angry Mom—caused me to hide there. Behind the sliding doors, I held Puppy, a yellow stuffed dog I had slept with since I was a baby, close to my chest. I wrapped myself in a blanket and pretended to be the little girl who was abducted by the big, friendly giant in Dahl's *The BFG.* But the giant never came to kidnap me and the closet doors couldn't muffle Mom's shouts, so I tiptoed to the shower where I hoped the water would drown her out. Alone in the white bathroom, my bare toes cold against the small pieces of off-white tile, I studied my reflection in the wall-to-wall mirror above the sink. I analyzed my ratty, brown hair and pale skin. Then I looked into my own blue eyes. There isn't anyone I can rely on but me, I told myself. I'm all I have. For a quick moment, I reconsidered. Maybe I would have Puppy forever. But what if he got lost someday? The sadness I felt when I realized I couldn't even count on my loyal stuffed animal overwhelmed me, as if the bathroom was filling with water, drowning me.

I admitted to myself that the limits the Air Force would place on my relationship with Mom were part of the appeal of the Academy. I wouldn't have e-mail for six weeks. No phone for nine months. I couldn't visit home any more than a few times a year. I was relieved to make the military my new family.

And that's exactly what the military promoted itself to be. Family. The other cadets would be "brothers and sisters in arms." The Academy had thirty-six squadrons total, each with its own traditions, commander, and corner of the dorms. I would live, work, and bond with my squadron for the next four years, and we would serve together in the operational Air Force. Waiting in formation to take the oath of office, I stood next to adopted brothers and sisters. When ordered, I raised my right hand and repeated the oath. "I, Lynn Miller, having been appointed a cadet in the United States Air Force Academy, do solemnly swear that I will support and defend the Constitution of the United States against all enemies, foreign and domestic." The parents at the chapel wall cheered.

CHAPTER 3

*How do you take young men and women out of high school, where
they have seldom experienced any adversity or deprivation, and turn
them into the kinds of officers who are ready for the demands of
the military profession? The answer is that you put them into such
a demanding environment, where, if they survive, they will have
developed the strengths necessary for the profession.*

—William L. Smallwood,
The Air Force Academy Candidate Book, 3rd ed.

I woke up the next morning to loud bass and heavy guitar chords,
with Guns N' Roses' Axl Rose screaming, "Welcome to the jungle!" Thud-thud-thud. Our wood door rattled as the upperclassmen
banged against it. "Pants on, doors open!" a cadre yelled. Jo flipped
on the lights, and my eyes stung. My body was heavy with exhaustion, even though it was only my second morning of Basic Cadet
Training.

"Pants on, doors open!" a cadre yelled again. I assumed women
should put on pants *and* shirts. Jo and I moved quickly and then
propped open the door. The music and yelling was deafening. Two
cadre, including the only woman, came running into the thresh-
old of our room. They wore impeccably neat blue uniforms, the
fold on their short sleeves crisp and the shirt tucked smoothly into
their pants so that there were no bunches. Their dark blue shoulder
boards were clad with embroidered white bars—code for rank I
didn't yet understand.

"Get your pajamas off the floor!" the woman yelled. "Make
your bed, brush your teeth, put on your boots!" Her hair was pulled

back into a bun, and she wore diamond earrings and mascara and blush. It surprised me to see a cadet so girly. The second cadre stood just behind the woman's shoulder.

"Hurry! It! Up!" he yelled.

"Yes, ma'am," Jo and I answered in near unison. One day in and we had already started to speak in chorus. I tucked my T-shirt into my camouflage BDU pants. I added a belt and sat on the floor to lace up my combat boots.

"Basic Cadet Miller, why are you sitting on the floor?" Startled, I looked up to see another cadre standing in my doorway. I almost answered the truth: I didn't know we weren't allowed to sit in our dorm rooms. Then I remembered the prescribed response and, in spite of myself, yelled, "No excuse, sir." At least the simple response kept me from needing to think. As the cadre walked away, I pulled myself off the floor to squat while I finished tying the laces and tucking the BDU pants into the boots.

"Get out here, basics!" A cadre yelled. The song had switched from Guns N' Roses to an unrecognizable rock song. It was so loud it throbbed in my eardrums. My male classmates across the hallway had opened their door and were shirtless. I brushed my teeth and pulled my covers tight across my bed, trying to straighten the hospital corners. The night before, Cadet Garcia had made us do flutter kicks under the sheets so that we messed up the covers. Making the bed in a hurry, while still paying attention to the perfection of the corners, was part of the training that would eventually mold us into competent officers. Multitask without losing focus.

"Ready?" I asked Jo. Neither one of us would brave the hallway until we could do so together. Jo nodded. Once our boots left the safety of our carpeted dorm room and took their first steps onto the linoleum, we straightened to the position of attention, cupping our hands at our sides and pulling our shoulders up, back, and down. I marched behind Jo and caged my eyes on the thin, blond hair at the base of her neck. We joined our classmates, who were forming one long line braced against the wall.

"While we are waiting for your slow classmates, what are the seven responses of a basic cadet?" one of the cadre yelled.

"Sir," we said together, "the seven responses of a basic cadet are as follows: 'yes, sir'; 'no, sir'; 'no excuse, sir' . . ." From there we each diverted into different answers as we struggled to remember the correct order.

"No!" he yelled. "Get it right!" We tried again, and then again, before we could answer all together: "yes, sir"; "no, sir"; "no excuse, sir"; "sir, may I make a statement?"; "sir, may I ask a question?"; "sir, I do not understand"; "sir, I do not know." Without being able to see each other, the only clues we had to getting it right were the more confident, louder voices of the basic cadets remembering correctly. "Remind the rest of your classmates that you are waiting for them!" he yelled. I wasn't sure what he meant. "Repeat, 'Sir, we are waiting for our classmates.'"

"Sir, we are waiting for our classmates," we shouted.

"To the floor!" the cadre yelled, and he dropped to his hands and toes in the push-up position. I dropped to my hands, and my elbow knocked against Jo's. I studied the imperfections in the polished, white linoleum. "Keep reminding your classmates!" the cadre said.

"Sir, we are waiting for our classmates! Sir, we are waiting for our classmates!"

"Down!" he yelled, and I felt my classmates dip into a full push-up. I dipped, too. "Down," he said again, and we did a second. I kept my back straight between commands, my arms fully extended and my palms and toes supporting my weight, but after a few minutes, my arms began to tremble. My back sagged. I had done push-ups on my bedroom floor between homework assignments in the last few months of high school, but I hadn't progressed to doing more than ten or twenty at a time. School had always come easier than athletics. Plus, I had wasted so many months of my senior year, a few lost to a knee surgery, a few lost to the depressed fog I felt during the winter months when my flight instructor forced me to have sex with him.

"Miller, get your ass up!" one of the cadre yelled. My lower back burned as I forced it straight again. "Up!" the cadre yelled. I scrambled to my feet, again taking deep breaths, this time to slow my heart rate.

All thirty-six of us had assembled in a long line broken up into groups by the alcoves to our dorm rooms. "That was pathetic! Tomorrow you better not take that long to get out here."

"Follow me," another cadre yelled. We followed him, single file, to the end of the hall and then down five stories. Outside there was no hint of the sun and the chilly air cooled my sweaty arms. Cadre broke us into groups, and four of us were ordered to do sprints. We took off running toward the dorm building wall at the opposite end of the quad. I followed after them, my boots slamming against the concrete. I dug in, but my classmates all slapped the wall before I came anywhere near it.

"Lunges!" the upperclassman yelled when we returned. "To the wall and back. Repeat 'Iron, Mike' with each step. Go!"

"Iron," we said as we took a step forward, our knees dipping nearly to the concrete. "Mike," we said with the next step.

"Louder!" the cadre yelled. The other cadre from our squadron yelled their own commands, plus other squadrons had also formed in the adjoining quads. So many staccato, overlapping screams sounded like a pack of dogs barking incessantly.

The sky to the east began to fade into a lighter blue. I had no idea how long I would have to keep going. Or if I could. When I ran cross-country with my high school for the first time my junior year, my teammates finished runs whole minutes ahead of me. But by my senior year, my mile time had dipped below six minutes, and I was no longer my team's caboose. If I pushed through then, I could push through now.

Finally we reformed into a single line to return to our rooms and wash for breakfast. I had survived, but only the first of many beat sessions—that was what cadre called this physical training. On the way back inside, cadre stopped us at the pull-up bars bolted to the wall just inside the stairwell. Many of the men did as many as ten or fifteen. All six of the other women did at least one, the minimum for us to pass the physical fitness test. I was nearly last to jump up on the bar. For a moment I dangled, all of my weight supported by my shoulder sockets. When I pulled, my elbows only bent a little before my arms trembled and stopped moving me upward. My right arm, strengthened by years of pitching back-to-back softball games, worked harder, heaving the right side of my body slightly above the left. I pulled my knees toward my chest, as if raising my legs would help me. My neck strained and tilted upward, but my chin wasn't anywhere near the same level as the bar. I flexed and flexed, but my biceps refused to pull me any higher. I couldn't will them to lie about my level of physical conditioning. I fell back to my feet.

Three cadre swarmed to me. "Miller, what was that?" the woman cadre yelled.

One of the men moved right in front of my face. He looked at me straight into my eyes, but I locked mine onto the peach skin of his throat, avoiding his stare. "Basic Cadet Miller," he whispered. For the first time, the words coming from one of the cadre's mouth wasn't a yell. His low, firm tone demanded my complete attention. "You are officially the most pathetic being out of every single one of your classmates. Each of them has prepared themselves to pass a fitness test. You are the only one who could not."

I had never before failed. My first physical fitness test would occur in four months, and I could only hope to catch up to my classmates in that time. Otherwise, I would be kicked out. But before then cadre could make my life hell and force me out during Basic Cadet Training. That was the upperclassmen's job, to single out those who weren't fit to be Air Force officers. What I didn't notice as I tried to recover from the cadre's threat was that there were two boys behind me, boys my classmates would later call Fatty Hughes and Betty Crocker, who couldn't do any pull-ups, either. The upperclassmen had scolded them just as scathingly, but I was already climbing the stairs back to the dorm.

Every morning of Basic Cadet Training, we woke before the sun and rushed outside to be beat. I was always the weakest, the basic cadet who made classmates feel better about their performance. Cadre warned me I wouldn't survive the second half of Basic Cadet Training, during which we would camp in the woods in a place called Jack's Valley and endure back-to-back beat sessions for three weeks. At least during this first half of the summer, cadre put as much focus on mental training as physical conditioning. This meant there were

some things at which I excelled. I was one of the quicker basic cadets to memorize knowledge, or quotes, from *Wingtips*. Although
my classmates waited for me to catch up to them on runs, and cadre
consistently singled me out for failing at pull-ups, I could help with
more psychologically demanding tasks, including remembering the
meal protocol. We studied mealtime rules out of *Wingtips*, but once
we were inside Mitchell Hall, we could only rely on each other to
remember every detail cadre required of us.

One evening, a week after our arrival, I marched single file
behind my classmates into Mitchell Hall while all 1,200 of us in
our class chanted, in unison, "2005: Full of Pride," our given class
motto. Mitchell Hall became thunderous as more and more basic
cadets flooded through its doors. Straight ahead, the two-story glass
walls gave views of pine forests to the south and west. As my classmates arrived at our four tables in the middle of the hall, nine of us
filed in behind chairs, standing at attention shoulder to shoulder. I
was in the center of the rectangular table. The smell of food wafted
from carts at the end of the aisle, but we would not be allowed to eat
for several more minutes. "What's the Code of Conduct?" Cadet
Garcia asked from the table's head. He screamed loudly enough to
be heard over the cadre and basics. We stopped chanting "Full of
Pride" to answer him.

"Sir, the Code of Conduct for members of the armed forces
of the United States is as follows: Article One, I am an American
fighting in the forces which guard my country and our way of life.
I am prepared to give my life in its defense . . ." We had already
recited the six articles dictating proper prisoner of war behavior over
and over. Just like when we answered any of cadre's questions, we
had learned to match each other's pacing and breaths to stay in unison. A few of my classmates still struggled to remember each word.
Confident that I had each article 100 percent correct, I answered
loudly so that they could follow after me: "Article Six, I will never
forget that I am an American, fighting for freedom, responsible for
my actions, and dedicated to the principles which make my country
free. I will trust in my God and in the United States of America."
As we recited, we poured drinks. We had to remember the drink
preferences for each of our cadre without asking: Cadet Garcia liked

one glass with juice and no ice, and another glass with water and ice. We poured so that the liquid was exactly one knife-width from the top of the glass. As we passed the drinks to his end of the table, we prevented our fingers from touching the top one-third of the glass. If one of my classmates misremembered the correct drinks, I returned it in the direction it came as a hint for them to try again. We couldn't ever speak to each other or talk to the cadre without being spoken to first. Then we passed around water for each basic cadet: two glasses of water with ice.

"Basics, take seats" came from the loudspeaker.

In unison we sat. I utilized only the front six inches of my chair, bracing my back as straight as possible. I kept my hands flat in my lap while not using them, and shoulders even further back and down than usual. My stomach was exactly one fist width from the table. I focused my eyes on my white, round plate's eagle emblem while keeping my chin level. As I strained my eyes downward, I tried to keep my forehead back and not bowed. The muscles around my eyes burned. My forehead wrinkled. Careful not to get caught, I nudged the plate with my thumb tip slightly further from me so that I didn't have to strain my eyes quite as much.

"Tuck your chin in, basics," a cadre yelled. "Pulling chins" was an Academy-specific haze that required cadets to awkwardly tuck their chin into their neck. Before I became a cadet, I had read that pulling chins had been banned because of a doctor's concern that it caused pinched nerves. But when the adult officers in charge weren't looking, cadre made us pull chins anyway. It wasn't as if any basic cadets would challenge their commands. We did whatever the upperclassmen said, whether it was legal or not. I tried to tuck my chin down to my neck as tightly as possible to create double, triple, or quadruple chins. Cadre circled around us, poking their fingers toward our chins.

"Further!" one of them yelled. "We pulled chins all the time in basic. Your class has it so easy." We heard that line constantly from cadre, that their training was harder than ours, that the Academy had turned soft.

The waiter moved down the aisle of tables, distributing serving trays. I snuck a look at the steak, green beans, and mashed potatoes on silver platters at the end of the table. "Mashed potatoes for the table commandant," my classmate said as he passed the dish to his right. We each repeated the phrase as we passed the potatoes to Cadet Garcia. He scooped some onto his plate and then returned the rest to the basic cadets. I tried to take a perfect amount so that all nine of us received the same portion. Cadre allowed us to uncage our eyes from our eagle emblem long enough to accomplish these tasks.

We waited for the basic cadet at the end of the table, the guy whose misfortune landed him in that position, to gain the courage to ask to eat. "Cadet Garcia, pardon me please, sir," he said.

"What?" Cadet Garcia barked.

"Sir, may I ask a question?"

"What?"

"Sir, all basic cadets have been served," the basic cadet tried.

"No!" Garcia screamed. "You can't eat until you say it correctly."

"Sir, all basic cadets and cadet have been served." Wrong.

Garcia shouted, "Still missing something! Better figure it out or your classmates won't eat!" My classmate struggled to find the words. "Anybody want to help?" This was a trick question: if we confessed we knew the proper wording, we were pimping our classmate. Pimping meant that we put our own needs ahead of our classmate's. Bragging that we knew what he should know would make him look bad, so it was better if we pled ignorance.

Finally my classmate remembered. "Sir, all basic cadets and cadet at the table have been served at this time," he said.

Cadet Garcia yelled, "Eat!"

We did, immediately. I carefully cut my food so that I could swallow it in seven chews. As I brought my utensil upward, I boxed the trajectory of the fork so that it created the perfect right angle in front of my mouth. I replaced the knife, fork, or spoon in their respective spot and angle on the plate before chewing a soft green bean. Sitting at the head of the table, Cadet Garcia watched us carefully. He had already eaten so that he could devote the entire meal period to training us. "Basic Cadet Clark!" Cadet Garcia's roar made arms startle. I could not continue to eat while someone was being trained. "Did I just see you take eight chews? Where the hell do you think you are? Thanks to you, you and your classmates will now only be allowed six!" Some meals we were restricted to as few as four chews. The limitation built self-discipline, the cadre claimed. I focused on the mashed potatoes rather than the steak.

"This is the end of the noon meal," I heard over the loudspeaker. I replaced my fork to its home. "Basics, have you had a full and satisfying meal?" In unison we gave the only correct answer: "Yes, sir!" But I was still hungry, and I knew my classmates were, too. It didn't matter how much we improved, the cadre always found enough mistakes to spend most of the hour correcting us.

"Cadet Garcia, pardon me please, sir," I said. While it was foolish to draw attention to myself and invite criticism, we would not be dismissed until one of us went through the proper procedure. As a physical weakling, I had to compensate by contributing to my classmates elsewhere.

"What?" Cadet Garcia answered.

"Sir, may I ask a question?" He said yes. "Sir, may the basic cadets at the table please be excused at this time?" My voice sounded high and uncertain despite my best efforts, but I was relieved to recite the exact phrase.

Out of the corner of my eye, I saw Cadet Garcia raise a shiny spoon two feet above the blue tablecloth. "Get up from my table!" We stood expediently to beat the spoon before it hit with a dull thud.

"Excuse me please, good evening sir." We said the line in a singsong tune that helped us stay in unison.

Meals became the mile markers for each day. Just survive to breakfast, I told myself when I woke up. Then, just make it until lunch.

In addition to beat sessions and learning dining protocol, during the first three weeks of Basic Cadet Training, we listened to briefings on the Honor Code, which said we couldn't lie, cheat, or steal; received more uniform issues; learned to march; and took academic placement tests for the school year. In the evening after dinner, cadre herded all 1,200 of us in a single-file chain across the Terrazzo to the largest auditorium for briefings with the entire class.

The wing commander, the highest ranking senior cadet, raged: "Never in the history of this fine institution has a class of basics been so pathetic!" I suspected cadre said the same thing every year in an attempt to "motivate" basic cadets to do better. In fact cadre used that word, "pathetic," so often it had begun to lose its meaning. Another night, we watched "air power" videos in which the Air Force fleet zoomed across the screen. My classmates cheered when a B-1 dropped bombs on barren land, but I preferred the films of high-altitude planes. During the movies, cadre prohibited us from going to the bathroom, even though they had made us drink pitcher upon pitcher of water at dinner, using high altitude and dry air as an excuse. As the Air Force videos continued, I became more and more uncomfortable with my swelling bladder. Most of us fidgeted to keep from wetting our pants. I had heard a rumor once that there was a woman years ago who had died of water poisoning during Basic Cadet Training. None of us were sure if it was true, but drinking water and not being allowed to pee was just another tradition that fell somewhere between sanctioned training and hazes inflicted by the cadre because it had been done to them. None of us ever wet our pants.

Other nights, cadre gave us the option to attend church. At dinner they'd say, "Stick out a paw if you want to go to the chapel." The alternative was to go back to our rooms to write letters home. Nearly all of my classmates projected their fists straight in front of their chest, the equivalent of raising a hand. I suspected some of my classmates used the chapel as an excuse to get away from the cadre. Inside they could talk, sit casually, or even sleep without repercussion. Pretending to be a Christian was probably no worse than using a Bible to smuggle pictures like I had. Instead of joining them, I returned to my room with the other "heathens," as cadre called us.

Unlike most of my classmates, I missed quiet time more than I missed socializing. The constant quotes and chants we regurgitated, plus yells from cadre, echoed across the Terrazzo during all hours of the day. I imagined the Protestant chapel, with the majority of the 1,200 basic cadets talking excitedly, and felt overwhelmed. I longed for a calm moment. I felt strengthened by my quiet dorm room. These moments during which I could actually think were so few and far between. When I was alone I could remember who I was. Not the teenaged part of me that failed at protecting myself from my sexual abuser, not the part of me that couldn't yet do a pull-up, but the part of myself that endured, never gave up, that was audacious enough to believe she could become an astronaut. I was so adept at turning off my own thoughts and opinions while cadre trained me, it felt as if I wasn't anything but what they told me. And at this stage of the Academy's process, I was still a SMACK, a soldier minus ability, courage, and knowledge. I needed to remember I was stronger than that, right there, in that moment.

After Jo returned from chapel, she said I should have come since "it's the only time we actually get to know one another." She was right—my classmates didn't know me and I didn't know them. Despite spending every waking minute together, we rarely had any conversations. Even Jo and I didn't talk much. Our brief snippets of exchange usually consisted of reminders to do this and that and whispers before falling asleep. I wasn't sure what most of my classmates looked like, though I could probably identify all thirty-five by their voice and the back of their heads. I knew the full names of all six of the women, plus a few of the guys, but most of my other classmates looked like little clone soldiers: the same shaved head, the same uniform, the same lean, muscular build. I suspected I was missing out on building relationships with my classmates by not going to chapel. Yet, I chose my room every time.

We weren't alone even when we showered. Typically one of our two women cadre would collect us seven women from our rooms, and we would stand outside of the bathroom in flip-flops and our USAFA robe, holding our shower bags in our left hands. "Three minutes ladies," the cadre would announce as she started her stopwatch. I liked the way the women cadre said the respectful word "ladies," rather than "females." The cadre waited in the hallway while we rushed into the bathroom, shedding our robes on a bench. If urinating wasn't urgent I held it, unwilling to sacrifice those extra few seconds. Then I raced to a showerhead where I doused my damp hair and body with soap. We all showered next to each other, short stalls dividing us but no curtains to create privacy. I had thought that showering with other women would make me feel horrifyingly self-conscious, but there wasn't time or energy for that.

But one morning, I found a way to steal a few minutes of freedom. In the July heat, our squadrons had broken up to play intramural sports mixed in with basics from other units. I had been selected for cross-country and that morning, by the time we finished our several mile run, sweat and salt covered my exhausted body. The upperclassmen who led practice dropped me off early at my dorm room and told me to stay there. I stood in the doorway and looked up and down the empty halls. My cadre were probably catching up on sleep. Jo wasn't yet back from swimming, nor were the other basic cadets in my squadron. I was actually alone. In an instant decision, I grabbed my shower bag and towel, and I raced down the hallway to the bathroom. For several minutes I did nothing but stand under the hot water, letting the pressure massage my sore shoulders and back, rejoicing in the quiet. For the only time that whole summer, I shaved my legs.

By the end of the first three weeks of Basic Cadet Training, I could no longer remember what it felt like to be anything other than a cadet. Memories of high school and my mom and even those of my former flight instructor felt like a different lifetime. The cadre told me to march, I marched. They told me to run, I ran. They told me how to dress, how to move, what to speak, and even what to think, and I obeyed. In the second half of Basic Cadet Training, we would march to Jack's Valley to camp. As soon as we left the Terrazzo, my ability to memorize quotes or pay attention to our room's tiniest details wouldn't matter. The only thing that would matter as we completed obstacle courses and beat sessions out in the middle of the woods would be our level of physical conditioning. While I had grown stronger over the previous three weeks, so had my classmates, and I still couldn't keep up with them. If anything was going to prevent me from graduating, it would be Jack's Valley. Our cadre were about to rotate out for a fresh set of upperclassmen to train us, and if the new cadre didn't respect me, they could single me out until I quit. Most of the other squadrons had already lost at least a few basic cadets. Ours hadn't lost a single person. Yet.

On our last night before the cadre switch, Cadet Garcia lightly knocked on our door. "Get on your uniforms and get back out here," he said in a normal voice, not a yell. My eyes had just fallen closed. Realizing that they probably wanted to beat us one last time, my gut knotted. We assembled in the hallway, but something was different: Cadet Garcia wanted us to be quiet rather than yell a chant or recite knowledge.

"Come on," he whispered. He led us down the stairs and around the backside of the Terrazzo to a large hill behind the Cadet Chapel. Called the LZ for "landing zone," the hill was steep with rocks and trees that seemed invisible in the night. We formed a single-file line as Cadet Garcia herded us up the side. Knee-high wild grass turned to a bed of pine needles. I scrambled up the hill behind my classmates. When I wasn't keeping up the pace, my classmate Nathan from Pennsylvania put his hand on the small of my back. The warmth felt like a whispered "hang in there."

Just before we reached the top, Cadet Garcia told us to close our eyes and hold each other's hands for guidance. I held Nathan's and Jo's hands with my sweaty fingers. From the front of the line, Cadet Garcia led us. I stumbled over rocks and tree roots. We leaned on each other so that none of us fell. At the LZ's top, with my eyes still closed, a gentle breeze smelling of pine blew off the foothill and rustled through my hair. When I opened my eyes we faced toward the cadet area, lit up with gold lights reflecting off the aluminum and glass buildings. Further below, Colorado Springs's twinkling lights interrupted endless, dark plains. I felt as if I could reach out and hold the glowing city.

"Ladies and gentlemen," Cadet Garcia's deep voice broke the silence. "This is the country that you have volunteered to serve. In this city there are thousands of sleeping civilians who will depend on you to protect their freedom. This is the reason why you are enduring. Tonight is the last night I will be your cadre. Tomorrow I will pass you off to my peers, and you will have to prove yourself to them as you have to me. But, ladies and gentlemen, I am proud to say that I will be honored to serve with each and every one of you in *our* Air Force when you graduate in less than four years."

Cadet Garcia hadn't brought us to the top of the LZ to beat us. He brought us there to return our respect. Listening to Cadet Garcia's praise, I could begin to see how the training would be worth it by Recognition. Garcia held up a thick chain that was as long as his arms. "It's time you claim part of this Academy as your own. Tonight, you will bury these seventy-two links. Nine months from now, when you are Recognized, you can recover half of the links, one for each of you. The remaining links will stay buried here at the Academy. I expect every one of you to make it until then. Nearly every other squadron has already lost several basics, but not a single one of you has left. I'm proud of you." A few of the guys used shovels to bury the chain while the rest of us huddled around them. Afterward we enjoyed candy bars and soda, and I looked around in the dark at my classmates' smiles. I couldn't believe what we had heard: personal claim to *our* Academy—not the upperclassmen's Academy—and a promise of graduation.

CHAPTER 4
————

*The "freeze" response is one of the three primary responses . . . the
other two, fight and flight, are much more familiar to us. . . . In
freezing, the impala (and human) enters an altered state in which no
pain is experienced. What that means for the impala is that it will
not have to suffer while being torn apart by the cheetah's sharp teeth
and claws. . . . It is a gift to us from the wild.*

—Peter Levine, *Waking the Tiger: Healing Trauma*

The Academy granted us one rest day before marching to Jack's
Valley. Hundreds of military families in Colorado Springs volunteered to pick us up, feed us, and provide a phone and couch. My
volunteer "sponsor" family didn't serve steak and baked goods as
I had fantasized, but instead tofu and watermelon. Nevertheless, I
sometimes took a dozen or more chews, simply because I could,
because there wasn't anyone there to tell me I was a worthless human being for lacking the discipline to swallow each bite in less than
seven chews.

After lunch I sprawled out on a guest bed and took out my Bible
to once again flip through my photos. I compared two of the pictures taken of me at the airfield. The first picture had been snapped a
year earlier, after I soloed an airplane for the first time. My skin was
baby-like, even younger than seventeen. My wide smile exposed
almost all of my upper teeth. Wisps of hair that had fallen from my
ponytail were tucked behind my ears. I wore a red Abercrombie
sweater belonging to one of my guy friends, the long sleeves folded
at my wrists. I didn't know it then, but within a few days, the owner
of that sweater would become my first kiss. The second picture

was from only a month earlier, the day I passed my check ride to become a private pilot. My bloodshot eyes drooped. My oily skin was broken out. I had already chopped off my hair, and I wore blue athletic pants with the words "Air Force" written vertically. Moments earlier I became a licensed pilot, but I barely smiled. I liked to tell myself that what had happened to me in the year between those two pictures hadn't mattered, but the proof of my denial was there in my hands.

For the first picture I had been at Niagara Falls Air Reserve Station. It was July before my senior year, and I traveled there to upstate New York for a Civil Air Patrol, or CAP, flight academy. About 10 percent of my Academy classmates had also been in CAP, especially the women who couldn't join Boy Scouts, another program highly regarded by the Academy admissions boards. I had joined a new CAP squadron in my hometown during my freshman year and earned my way to become its cadet commander, and I hoped that through the organization I could earn my private pilot's license.

A few days into the flight academy, I watched from the backseat of a tiny Cessna as another student took his turn in front of the yoke. Jack looked lost among the panel of controls and instruments. He laughed nervously into his headset when he couldn't keep up with our instructor's commands. After the plane bounced back to the runway, our instructor soothed, "It'll come."

During my landing sequence, our instructor remained silent. I lowered the flaps, kept my airspeed low, made the radio calls, and finally lowered the wheels smoothly to the runway. "Perfect," our instructor said. Jack slammed his fist playfully into the backseat's blue vinyl. I couldn't tell if he liked or loathed that a girl could nail landings better than he could.

Our instructor left Jack and me to finish the postflight checklist, and Jack climbed up onto the wing's strut to reach across the front of the windshield to wipe off bugs. As he twisted back to me so that I could hand him the paper towels and Windex, he pulled his aviator sunglasses up over his blondish-brown hair. He winked. I couldn't help but smile. Until then, I hadn't dated. I told myself that boys didn't fit into my crammed schedule. I didn't acknowledge that until Jack, I didn't think anyone would like me enough. I trusted I could kick most guys' butts at anything from calculus to running a mile to landing an airplane. But dating one? I didn't know anything about looking cute or being girly.

Later that night in the base dining hall, Jack plopped down onto the cushioned bench across the table from me, next to my roommate. We chatted about upcoming tests as we ate. After we had cleared our plates, Jack pulled out a bag of M&M'S from the cargo pocket of his shorts and emptied it out onto the table. My roommate and I giggled as he wrote in the multicolored candy: "Lyn is a cute girl." He ran out and had to steal an *n* to finish the sentence. I stared at the M&M'S in shock while my roommate left us to be alone. Jack asked me questions about why I liked to fly, my goals, and my home life. By the time we had eaten all the M&M'S, the dining hall was empty. I wanted to play it cool, to pretend his interest didn't excite me as much as it did, but I smiled too much and gave myself away. Jack was the kind of popular kid who wouldn't know my name if we went to the same high school.

The next morning my instructor endorsed my black leather flight log book, signing permission for me to become the first student in the class to solo. As I waited for a massive C-130 to land in front of me, I tugged on the long sleeves of Jack's red Abercrombie sweater. Its smell of aftershave distracted me from the responsibility of flying by myself for the very first time.

Once the runway was clear, I maneuvered the Cessna at the end of it and pushed in the throttle. The airplane rolled faster and faster until I pulled back the yoke. When the wheels lost contact with the ground, my elation made me feel weightless. I loved that I sat alone at the controls of an airplane. I had never felt so powerful. I had never done anything so brave. I completed three laps around the airfield before returning to the ground where my instructor stood on the grass, waving his arms over his head. It wasn't until I reached him, when I stood on solid ground again and the adrenaline and fear pushed from my system, that I felt fully ecstatic, too. The Air Force pilots at the airfield with whom I flew were living my dream, and I saw myself becoming like them in a few short years. As I hopped out of the plane, Jack congratulated me.

That weekend we took a field trip to Niagara Falls. Jack and I followed behind the group, inches apart from one another, as we walked to a lookout deck. I leaned over the handrails and watched the water blast over the edge. The massiveness and intensity of the falls both amazed and scared me. Jack took my hand and led me away from the group. He slowly kissed me on the mouth. I didn't expect making out to feel so soft and tender. The longing that came with it surprised me. It wasn't enough for Jack's tongue to explore my mouth. I wanted him to explore all of me. For the first time ever, I felt beautiful and sexy. "We better get back," Jack said between kisses. I followed him back to the trail, my head fuzzy with feelings of which I hadn't known I was capable.

At the end of the two-week flight academy, Jack accompanied me on the airport shuttle, even though his mom would pick him up back at the base. I lived in Missouri, and he lived in Albany. I wanted to go to the Air Force Academy, and he wanted to enlist. We weren't likely to see each other again. Besides, it felt perfect to end our relationship while we still liked each other. While he still liked me. Jack and I kissed one last time before I walked into the terminal.

I was still thinking about Jack's kiss as my plane landed in Saint Louis, but Mom yanked away my attention. It wasn't Devoted Mom or Angry Mom waiting for me at the gate, but Helpless Mom. She cried for much of the hour and a half drive to our house in the country. She said of my stepdad, the Hobbit, "Pat won't let me go to the doctor anymore." Doctors had removed a foot-long, cancerous tumor from Mom's colon the year before. They had declared she was cancer free, but now she was bleeding again. She wiped the tears away from her eyes so that she could see to drive. I wanted to be back at Niagara, flying, not here with my mother, who seemed so obedient to a man. I couldn't help but judge her.

I finally said, "Mom, he can't keep you from going to the doctor." Then she told me he asked her to spell-check an obituary he wrote for her. For the first time since we started driving, I gave her my undivided attention. I couldn't imagine what she was saying could be true, that my stepdad could be *that* crazy.

"I'm afraid," Mom said.

"You need to kick him out."

"I can't do that."

"Yes you can, Mom. You have to. And if you don't, I won't go to the student council retreat this weekend." I was supposed to be leaving for four days to lead the retreat. My threat was a trump card; if her husband's threat was costing me in my school career, Devoted Mom would do what she needed.

Mom changed the locks, filed a restraining order, contacted a lawyer, and called my middle sister, who lived two hours away. Megan came immediately. "I'm sorry I let that man come between us," Mom told Megan. We had missed Megan's wedding and her white-coat ceremony marking her entrance to medical school, but now I had my sister back. Megan and I had the same cheek bones, brown hair, and smiles. If Megan could follow her dreams, could start medical school even while she dated her now husband, a half-Thai man whom our stepdad had denigrated, then maybe I could be successful, too.

As I began my senior year of high school, I maintained focus on my perfect GPA; the Academy admissions package, including applying for Congressional nominations; and my private pilot's license. I woke early to finish homework, ran with the cross-country team after school, and often stayed up late to write papers. Twice a week, I went to the Saint Louis airfield to take instructions from a local CAP instructor. All the busyness distracted me from the divorce and the cancer scare.

After a weekly CAP meeting in October, instead of eating at Steak 'n Shake with my squadron, I went home to study. I blasted the sound track to *Top Gun* as I pulled onto the dark country highway. A truck's taller headlights approached in my rearview mirror. The reflection burned my eyes. I slowed down to let the truck pass, but it didn't. I sped back up, but the blinding headlights stayed so bright I needed to adjust my mirrors. Making my usual two turns through my small town, I followed another windy country highway, and told myself it was a coincidence that the headlights stayed behind me—but the pit in my stomach knew better. After twenty minutes and two turns, the headlights remained. I punched off the stereo. I drove past my house to loop around the neighborhood. Houses became scarcer, and it was just me in my car, the woods, and the blinding lights. After three circles through empty roads, I didn't have a choice but to park in my own driveway. I pulled in and waited, doors locked, hoping the headlights would pass without stopping. In the side mirror I watched my stepdad's red Toyota roll past the house, illuminated by the porch light. I had never been so afraid of my stepdad.

Since Mom kicked Pat out and changed the locks, he had been disturbing us nearly every day. He left a note in the mailbox threatening to burn down the house if Mom didn't give in to him. Sometimes I could tell Pat had been in my car while I was at school because of the way my CDs were rearranged. When it snowed I woke up to find his footprints in fresh powder in front of all the windows, including those for my bedroom. I had lived with Pat since the age of nine. While I thought he was repulsive and crazy, I never thought he would hurt me—until I saw the print of a man's boot a few feet from where I slept.

The police said that, despite the restraining order, they couldn't do anything without proof. As Pat crept by the house in his red Toyota, I knew there wasn't anything I could do to keep him from following me again.

The next week after the CAP meeting, while the other kids filed past me to their cars, I hesitated before walking to mine.

"What's wrong?" Colonel Thomas asked. Arthur Thomas was my flight instructor, a man with whom I squeezed into a Cessna twice a week. He was a Vietnam veteran and a high-ranking CAP officer. The other adults told me I was lucky—he was the best flight instructor.

"It's my stepdad."

Thomas was tall enough that when I explained, I had to look upward into his eyes, hidden behind wire-rim glasses so large they covered half his cheeks. Thomas offered to follow me home, then pick me up and take me both ways starting the week after.

As we drove, Thomas asked about my stepdad. "He's pissed because Mom kicked him out of the house."

"What about your real dad?"

"He's in Colorado. Mom left him and took us with her when I was five. I haven't talked to him since before high school."

"He doesn't know how successful you are, does he?" The reference to my achievements felt nice.

"Nope, I guess he doesn't," I said.

"That's too bad. He has a lot to be proud of."

Even though his car was dirty and smelled like old coffee, I liked Colonel Thomas taking me to meetings each week. Thomas was a pilot and an Air Force veteran—exactly what I wanted to become. Between weekly CAP meetings, lessons at the airfield, and attending an aviation class he taught at a Saint Louis community college, I saw more of Thomas than I did any of my friends. He knew more about my life than anyone, too. He knew little details like how I did on school tests. He even knew about my frustrations with my volatile mother.

Thomas's wife was an airline pilot who traveled often, and his adult daughter hardly spoke to him, so sometimes Mom invited Thomas over for dinner. He was fifty-three, just a few years older than Mom. I liked it when the three of us ate together; I could almost imagine him becoming my stepdad.

I had known Thomas for six months when he took me to his company picnic at Boeing. His invitation was a celebration, he said, because I completed the Academy's long application process. The company tarmac was filled with jets. Colonel Thomas and I sat on the ground next to my favorite, the F-22 Raptor, and ate hamburgers from paper plates on our laps. The unusually warm November sun had heated the asphalt under my legs. Thomas put his arm around my shoulders. I flinched, not used to anyone touching me. Once three years earlier, my softball coach patted my arm after a winning game, and I startled.

"Just trying to say congratulations," my coach had said, confused by my reaction. But even though I was startled by contact, I longed for it, too. It was my "little-girl me," that part of me I hadn't ever let anyone see, the part of me who crawled into my giant teddy bear's lap, who craved it. On the tarmac I let Thomas's arm settle across my shoulders.

"You know, I care about you," Thomas said. "I love you like you were my own daughter." I stared down at the asphalt under my knees.

"I love you, too," I said, still looking down.

"I know you miss having a dad. I hope I can help you with the kinds of things you need a dad for."

I rested my head on his shoulder. "Will you always feel this way? I mean, ever after I leave for the Academy?"

"I'll feel this way forever, just like you were my own daughter. If it would help you remember, you could call me Dad if you wanted."

No one had ever known about the part of me beneath my ambitious front that longed for affection. It felt too good to be true. "Okay, Dad," I said.

After the Boeing picnic I saw Thomas even more frequently. He came with my mom when I needed knee surgery. When I woke from anesthesia, he surprised me with a stuffed dog. Thomas told me I could accomplish anything. He told me that I was funny and beautiful. He hugged me a lot. I went from never receiving affection to having it as often as I wanted. Plus, he was as steady and constant as the math and physics I studied; he never flipped from devoted to angry.

To celebrate my Academy acceptance, he gave me diamond earrings that I would be allowed to wear with my uniform. I wasn't the kind of girl who liked flashy jewelry, but I liked his thoughtfulness and the idea of taking the earrings with me. They were a reminder of Thomas's intangible gift: the knowledge that I could have both a career *and* people in my life who cared for me. I was loveable as much as I was successful.

The day before New Year's Eve, Mom called the police when we again woke to fresh footprints in the snow. The mumbling policeman who stood in our family room said—again—he couldn't verify that the footprints belonged to my stepdad and that the only way they could press charges was if we had evidence of the restraining order violation. After he left, Mom asked what he said. She hadn't been able to read the policeman's lips. I answered, "They need proof."

Mom walked out the front door and sat on the edge of the front porch, bundled only in a sweater, her red plaid slippers pressed against snow. I didn't know what advice to give. So I called the only person I knew who could help: my adopted dad. Thomas came over that night with three video cameras. He and I set up each one in a different window of the house, hoping to catch Pat. Mom cooked upstairs as we arranged the last camera in the guest bedroom in the basement. Thomas flipped off the light and we waited for it to capture a few minutes of tape to confirm that it wasn't just picking up a reflection in the window.

I sat on the bed to wait, looking outside at the oak trees lit up by the back porch light. Was my stepdad beyond the light, in the dark woods, watching us? Thomas stood next to me and put a hand on my back. Mom always needed me to be strong, but with Thomas, it was okay for me to admit that I was scared. I rose to kneel on the bed so that I could hug him. He squeezed me, and I hid my face into his collared shirt, as if I were five rather than seventeen. Ever since we ate lunch on the tarmac at his company picnic, I felt like I finally had a second parent, a loving and stable one.

Thomas's hot fingers pressed against the bare skin of my sides, just above my hips. Then he slid his hand under my shirt. His hand isn't really against my skin, I told myself, while he worked his hands higher and higher. His hand isn't really that close to my bra, I told myself next. I didn't believe the messages my body sent my brain as his fingers slid between my skin and my bra's underwire; I didn't believe he was actually touching my breast. I trusted him more than I believed my own skin's sensations.

His fingers moved downward, inside my sweatpants and underwear. Maybe he doesn't realize where his hand is, I thought. "What are you doing?" I finally said. His hand stopped moving and pressed against my hip.

"I love you so much. I just want to be closer to you."

My mind couldn't process what was happening. I liked being close to him, too, but I didn't want him to touch me like that. Dads weren't supposed to touch daughters inside their bras and underwear.

"Dad, I don't want you to do that." My voice came out in a soft but firm whisper. Thomas didn't listen. His hand went the rest of the way down my underwear. He pushed his fingers against me. Bile flooded my stomach. I couldn't move any of my limbs; my body felt like it didn't belong to me. My hands, the only muscles in my body seemingly able to fire, wound my fingers into fists around his collar. The rest of me felt paralyzed.

I heard my mom's footsteps coming down the stairs. Each was slow and heavy. Her announcement that dinner was ready would make him stop. Her silhouette appeared in the doorway, but the only lights came from the hallway behind her and the porch light that shone through the window, so I couldn't clearly see her face. She stood still, staring at us, at our bodies pressed into one another at the foot of the bed. Say something, Mom, I plead silently. I wanted her to scream at him. Say something, Mom, I plead again in my mind. Say anything. But she remained quiet. Then she turned around and walked away. It wasn't until her footsteps resumed on the stairs that Thomas removed his hand from inside my underwear. Thomas didn't say anything as he rewound the video camera, checked to make sure it was recording, and led me up the stairs.

Thomas sat at the head of our dining table, and Mom served our plates. Mom asked him about work. He began discussing a project in a calm, steady voice while Mom uh-huh'd and laughed. I picked at the mashed potato and beef casserole, my best attempt at mimicking the adults who pretended nothing had just happened.

The next night, I went to a friend's house to celebrate New Year's. I curled into a couch corner as the girls talked about friends, colleges, siblings. I didn't care about any of these things anymore. I felt separate from their conversations and from our inside jokes. Something changed. In one small moment in the basement of my home, I crossed over into a world that no one else could reach. But at the time I didn't think of it that way. I couldn't name why I felt so alone and different. Watching the ball drop over Times Square and the year—2001—light the screen, I reflected on the months to come. I was about to turn eighteen, graduate, and launch my adult life, becoming a cadet and beginning my career as a pilot and astronaut. The year 2001, my space odyssey, when I would steer my life in the direction I wanted: up.

Curled on my friend's couch, I remembered listening to the hum of a Cessna's single engine, feeling the yoke's smooth black plastic under my fingertips. The memory reminded me I was brave. I was strong. I thought of the times in my childhood when I failed to speak up for myself. When I was in second grade and my teacher, irritated with incessant requests to use the bathroom, warned that none of us would be allowed to go again until lunch, I wet my pants rather than risk my teacher screaming at me like Mom yelled.

I could solve problems for myself now. All I needed to do was talk to Thomas, to Dad, and he would listen. Of course he would.

I'm seventeen now, I told myself as I watched the New Year's celebration on my friend's TV. Time to be an adult. Time to verbalize my needs. I decided that when I saw Dad for our flight lesson, I would be honest. The next morning as I drove, I rehearsed what I would say to Thomas. "I love you like you are my dad, not like a boyfriend," I said over and over out loud. I planned to meet Thomas at his house, our usual meeting spot, because it was between mine and the airport. When I got there his garage door opened. He stood in the back, wearing worn, black sweatpants, waving me to pull in with two hands, directing my car like planes are directed on a tarmac. I did as he ordered, not questioning why he wanted me to park in the garage or why he was wearing sweatpants rather than our CAP uniform. He took my hand to lead me straight through his house to his bedroom. Like a puppy on a leash, I followed him without a single protest. All of the blinds were closed and the room was dark. He sat down on the king-sized bed that he shared with his wife and motioned for me to sit next to him. Still obedient, I sat. He hugged me sideways.

Finally I said, "I want you to always be like my dad, as you promised, not something else." I breathed in relief. I had said it. He wouldn't touch me again.

"You know I love you, too, don't you? Don't you know that I love you?"

"Yeah, I do. But I want you to be like my dad."

"I can still be a dad to you, Lynn. Nothing is going to change that." He put his arm around me, squeezing out my relief. He tugged at the zipper on my blue, CAP-issued flight suit.

"Not even *this*?" I said while he continued to work the zipper. "I love you like you were my dad," I said my rehearsed line again.

Thomas stood and walked out of the room. I heard a door slide open down the hall, then his footsteps coming near again. When he returned he held a small gun. He pulled my wrist toward him. His other hand placed the ivory handle in my now open palm.

The gun said, I dare you to do something. My pulse pounded through my limbs as I thought of its bullets. Everything clenched— my jaw, my legs, even my toes curled under themselves. In the palm of my hand, I had the power to stop Thomas from hurting me again. But my hand stayed open, my fingers unwilling to touch the handle. Gripping the gun would be threatening the only consistent love I had ever known. Thomas and I both stared at the gun idle in my palm.

He yanked the gun away and returned it to his closet, almost as if to say, "See? I knew you were too weak to stop me." I wasn't angry with Thomas for putting the gun in my hand. I was ashamed because of my inability to help myself. I was as feeble as my mother was. The version of me who had soloed a plane was a fake. The real me was the little girl who once peed all over her blue chair in second grade, a puddle forming at her feet.

I lay motionless as Thomas took off my clothes and tore into my body with his fingers. I began to feel like I did when my mom yelled at me. There were two of me, the girl Thomas groped and the girl who felt fear and betrayal. The girl who felt the pain didn't live inside me, but rather someplace far, far away.

By the time he took off his own clothes, I felt lifeless, as if nothing in the world could ever shock or disgust or make me happy again. "I can't have an erection anymore," he said. He guided my fingers to wrap around his limp penis. I felt like I was in kindergarten at Halloween, when the teacher put a blindfold around my eyes and led my hand into different bowls of squiggly worms and squishy spiders, and I was supposed to trust them that it was all pretend and wouldn't hurt me. He pulled my body on top of his and toward his penis. "Suck it," he said. When I hesitated he used his palm to easily push my head toward his groin.

I tried not to look at his penis as I put it inside of my mouth, turning my face away from his so that he couldn't see me gag. Even though he couldn't get hard, it filled my mouth like a rotten piece of meat that I couldn't spit out. He moaned and at first, I didn't understand why hot, sticky goo covered my tongue, not knowing that it was possible for men to ejaculate without an erection. "I love you so much, little girl. I love you so much."

After Thomas put the gun in my hand, telling on him would have equally exposed me for my own inaction. He had given me the gun, not threatened me with it. If I felt so afraid, why hadn't I used it to get out of his house and away from him?

From that point on Thomas began touching me or forcing my mouth to his penis nearly every time I saw him. He couldn't have an erection, but when he took off my clothes, he would rub his penis against me, between my legs, like he could will it to penetrate me. After he finished I reached for my clothes as quickly as possible.

His cluttered dark bedroom made me feel claustrophobic, and once, when I was in a hurry to breathe fresh air, I forgot my barrette that I had set on his nightstand. I didn't remember it until we were fifteen minutes down the highway. "Dad, I left my barrette in your bedroom," I said. I still called him Dad, that's how screwed up I was. That's how badly I wanted to cling to his love. The sex wasn't a big deal, I told myself.

But the barrette was a big deal. Without talking or looking at me, he turned around at the next exit and drove back to the house. He ordered me to stay put and slammed the door so hard that the Bronco rocked. He returned and plopped the barrette, with stick figures of girls and the word "Friends," into my hands. "Do you realize what you could have done to me?" he screamed. I really didn't. I couldn't think outside of myself to wonder what his wife would do if she found the barrette. I could only think of my shame. It was the first time Thomas was furious with me, and I felt his anger like stabs into my chest.

Back at home, I collapsed into my bed and pulled the comforter over my head. When I got up in the morning, it was like a part of me stayed curled between the flannel sheets while a ghost version of me walked around my high school. As the days turned into weeks, I morphed into more and more of a zombie. I didn't talk to friends or raise my hand in class. I kept my straight A's despite not studying. But when I stopped working out, I went from being able to run for miles and do a fair number of push-ups to none at all.

I have few memories from those months: a tiny portion of my history professor's lecture to which I managed to listen, a rush of embarrassment after gym class because I suddenly didn't want the other girls to see me naked, a moment during which I stood in front of my locker, unable to think through which books I needed for my next class. But I can't reconcile the girl in any of those memories with the girl Thomas molested. After the first time, I hadn't been able to stop thinking of Thomas's fingers in a desperate attempt to make sense of what he did. But in the months that followed I didn't dwell on the sex at all, as if I understood somewhere deep within that I couldn't face what was happening to me. I wasn't sure why I couldn't focus in class, or why I couldn't engage with my friends' attempts at conversation, or why I dressed in as many layers as I could so that no one would see my bare skin. I didn't connect those new problems with my "dad's" violations.

Each time I let Thomas touch me, the secret multiplied. The longer I went without telling someone, the more I had to confess. Someone would want to know why I had let him do this to me again and again and again, and I wouldn't know how to answer them. Plus, if Thomas had become so angry over my barrette, what would he do if someone found out about us? What would he do to me? I couldn't tell anyone. Ever. I would graduate high school, and once I was at the Academy, I'd be away from Thomas. I'd be safe from him there.

By the third month of sex with Thomas, my body went numb. Lightness replaced the aching in my jaw. Wherever Thomas touched me on my skin, I couldn't feel it. If I closed my eyes, I could believe he wasn't in contact with me at all. He touched me, and my mind took me someplace else. It wasn't that I fantasized about hiding in a field of flowers and butterflies, it was just that I stopped thinking and feeling. For those hours I didn't exist at all.

I felt detached from my body long after I was safe in my bedroom again. When I showered I didn't realize the water was too hot until my skin turned red. A few times I nearly wet my pants because I hadn't processed the sensation of needing to urinate. I rarely retained the information during my flight lessons that I needed to progress toward my license. Of those months, I don't have a single memory of flying an airplane.

But the memories of being stuck in Thomas's bedroom or the airplane hangar's frigid concrete ground remained fresh even more than six months later. The pain remained evident on my face in the picture I held. I tucked the picture away into one of the last pages of the Bible. In only a few hours, I would return to the Academy for my march to Jack's Valley, and I needed to remember the strength of the younger me, the me who hadn't been forced to have sex, the me who only saw the world in terms of its possibilities.

CHAPTER 5
_____

They are going to yell in your face. Loudly. You are going to be
criticized more harshly than you can ever imagine. . . . They will
take away your freedom. All of it. You will have to perform like a
robot. You will do everything they tell you to do, when they tell you
to do it, no matter how stupid or irrelevant or trivial or silly the
tasks seem. There will be no questioning of their orders.

—William L. Smallwood,
The Air Force Academy Candidate Book, 3rd ed.

That night after our visit to local families' homes, Cadet Garcia escorted us to our dining tables. Then he vanished. The entire class of
1,200 basic cadets—minus the dozens who had already quit—stood
at attention waiting for the new set of cadre. At my table none of
my eight classmates dared to fidget. I hadn't heard such silence since
arriving at the Academy. Seconds turned to minutes. My stomach
had pangs in it that had nothing to do with mealtime hunger.

Heavy boot steps thundered into Mitchell Hall. Four cadre in
BDU uniforms, all men, appeared at our table. They screamed a litany
of demands and questions: "Recite the code of conduct!" "Pour my
drinks!" "What's my name?" All at once, the uncomfortably quiet hall
transformed into a madhouse. Cadre yelled louder than I had heard
since our first few days of Basic Cadet Training. Between the nine
of us, we scrambled to keep up with our new cadre's demands, even
though we could hardly understand them over the raucousness.

Cadre corrected my classmates for taking too many chews, utiliz-
ing too much of their chair, not placing their utensils in the correct
order on their plate, and any other detail they could nitpick. Each
time someone at our table was corrected, we all stopped chewing.

As we stood from the table to march back to our dorm room, one of our new cadre approached me. "Miller, you're the one who's not going to survive Jack's, right?" The other cadre laughed. My former cadre had singled me out to the new set. An hour: that's how long it took to become my new cadre's target. In the previous few days, I had snuck a long shower, eaten a candy bar with my classmates on top of the LZ, and used an actual telephone to call home. None of that mattered now.

The next morning I sweated in the long sleeves of my thick BDUs, waiting to march the five miles to Jack's Valley. I stood at attention in a long formation that stretched across the Terrazzo. My M14 rifle, the firing pin removed, rested across my right shoulder. The top three-star Academy general led the formation down the Terrazzo's ramp. To the beat of drums, we marched through the tunnel that bore the words "Bring Me Men" engraved at the top, though with my eyes caged, I couldn't see them. My rifle bounced against my collarbone. We turned off the main road and marched deep into the woods. My legs fatigued, but I willed them to continue. During a rest break halfway, I gulped warm water from the canteen slung around my waist, but my mouth still felt dry. My eyes burned from squinting against the sun. The paved road turned to dirt and eventually we came to a large wooden sign that proclaimed Welcome to Jack's Valley. The dirt under my feet turned to a thin powder. My skin felt gritty, a combination of sweat and dirt.

Tent raising and equipment issue took all afternoon. I received a cot, a sleeping bag, and a trunk. Our squadron of basic cadets divided into three ten-person tents: two for the men and one for the seven of us women, which we shared with a few women from another squadron. A grid of permanent wood walkways connected the rows of tents.

At dinner we loaded our plates in the buffet line, not worrying about remembering protocol. We sat at attention, but not the kind of strict position to which we had grown accustomed. Uninterrupted, I piled food into my mouth. I had heard commanders wanted the rules during meals in Jack's Valley to be softer because, with so much more physical training, our bodies would require far more calories. Each bite of food I enjoyed reminded me that there would be a price for this luxury.

As the sun set, we changed into blue athletic shorts, USAFA T-shirts, and flip-flops to go to the showers. Instead of having only three minutes, cadre granted us thirty and left the seven of us women on our own to find the shower house. We marched gleefully unattended along the dirt road.

The shower house was so packed I could only open its door partially until a few women on the other side moved. Only three showerheads were open. Jo and I took turns rinsing along with Charlotte—Charlie, for short, who bunked next to me in our tent—while we tried to respect each other's privacy. The water was frigid. My lungs refused to breathe in air as long as the coldness battered my scalp, so I could only rinse for a few seconds at a time. As I tugged my clothes back on, I still felt sticky with soap. We ran in a single file back to our tent. Dirt caked my damp feet and ankles on the way.

Clattering on metal trash can lids catapulted me awake the next morning. The loud cacophony sounded like one of the cadre banged one right next to my head on the other side of the tent wall. "You have three minutes, basics!"

I rushed out of my sleeping bag that I had cinched up to my chin. I slept wearing my BDUs, so I only needed to put on my combat boots, tie them, and correctly roll my sleeping bag into a canoe shape in the dark. Charlie finished seconds before me. Then we sprinted down the wooden walkway to meet our male classmates in front of their tent. We arrived first.

"Feed your faces!" Cadet Pratt, the new squadron commander, yelled. Pratt was tall and stocky, with cheeks that made him look like a chipmunk. We dropped to our hands and toes for push-ups, flipping our rifles so that they rested on the top of our hands and not in the dirt.

"Sir, we are waiting for our classmates!" the seven of us women yelled in high-pitched voices. "Sir, we are waiting for our classmates!" We did push-up after push-up. The guys' tent stayed quiet.

But instead of harassing the men to hurry up, the cadre circled around us women. My rifle rolled from the tops of my fingers and into the dirt powder.

"Miller, get your rifle off the ground!" Another yelled, "lower!" evidently thinking we weren't doing the push-ups well enough. As usual, my back sagged and my arms nearly gave out. I was already spent by the time the men streamed out of their tent in masse.

"Up!" Cadet Pratt yelled. I jumped to my feet and struggled to catch my breath. "Form up!"

We hurried into a rectangular formation and rearranged so that the taller were in front, our usual protocol. I ended up in the back row, on the end, by most of the women and a few shorter guys.

"I wanna be an Air Force pilot," Cadet Pratt sang as we began running away from the tent city. The chant to help us stay in step was called a jody. Our left foot hit the ground on the heavy syllables he emphasized.

"I wanna be an Air Force pilot," we echoed together.

"I wanna fly that F-16," he continued.

"I wanna fly that F-16," we echoed again.

"I wanna fly with the canopy open . . . just to hear them commies scream."

Once we ran a mile or so away from the tent city, another cadre asked if we wanted to learn a new jody. We listened and echoed as one of the shorter cadre sang about Yogi Bear stealing a jar of honey from Boo Boo. I imagined this cadet with a bow tie and how he would look just like Boo Boo. Instead of echoing, we all laughed together, even the cadre, making me feel like we were momentarily on the same team.

"How about a song we can't sing in the middle of Jack's Valley," Cadet Wilson said when we had stopped laughing. Cadet Wilson, one of the senior cadre, was tall and had squinty eyes. "Hey, mamacita," he sang.

"Hey, mamacita," we echoed, still running in step down a dirt road that twisted through the forest, now becoming light with the rising sun.

"I wish that all the ladies . . ."

"I wish that all the ladies . . ."

"Were bricks in a pile," he sang and then we repeated. "And I was a mason . . . I'd lay them all in style." I didn't process the song's meaning at first. He continued, "I wish that all the ladies . . . were holes in the road . . . and I was a dump truck . . . I'd fill 'em with my load." The men laughed. The song shocked me. I looked at the woman next to me, but in the early light, I couldn't tell if she was as disgusted as I was. "I wish all the ladies . . . were statues of Venus . . . and I was a sculptor . . . I'd break 'em with my . . ." He didn't finish that sentence. I noticed that the other male cadre like Boo Boo Bear and Pratt didn't sing along with him, but they didn't stop him, either. "You fe-males in the back, louder," he screamed. Cadet Wilson had a funny way of saying "females" so that it was two words. It felt as though instead of saying "fee" and then "male," he was really saying "not male," marking women as different, as less. I mumbled along with the jody, as ordered. I didn't have a choice, and rationalized they were just words, anyway.

We ran until the sky turned a lighter blue before we began to circle back around to our tents. My rifle grew heavier and heavier in my hands, and it dropped to waist level. "Get your rifle up, Miller! Stop being weak!" The rifle only weighed a few pounds, but my shoulders throbbed. Distance grew between my row and those in front, but I couldn't lengthen my stride, and neither could a few of my classmates to my side. Charlie was one row ahead, and she held her rifle high, taking long, solid steps.

"Miller, you're really struggling with that rifle, huh?" one of the male cadre asked as he jogged next to me. He convinced me that he wanted to help me by carrying it, and after passing the rifle, he yelled, "Look what I have!"

"Woo-hoo!" they cheered. I realized the seriousness of my mistake. Cadet Pratt halted the squadron, and all five of the cadre came running toward me. I locked my eyes on Charlie's short brown hair as they all started yelling at me.

"Miller, are you some kind of pathetic baby who needs someone to carry her rifle for her?" "Are you really that broken?" "If you were in combat, would you need a buddy to bail you out then, too?" "You want to be an officer in the United States Air Force, and you can't even run with a rifle?"

Back at home, when Mom yelled at me, I had become practiced at picking out something to stare at and not responding to her
insults. I remembered the time I was fourteen and she found out I
was friends with a boy my Hobbit stepdad called "nigger," and she
slapped me. Even as my cheek stung, I kept my eyes focused on the
leafy wallpaper pattern on the kitchen wall—intricate vines against
a cream color—still not acknowledging her. The better I got at not
responding, the more I won. It made me feel stronger than her, and
without an emotional reaction, Mom couldn't respond. It was the
last time Mom slapped me.

The cadre were the same way. Other basics would tear up or answer in shaky voices whenever they were singled out. I refused to be
like them. I wasn't about to let them see my embarrassment. While
all five cadre flung different insults at me, I kept my eyes locked on
the back of Charlie's head and my mouth shut. Without a reaction,
the cadre's anger deflated. I won the battle, just as I had with Mom.

Realizing my power in not giving cadre an emotional response,
I worked even harder to remain stoic. Eventually they stopped tar-
geting me as much and moved on to Fatty Hughes or Ben Crocker,
the skinny, weak boy nicknamed Betty Crocker. When cadre yelled
at them, both tended to develop cracked, high-pitched voices. I
wasn't the only one who was struggling.

While I had found a way to outmaneuver the cadre, I still needed to
complete a required series of obstacle courses, all of which would be
physically demanding even for the stronger basic cadets. Twice a day
cadre marched us to one of the many courses—the Assault Course,
Obstacle Course, Leadership Reaction Course.

The Assault Course was the most notorious and had a fixed staff
different than our usual cadre, plucked mostly from the Academy
football team. When we were in earshot marching toward the Assault Course, my classmates started chanting: "A-Course is a gay
course. A-Course is a gay course." One of the cadre had coached
us that the expression was a tradition to express a lack of fear and
intimidation. I found the words offensive, and I didn't think I was in
a position to belittle a course that cadre had warned me would "tear

me apart." But in keeping with the pretend-to-go-along-with-it, even-though-I-don't-agree mindset, I mumbled the words anyway. A tall, burly guy at the front of our formation shouted through a megaphone, "The affirmative on this course is 'assault course, sir.'" In other words, that's how we were to say yes. "Do you understand me, basics?"

We answered, "Assault course, sir."

Sirens wailed. I wore a clunky Kevlar helmet and a blue mouth guard as I followed my classmates under the sign that read Welcome to Hell's Half Acre. Thick mud already coated my BDUs from an earlier beat session, and my arms ached as I carried my rifle high over my head. More burly cadre in BDUs funneled my classmates and me into two-foot high barbed-wire chutes that led up a long hill. I followed the heels of the muddy boots in front of me as I used my forearms to drag my body. Fake bombs exploded hazy, red gas. The cadre stood to the sides, pilling sand on top of us as an extra hurdle. The sand clung to my wet, dirt-covered face while more of it landed on my back.

On the other side of the tunnel, a group of us gathered around a linebacker who wore a blue beret, like all cadre, and had his foot casually propped on a log. He blew a whistle every few seconds, signaling us to do an up-down, and I crashed my body into the ground, bashing my chest and shoulders, only to pop back up and continue running in place. The classmate to my right collapsed, his helmet slamming against the dirt. Was it exhaustion? Or heat? Medics with crosses on their sleeves came running. Ordinarily I would be worried about someone who had just passed out, but just now I was only relieved that it wasn't me showing signs of weakness.

"Crawl through my tunnel," a cadre yelled when I reached his station. Sliding on my stomach, my elbows drove me through the sand. I carried the ends of my rifle in my hands, trying to keep it clean. The sand clung to me, making me heavier, and making it harder to move forward. I made slow progress up the long hill. Bombs exploded again to my side. My ears rang and red smoke filled the tunnel. Unable to see, the barrel of my rifle tangled in the netting over my head just as the sirens that indicated the end of the course wailed in the distance. The harder I tried to free my weapon, the more entangled it became. To my side, my classmate kept crawling, and I found myself in violation of a cardinal rule: never be alone. "What's wrong with you, basic?" the cadre screamed when he saw my predicament. "Can't you get out, fe-male?" He pronounced it just like Cadet Wilson, the guy with the squinty eyes who liked to sing misogynistic jodies. I hated how they called me out, not as a basic, as they did the men, but as a female, like that was my entire identity—like my being "fe-male" was the reason my rifle was tangled. I heard the boot falls of other cadre escorting basic cadets back to the base of the hill, but I still couldn't budge. More cadre rushed toward me. One of them finally bent down and with one swift move freed my rifle.

"Get up, basic!" They hovered around me as I carried my rifle high over my head. I joined another lone woman whom I didn't know, and they led us slowly down the hill. She and I glanced at each other, our eyes connecting in camaraderie. "If either of you drop your weapon, we'll start back at the top of the hill," one of them warned. My arms burned, and I could barely hold my rifle. But I held it high above my head until I passed under the entrance sign that read Only the Strong Survive.

That night I woke up with a startle. My toes and hands were nearly numb with cold, but my hair dripped with sweat. My elbows hurt. I realized I was on the floor on the tent's far side. I had so much anxiety about my physical performance, I had been low crawling in my sleep. Plus, the memories of Thomas's penis shoved in my mouth felt fresh in my mind, as if it had just happened not months but minutes earlier. The nightmares about him had stopped after I became a cadet, but the next night, I woke once again with the memory of him at the forefront of my thoughts.

Fear combined with the physical discomforts of Basic Cadet Training to make me miserable. I chilled at night after the sun dipped behind the mountains, but during the day, I baked. Under the frigid shower, I failed at getting the chunks of dirt off of my scalp. We only had four issued black T-shirts to go under our BDU tops, and we sacrificed two at a time to the mail-out laundry service.

I wore the same T-shirt three or four days in a row. We all stunk. I was so hungry, even bugs looked appetizing. My muscles screamed at me when I rolled off the cot in the morning. My arms and legs quivered while sitting during meals. The accumulated exhaustion of being beat nearly all day was worsened by sleeping what I guessed was six hours at night. But my classmates grew fatigued, too. I could tell by the way they also seemed to be in a fog. None of us were becoming stronger; often we did fewer consecutive push-ups before we all were "broken" and various parts of our bodies fell into the powdery dirt. The cadre now had plenty of people to chastise for being weak.

My refuge was mail call. Day after day I collected a stack of notes from my sister Megan and my high school friends, reminding me to stay tough. Each minute I survived, I came closer to graduating Basic Cadet Training. Though our squadron had lost only one—a guy who received news that his girlfriend was pregnant—many squadrons had already lost many.

The cadre, I had realized, were as sleep deprived and exhausted as we were. They too were counting days until it was over. Their daily fuel: mocking us. Some pranks were harmless. Once, while we waited in formation for dinner, a higher-ranking woman cadre singled me out: "Basic Cadet Miller," Cadet Logan said.

"Yes, ma'am," I answered.

Logan was short and petite but had a louder voice than many of the cadre. I hadn't ever seen Logan insult anyone, and I respected her for it. "You have up dog on your shirt," she noted, pointing at my chest. I looked down at my BDU blouse but didn't see anything.

"Ma'am, what is up dog?" As soon as I said it, I realized the set up. My face flushed.

"Am I your buddy, huh, Basic Cadet Miller?" She pretended to scream but then roared with laughter as did everyone else. Logan slapped me on the back. She just wanted to make us all laugh. I didn't feel like the butt of her joke.

But that's exactly how I felt when cadre made us carry sandbags to a hill off to the side of the tent city. Cadre broke open sandbags and made a beach on top of the pine needles. The next time we didn't have anywhere to be, they lined us up at the bottom of the hill. "The affirmative on this course is 'Golf Course, sir.' Do you understand me, basics?" We barked, "Golf Course, sir." I guessed that they named it the Golf Course to mimic a sand trap. We low crawled around the track they had created: up the hill, around a circuit that included tunnels and moguls, and back down the hill, only to repeat the cycle immediately.

Cadet Wilson loved taking us to the Golf Course more than most. He screamed at one of my classmates: "Basic Cadet Lake, are you having fun yet?"

"Golf Course, sir!"

"Let's have some more fun, 'K? Open your eyes and mouth as wide as you can!" I was two basic cadets behind her on a curve, so I saw clearly as Tiffany Lake opened her mouth just as he kicked a pile of sand at her. She rolled on her side, coughing and spitting up while Wilson laughed. I noticed Wilson only kicked sand on us women. "Gentlemen, the fe-males of the unit are slowing you down once again," Wilson said often to the men, whether it was true or not. He kept his mouth shut during the times it was the women waiting for the men.

The night after Wilson kicked sand on Tiffany, the six other women whispered in our tent. "It's not okay how Wilson singles us out," Tiffany said. She came from a rich Texan family and wore Victoria's Secret lingerie, which by this time was all stained with mud. Rachel said we should do something. I didn't think what Wilson did was okay, either, but I had expected to put up with crap; we were all miserable, and if we wanted to survive, we had to outlast the kids who couldn't handle it. I was already a target because I was physically weak and didn't want to be the one who complained. But as much as I wanted to stay quiet, I respected the other women and their strength, especially Rachel and Charlie. These women were tough, independent, and smart, not like the women from the squadron with whom we shared a tent: the ones who cried at night, whined, and pretended to be injured. So if Rachel and Charlie thought that speaking up about Wilson was the right thing to do, I'd follow them, even though I suspected it would be futile.

The next morning we asked the most decent cadre, the guy who reminded me of Boo Boo Bear, if we could talk to him. "We don't like how Wilson treats us," Rachel shared. "We don't like how he calls us fe-males and berates us, and how he kicks sand on us, especially, when he kicked sand in Tiffany's face." We all turned to Tiffany's still-red eyes.

Boo Boo stared at us with wide eyes, like he couldn't believe our audacity. It probably sounded ridiculous that we were complaining about how someone pronounced the word "female." But it was offensive, and not just to me. I had developed a visceral reaction to being called "fe-male," a tightening and sickness in my gut. Besides, the sand in Tiffany's eyes could have hurt her eyesight, which could cost her a pilot slot. "Look, ladies," Boo Boo answered in a gentle voice. "There are just some guys here who are that way. Ignore them." His comment made me first realize that some men at the Academy didn't want women present.

We did our best to ignore the slights and didn't talk about Wilson again.

There was one final course I needed to complete to graduate: the Obstacle Course. The thirty-five of us would be timed as a unit. I imagined that for the stronger kids crawling along logs, climbing towers, and swinging jungle-style across muddy ponds could be exhilarating. But I worried that I would slow my classmates so badly that they would resent me for it. The sirens wailed, and most of my classmates ran toward the first obstacle, leaving me, Fatty Hughes, and Betty Crocker in the back. We waited for them to shimmy across rolling logs before moving onto the next. Our line of classmates spread out among the obstacles, the guys in the lead surging ahead, while those of us in the back dragged.

About halfway through the course, I crawled behind Betty Crocker in a sand tunnel covered with barbed wire. He wiggled and rolled from elbow to elbow, barely making progress. We were in the center lane, and classmates crawled on either side of us. But since Betty Crocker took so long trying to get through the obstacle, everyone else had long since made it through, and I was stuck behind him. "Crocker, get going!" I screamed. I felt bad turning on him, but I didn't understand what was taking so long. Finally he reached the end and scrambled to his feet, emptying the tunnel so that I could get through, too. By the time I stood up, Betty Crocker had climbed the next tower like a little monkey, and I was alone.

I followed the obstacle course and swung on ropes and jumped off towers without looking too pathetic for the cadre, who silently watched, their arms folded across their chests. I was now at the last obstacle: a ten-foot wall. Even if I could jump high enough to grip my hands at the top, I would need to be able to do a pull-up to get over it. I ran and took a jump, but missed. I smacked my shoulder into the wood planks. I tried again and again, each time slamming against the wall rather than moving gracefully up it. "Just go ahead, you've given it three tries," the cadre moderating the course waved to me.

"Not bad, not bad," Cadet Pratt reflected. "The best part was when all we could hear was the 'thuds' against the wall. Basic Cadet Miller, at least you don't give up." Cadet Pratt laughed, bending at the waist and throwing his hands to his hips. The other cadre laughed, too, and sensing the ease of the moment, my classmates turned to look at me. They didn't stare at me with contempt or resentment, just a nod in my direction that they agreed with Pratt. He was right; I was a fighter, but I still wished I'd gotten over that wall. Watching Betty Crocker struggle through the tunnel had made me appreciate, again, that I wasn't the only one at the bottom. Every single one of us basic cadets were targeted for some type of deficiency. And as much as I had my weaknesses, I had strengths, too, most notably my perseverance.

That night on our way back from the shower, I asked Jo to hold my wet towel and toiletry bag. When I was sure my only audience was the other women, I jumped up on the metal pull-up bar. The splinters, dug deeply into my palm from low crawling, stung as I gripped the metal. But without hesitation, I hoisted my chin to the top of the bar. Easy peasy. Maybe I had grown stronger over these six weeks, or maybe all this time I had been mentally sabotaging myself. I believed Arthur Thomas and my cadre so wholeheartedly each time they made me feel weak. I paused at the top to look out over the rows of army-green tents and the midsections of the pine trees. "Niiiice!" Jo and Charlie and the others cheered and clapped for me. I jumped back down, nonchalantly saying "no big deal," though triumphant inside.

After nearly three weeks in Jack's, we disassembled our tents and packed our gear. The entire class assembled into a massive formation broken up into blocks. Around 150 of my classmates—more than 12 percent—had quit over the 6 weeks of Basic Cadet Training, so now there were just over 1,000 of us. Top Academy generals marched with us back to the Terrazzo. My rifle continuously fell from my shoulder. My quads throbbed. My heels were bruised from running in my combat boots. Like all my classmates, I coughed every few minutes from inhaling the thin powdery dirt of Jack's Valley, which hung over our tents in a cloud. Cadre called it Jack's Hack, another rite of passage. They joked it would go away before Thanksgiving. It was now barely August.

Of the basic cadets in front of me, several wore bright yellow arm bands velcroed around their upper arms—the "broken basics." Some had joint or muscle injuries. Others had the flu. Regardless of their malady, cadre blamed them for their deficiencies. I may have been weak and exhausted, but I wasn't broken. I had survived Jack's Valley. I would graduate from the Academy and become a pilot, even if I did arrive unable to complete a single pull-up.

Rain poured down on us in the last stretch of the five miles, drenching my BDUs. The wet, heavy cloth clung to my skin, and raindrops fell from my short hair. Thunder cracked a few miles away. I started to shiver, but then our tempered pace turned into a run. We cut across the parade field toward the cadet area, where we reached the ramp to the Terrazzo and toward the welcomed transition to the academic year.

CHAPTER 6

You save yourself or you remain unsaved.
—Alice Sebold, *Lucky*

After a long, hot shower and a night in a real bed—gifts for surviving Jack's—my classmates and I assembled in formation for our
Acceptance Parade, a welcome into the Cadet Wing. We wore our
dressier blues uniform, with crisp pleats along the front of the pants
and on the edges of my short sleeves. I smelled of Dove soap, and
my scalp was dirt free. I felt fresh mentally, too. We were about to
begin academic classes, which would surely be my forte.

We marched toward the parade field to the beat of drums. Once
on the field's manicured grass, the thirty-five of us basic cadets
merged with ninety or so upperclassmen, who felt much older. Together we formed Squadron Four, and only three of the thirty-six
squadrons marched around the parade field in front of us. Later I'd
have a cloth emblem sewn on my uniform, signaling my membership in the "Fightin' Fourth." During our turn passing the bleachers,
I brought my right hand's fingertips to the edge of my eyebrow in a
salute to the three-star general who oversaw the Cadet Wing.

That afternoon I watched from my new dorm room as a herd of upperclassmen moved into the squadron. They loudly swapped summer stories and whooped and high-fived.

Though many of our classmates changed roommates, Jo and I
had been assigned to stay together through the fall semester. I didn't

consider Jo to be a friend since we rarely talked about anything personal, but we had grown used to helping each other, so staying together was fine by me.

As we watched the upperclassmen, Jo admitted she had to pee, as did I. Neither of us wanted to brave the hallway since the upperclassmen could stop us to correct whatever tiny mistake they witnessed. "C'mon," I said. "We have to go out there eventually." I inspected Jo's uniform while she analyzed mine. Her shoes were polished, uniform free of any dirt or stains, nametag straight, and belt aligned just perfectly with her pants' zipper and shirt's buttons. I helped her tuck the back of her shirt tighter into her pants so that there weren't any bunches, and she did the same for me.

"I'll lead," she offered. I followed her into the hallway. Jo pivoted with her right toe to make a clean ninety-degree left turn—called "squaring corners"—to march alongside the wall. I caged my eyes ahead and kept my body rigid, but in the periphery I saw two men approaching.

"Good afternoon, sir, Fightin' Fourth!" we yelled. Somebody had told us that's what we should say whenever we passed an upperclass cadet, and we managed to do so in unison.

"Stop!" one of them yelled at us. "What's my name?"

Jo and I stopped marching. My heart beat faster. I stole a glance at the man's nametag. "Good afternoon Cadet Smith, Fightin' Fourth!" we yelled in unison. Jo must have looked at his nametag, too.

"What about me, huh?" the other guy said, but he covered his nametag with his hand. "I asked you a question! What's my name?"

"Sir, I do not know," we yelled.

"Why don't you know?"

"No excuse, sir."

"You better figure it out," he said. "We expect that anytime you pass an upperclassman of our own squadron, you have the decency to identify him by name." The pressure of immediately learning ninety names flooded my mind.

"Yes, sir!" we yelled.

"Feed your faces," one of them shouted as he lowered himself into a push-up position. Next to Jo, I dropped to my hands and toes, my back straight and my bladder feeling even fuller. "Down," he yelled. We dipped into a push-up.

Because of this one encounter in the hallway, it took five minutes to reach the bathroom. I knew exactly how long it had been because for the first time in six weeks, I had a watch. From then on Jo and I planned our bathroom breaks around other tasks, like when we went out to the Terrazzo to pick up our new laptops, or when we went to the Cadet Store to buy our textbooks. That we were on our own to accomplish these errands was the biggest difference between Basic Cadet Training and the academic year. Upperclassmen no longer babysat us, but could still stop and train us at will. Traveling around the Academy felt like playing freeze tag when I was a kid. Our dorm rooms, the bathroom, the library, the academic building, and the athletic facility were the safe zones where we were off limits. Everywhere in between, plus in the dining hall, we had to be at attention and were at the mercy of the upperclassmen's mood swings.

On the Terrazzo we were required to run in one long line between buildings, traveling not in direct routes but rather along the white marble strips that bordered the giant quad. "Running the strips," they called it. As freshmen, we were now called Fourth Class Cadets, or four degrees for short. In three years we'd become First Class Cadets. But well before that, we still had nine months as four degrees to abide by these demanding rules before becoming a fully human being, marked by a Recognition ceremony at the year's end.

At least now I had the comfort of textbooks, Twinkies, and a new laptop. Already my e-mail was full of messages from my sister Megan, my mom, my CAP friends, and high school girlfriends.

I was busy comparing my class schedule against an online map of the maze-like academic building when I heard the chime of an incoming message. That's when I saw his name: Arthur Thomas. At the top of my inbox. My stomach clenched, and memories of his marble gun and Smurf-blue flight suit engulfed me. My hand shook as I clicked open Thomas's e-mail. "Lynn, I hope things are going well for you and life is starting to settle into a livable routine. I'm sure it has been tough but you can make it, so don't despair."

I hadn't seen Thomas since March, five months earlier. At that point he had been sexually abusing me for three months. But I never thought of that expression, sexual abuse. I never defined his actions, because the better I got at enduring sex with Thomas, the easier it was to deny its impact, and the more engrained my resolution became to keep my secret. I told myself that as soon as I stepped onto a Colorado-bound plane, he wouldn't be able to reach me. I would be safe at the Air Force Academy. I could survive another few months, I thought.

But then another adult in CAP raised the question no one else had thought to ask, a question that would end my silence. I had met Roger Clayton in February of my senior year, at a state-wide CAP conference where I taught a seminar. Other squadrons wanted to mimic the mentorship program I implanted in my unit as cadet commander, and the conference room was packed. I began with an ice breaker that illustrated different learning styles, speaking confidently. I wasn't the scared little girl afraid to fight for herself; I was bold, ambitious, and spoke with authority. It was like I could hide my real self, that vulnerable "little-girl me" from everyone but Thomas.

When the classroom had cleared out, many thanking me, a man who seemed vaguely familiar approached me. Lieutenant Clayton was about eight inches taller than me and had a flattop haircut and a mustache. He looked to be about in his late thirties. He introduced himself as Roger, and I remember he was friends with one of the adults in my unit. Then he said he loved my presentation and asked if he could he get my e-mail. Flattered, I tore a piece of paper in half, and we swapped addresses: mine began with "AstroGirl" and his, "RescueGuy." As Thomas walked into the room, I put the slip of paper in my pocket and returned to packing up my laptop. I felt Thomas's eyes on me and when I looked up, he was glaring.

"What was that all about?" Thomas asked. I explained that Roger was interested in my mentorship program, but instead of listening, Thomas's eyes followed Roger.

Within a week of the CAP conference, I swapped several messages with RescueGuy Roger. Besides asking my advice on implementing a mentorship program in his Kansas City unit, Roger told me that he had been in the Army Special Forces. I told him about school classes and my plans to go to the Academy. Roger always responded with a string of compliments, which felt nice. By March superficial topics had turned to more serious ones. Roger confided that his wife had miscarried the year before. I felt honored that he told me he was still grieving, like he trusted me as an adult. I told Roger about struggles with my mom, my stepdad stalking us, and how I worried about getting into shape for the Academy. I liked reading his responses just before bed, and having the chance to share my inner thoughts. My mom never wanted to know anything beyond school grades and the latest gossip. Thomas had stopped asking. Plus, Roger lived four hours away, which made the conversations feel almost anonymous. I couldn't have a friendship with someone who lived so far, so I wasn't risking anything by becoming vulnerable again as I once had with Thomas.

I knew better than to share my secret with Roger. Instead I said, "I can't say there are things in my life that I regret. If you regret something, it means you don't appreciate where you are because of it." I was still grateful that Thomas taught me to fly, acted as a dad, and helped my mom. I couldn't acknowledge then that the deeper wound he created every time he forced me to have sex negated those gifts. "But there are things I wish had never happened." Roger let my comments sit without further question.

On the day in March that Mom and I moved out of our country house as part of the divorce agreement, I carried clothes from my bedroom to my trunk while Megan and Mom finished packing the kitchen. Thomas pulled up with the moving van that he had rented for us. Three of my girlfriends arrived soon afterward, and I thanked them for giving up a day of sleep during spring break. Roger had surprised me with an offer to come help as well, and I met him at the easy-to-find gas station across the street so he could follow me back to the house. I parked in the space next to his, where he stood against the bed of his pickup truck, arms crossed, watching traffic. He was so much taller than me that when we hugged, my head only came up to his armpits. It was weird seeing him again after getting to know him via e-mail.

When we pulled up to the house and climbed out of our cars, Thomas stared at Roger. My friends walked out of the house and saw the two men's faces: Thomas's wrinkles around his narrowed eyes, Roger's neat mustache and damning glare. Roger made Thomas look like an old man in comparison, even though there were only fifteen years between them. My girlfriends looked to me, but I didn't know how to explain the two men's palpable hostility.

Roger dropped eye contact first and went inside. Thomas pulled my arm and jerked me around to the side of the house. "What is he doing here?"

"Roger? He's just here to help." Thomas's face turned a dark shade. He looked even madder than the time I left my barrette in his bedroom. He big glasses were inches from my face.

"You mean he drove four hours to help us move a few boxes? Do you really think that's all he wants?" That's really all I thought he wanted. When I didn't answer, Thomas let go of my arm with a hard squeeze and walked away.

While everyone worked, I shut myself up into my old room. I needed a few minutes to say good-bye to the only safe space I had. The room was empty now, only debris littering the carpet. I sat against a wall with my legs curled into my chest, numb.

After the van was packed, I was the last one to leave the house. As I shut the front door, I saw Thomas and Roger alone behind the moving truck. I couldn't hear what they were saying, but they flung their bodies toward each other as they spoke. Roger turned to look at me first, then Thomas glared at me. I ran to my car where my three friends waited for me. "Everything all right?" one of my friends asked. I nodded impulsively. Fear took over my numbness. I didn't understand why Roger and Thomas were fighting, but it had to be about me. Light headed, I shut my eyes to compose myself before I started the car.

I followed the truck, last in the caravan. Finally away from Roger, Thomas, and Mom, I felt tears rise. Months' worth. All three friends remained quiet as I cried, probably thinking I was sad to leave my house. I couldn't possibly explain otherwise. My tears turned into sobs. A weight as heavy as the moving truck was resting on top of my body, and I could barely breathe, let alone stop crying. I didn't try to contain my hysteria. I wept loudly. I slowed down my speed so that I was a good distance behind the truck Thomas drove. I didn't want him to be able to see me in his mirrors. We were twenty minutes down the highway toward our Saint Louis condo before I stopped crying. Taking deep breaths, I wiped my face and nose of tears and snot. In the rearview mirror, my eyes and nose were bright red. I switched off the emotion and let numbness take over me again. I felt my safety depended on it.

Emptying the moving van only took a few hours. Our new home was tall, with several floors, and skinny, squeezed among a row of townhouses. Boxes filled the garage, the hallways, and my bedroom.

After a break everyone but Roger and I went back to the old house to get a few last things. I wanted to start transforming my new room into the haven I needed, and Roger needed to get home. Before he left, I followed him out to his truck to grab the last few boxes. We chatted as we walked. "Is everything okay with Thomas?" Roger asked.

"Yeah," I lied. I guessed earlier that Roger hadn't noticed me as I watched them fight.

"I know you guys are really close. I bet you really like having him around."

"Mostly."

"Not as much as you used to?" I didn't know how to answer his question. We stood on opposite sides of his black truck. Roger had stickers in the back window of the cab that looked like bullet holes. I counted them slowly instead of responding. "Is something wrong?" Roger put a box back down and rested his elbows on the truck bed. I didn't answer. "Lynn, has Thomas kissed you?" Confessing my secret was as easy as nodding my head. I surrendered my fear and shame as I made each of the slow up–down motions. Roger looked away. I held my breath waiting for his judgment. "Has more than that happened, too?" I nodded again. "Does anyone else know?" I shook my head. "Okay." His calm made me feel calm. I didn't wonder, at least not then, why Roger was the only person in all of CAP to see the truth about me and Thomas. All I cared about was that Roger knew how to make it stop.

When Roger called me a few hours later, he asked me yes/no questions about what Thomas did to me. Did he have intercourse with you? *No.* Did he touch you? *Yes.* Did he make you give him oral sex? *Yes.* By the time he asked me these specifics, he had already reported the accusation to Civil Air Patrol. He said they would start an investigation against Thomas. Then, he coached me on what I should tell my mom about why I didn't want to see Thomas anymore. I never needed to explain to Roger why I couldn't talk to my mom. He just knew and understood. "Tell her that Thomas isn't teaching you what you need to learn," Roger said. It was true that I had more than fifty flight hours but was far from being able to test for my license. I could only hope that the excuse would suffice and that she would agree to pay far more money for private lessons outside of CAP.

Later that night Mom and I were alone in the house. She was in a good mood, so I recited the script as calmly and as matter-of-factly as I could: "Mom, I don't want to fly with Thomas or see him anymore." I didn't give her much time to contest, talking quickly, decisively, and stoically.

"Fine, Lynn, if that's what you want." I thought she'd put up a fight and defend our new friend. She shocked me when she didn't.

"I still want to finish my license, and it's just not going to happen with Thomas. I need to get private lessons."

"If that's what you think is best." Her reaction stunned me. Maybe, despite her seeming unwillingness to intervene with Thomas in our dark basement, she wanted to protect me after all.

The next night, Mom and I were eating her chicken and rice soup when the doorbell rang. I knew who it was. Thomas had found out about Roger's allegation to CAP. "I don't want to get it," I said to Mom.

"Do you think it's Thomas?" I nodded. Mom got up from the table, climbed the half flight of stairs, and rounded the corner to the front. Thomas started banging on the front door. Repeated, forceful bangs. Mom opened the door.

"Can I come in?" Hearing Thomas's voice made the reality of what I had done sink in. If he came into the house, I'd have to face him. I thought of his guns. He had one in his car just like he had one at home; twice, when I refused to suck his penis in the Bronco, he had threatened to immediately kill himself. I started to feel dizzy again. My ears rang so loudly I couldn't understand their yells, like I was trapped in an aquarium and they spoke on the other side of the thick glass. My lungs felt like I was drowning in an aquarium, too. The only thing I could gather was that Mom wasn't letting him into the house.

Mom sat back down without saying anything. I still felt ill. "May I please be excused?" Mom nodded. For once she remained in Devoted-Mom mode. She didn't make losing Thomas about herself. She didn't call me selfish for ending our relationship with him.

I climbed the stairs to my room and curled up in the lap of my largest stuffed animal to pretend, just as I used to, that it was real. Except now, I needed to add extra layers to my fantasy. My stuffed bear was my parent and I was a little girl again, and I hadn't ever had a penis inside my mouth, and the walls of my bedroom were like a fortress. Maybe there wasn't even anyone else in the world, like maybe they had all died in an apocalypse, so there was just me and the bear. So who could judge me for what I had let happen in Thomas's creepy bedroom, anyway.

On Friday, a few days after we had moved, Roger and his wife, Ruth, made the four-hour drive to Saint Louis to spend the day with me. They showed up at my door after Mom left for work. I spread a brown afghan on the hardwood floor in the family room because we didn't yet have a couch. Roger and Ruth sat down on either side of me. Between them—both so much taller and bigger than me—I felt like a baby inside the body of a near grown-up. "I know I'm almost eighteen, but I feel like a child right now."

Ruth spoke softly: "I know this hurts right now. But it'll get better."

"Ruth understands what this is like," Roger said. "She was molested when she was a kid, too." I looked up at Ruth's long, dark, wavy hair, fair skin, and calm eyes. In looking up at her, I felt pulled in two directions. She gave me hope that maybe someday I wouldn't still feel like this. Yet, I felt guilty for making them believe I was molested. Molested would mean I was a victim. Innocent. But I hadn't helped myself. I hadn't stopped him. Surely in whatever happened to Ruth, she wasn't as culpable. "Sweetheart, you don't have to be an adult today," Roger said. "We're here to be by you, and you can be however young you need to be. I'll treat you just like I would my little sister." I lay down on the blanket between Roger and Ruth. My legs were inches from Roger's, and his being so close reassured me, as if his proximity gave me all the comfort of my stuffed bear, except he was real. I didn't have to pretend to be anything other than my "little-girl me." I closed my eyes and curled my knees into my stomach, telling myself on Monday when I went back to school that I would be over it.

Beginning the next morning, I threw myself wholeheartedly into studying again, working out before class, and flying with the only woman instructor at the airfield. I only had three months. I woke up at 4:00 a.m. every day in a vain attempt to make up time.

In April, days before my eighteenth birthday and two months before reporting to the Air Force Academy, CAP asked to interview me. When Roger had reported my confession to him they opened an investigation into the allegation of misconduct. Just like in the active duty military, CAP had appointed an inspector general to investigate. The two inspector generals, a married couple both retired from the military, interviewed Thomas, our friends, and now me.

I didn't want to do the interview, to confess to anyone else what I had done.

I had asked Roger if what Thomas had done was a crime. "Technically sweetheart," he had said, "in the state of Missouri the legal age of consent is fourteen." In other words, I was correct in feeling so guilty. I didn't know that Thomas's position of trust over me as a minor, plus the coercion that he used—the gun, the threats, the physical force—made my age irrelevant. I didn't realize someone should have notified the real police. The only reason I cooperated with the investigation was because CAP had suspended me. I couldn't attend CAP events until their investigation was complete.

Roger drove me to the investigators' hotel. He waited in the car, but a woman named Stephanie, a mutual friend and adult in my CAP squadron, went in with me. Stephanie was twenty-eight and had been raped in the Army. Sometimes I wished I had called her after that first night Thomas touched me, but we argued just a few days prior. What had started that fight, anyway? It had something to do with Thomas. Actually *Thomas* had been the one to tell me she was mad at me.

Stephanie and I waited in two rose-colored armchairs in the hotel lobby. I stared beyond plastic greenery to the parking lot, wishing I could leave. The elevator opened and an older man and woman stepped out of it. They headed straight toward us. Both of them wore slacks and collared shirts. As the man shook my hand, I felt the wrinkles on his skin. I looked him in the eyes, at the man to whom I would have to relay the details of how I gave Colonel Thomas blow jobs.

"We thought it would be best if we had the privacy of our hotel room," the woman said. The four of us started walking toward the elevators, but the woman stopped Stephanie. "You can wait down here, please."

"I would like her to be with me," I said. I was proud of myself for stating my needs for once.

The lady turned to look at me. "You are a big girl now, and there'll be plenty of times you'll have to do interviews all by yourself, especially if you *actually* go to the Air Force Academy." I stepped back, unable to hide my shock. I couldn't see how she could compare this interview with anything I would face at the Academy. I felt ashamed, too, like it was wrong to want support. Stephanie put a hand on my shoulder just before I stepped into the elevator alone with the couple.

The bed in their hotel room had been hastily made, the comforter still wrinkled and pillows out of place. The shades were drawn, and the lamp barely lit up the room. I sat in a wooden chair a few feet from where they sat on the bed. When I crossed my legs, I had to be careful to keep my toes from brushing up against the man's. I looked back at the closed, locked door and I was back in a hotel with Thomas. My chest tightened.

"So what is it that you say happened between you and Colonel Thomas?" They both watched me fidget as I tried to shake the memory of him. I couldn't stop looking at the man's shoes inches from mine. I told them, slowly, about the first time Thomas put his hands down my pants. "If you didn't want it to happen, then why didn't you tell someone much sooner?" I didn't know how to answer the question. "Well then how come it was Lieutenant Clayton that you told first? How come you didn't tell any of your friends?" They were talking about Roger.

"Lieutenant Clayton is the only one who asked," I said.

"Surely there were others you could have told." I shrugged. I couldn't confess to them that my own mother had seen Thomas touch me and had turned her back on me, because I thought it said more about my own worth than anything.

They asked more—much more—about where it happened and when and how many times and what, but always the questions came back to why I hadn't done more to help myself. When I failed to adequately answer the investigator's questions, they handed me a stack of lined paper to write a statement. I turned to face the desk behind me. I felt the couple's eyes burrowing into my back. After filling only a few sheets of paper, my hand cramped, but I still couldn't justify my silence or helplessness. I handed them the papers and left.

It would be months before the investigators would announce their findings, probably not before I left for the Academy, yet I was still not allowed to attend CAP events. I steeled myself and tried to move on.

————

I chopped my hair the day before I gave my high school valedictorian speech. I was proud of my new militant look. I was tough now. Days later, just before I was to become a cadet, Roger and Ruth drove me to Colorado Springs to stay for a week. Roger had offered to take me because I wanted to acclimate to the higher elevation. We hiked in the Rocky Mountains foothills, and I wore my new combat boots to break them in. The three of us shared a room, went out to eat together, and talked about anything other than Thomas. When I returned home, I passed my check ride—my test to become a private pilot. Earning my license despite Thomas gave me more proof that I had put that episode of my life behind me.

But now, now as I was two months into my cadet tenure and I stared at Thomas's e-mail on my new laptop, the ordeal didn't feel behind me. I still hadn't heard the results from CAP, and Thomas apparently felt he had the right to contact me. The e-mail's last line caught my attention: "I want more than anything to be your dad again and I don't suppose that will ever go away."

What I felt in reading his last line was something slightly different than anger; it was clarity. I hadn't told on Thomas for all those months because I was ashamed. I was ashamed that, even at the age of seventeen, I acted like a five-year-old and wanted to climb into a grown man's lap, as if it was possible for a stranger to become my father. I had believed I brought everything Thomas made me do upon myself. But there was something about reading Thomas's words about wanting to be my dad again that helped me see straight through his manipulative bullshit. He didn't want to be my dad. He never wanted to be my dad. He had only wanted to fuck me as best he could with his limp dick. And now he wanted to keep me quiet, maybe hoping I would suddenly regain my needy affection for him.

For the first time I understood how calculated Thomas was. Putting his hands down my pants in my mother's basement wasn't an accident; it had been a planned move, choreographed among his efforts to exaggerate my dependence on him: the way he helped my mom with my stepdad, the gifts of stuffed bears and diamond earrings, the compliments, the never-ending hugs, his sabotage of my friendship with Stephanie. Fucking asshole. What a fucking asshole to deliberately abuse me. I had thought he loved me. I wondered if he ever laughed at my foolishness, if he thought it was funny how easily he lulled me into a sense of complete trust.

Then I thought of his daughter. Why did his daughter so rarely speak to him? I had met her once. She was a heavy-set blond in her thirties. The three of us once had lunch together, though she hardly spoke and was subdued. Had he touched her just as he had me? Did he bring me to lunch to show me off? My god, I thought, he abused me so badly. My next thought: worse, I let myself be abused.

Anger grew and grew and grew in my chest, until it became too much, and numbness coursed through me. I had calculus to study and uniforms to iron and "knowledge" to memorize and papers to write; I didn't have time to deal with the anger or sadness or disgust I felt at Thomas. I had to shove him away. So I did. Or at least I thought I did. But that night it was his gun that I dreamed of.

PART II

Broken

CHAPTER 7

Those who have a "why" to live, can bear with almost any "how."
—Viktor E. Frankl, *Man's Search for Meaning*

On our first morning of class, Jo and I woke at 5:00 a.m., not from rock music, yelling, or banging on metal trash cans. The alarm clock's tedious buzzing almost sounded pleasant. Our room needed to be perfect, down to the folds of our shirts in our drawers and the arrangement of our textbooks in height-descending order. Instead of sleeping between the sheets, as we had during Basic Cadet Training, we slept on top of the silver wool blankets to make less work for ourselves in the morning. We still had to refold the comforter at the foot of our beds so that none of the trim showed, which had taken considerable practice to master. I had also organized my pencils, highlighters, and notebooks in my metal desk drawers, and I had tacked up pictures that had lived in my Bible all summer onto the pin board behind my laptop. I liked the one of Roger and me hiking the week before I became a cadet. But my favorite picture was of Jack, taken just before our first kiss at the top of Niagara Falls.

Before leaving for class, Jo and I checked each other's uniforms to make sure they were as perfect as our room. This time Jo marched behind me, and we caged our eyes and squared our corners. Every time I saw an approaching upperclassman, my heart beat faster. Jo and I could still only identify about half of them. Many upperclassmen acted as if it was a personal insult if we failed to greet them with their correct last name, and they'd stop to yell at us. Sometimes we carelessly switched the names of the only two upperclassmen in our squadron who were black. They looked at us with such contempt, they didn't need to open their mouths to express their hostility. I was so caught up in my own daily struggles, I didn't analyze what might have been behind their strong reaction.

Once on the Terrazzo, Jo and I ran along the marble strips, carrying our identical backpacks in our left hand. Other lines of four degrees in front and behind us melded with Jo and me. The sun had barely risen, and even though it was August, the air was chilly. When an upperclassman yelled at a four degree ahead of us for gazing, he dropped him for push-ups and we all fell to our hands and toes, too. "Collaborate to graduate," cadets said. The bumpy Terrazzo stone felt cold under my fingers. After a few push-ups, I began to sweat and breathe heavily. To my side, Jo did, too. My arms were still exhausted from Basic Cadet Training, and they burned immediately.

Running to class should have only taken five minutes, but instead it took fifteen. My calculus class was somewhere on a top floor, and by the time I sat down, I was already drained like it was eight at night, not eight in the morning.

The textbook's glossy pages and endless practice problems dealing with triple integrals, vectors, and coordinate systems reinvigorated me. I had performed well enough during the placement tests we took earlier in the summer to skip ahead to Calculus III. In my chaotic childhood, math was always my constant, and I had competed in, and won, county-wide math contests all through high school. All I needed for complicated problems was a bit of logic, and the answer always added up the same. Math would be my comfort as it always had been.

Jo and many of my other classmates were panicked now that the academic year started. Academy classes were often compared in difficulty to those at an Ivy League school, and Jo feared not being able to pass, just as I had feared Jack's Valley. I offered to help her with her homework, and she would go to the pull-up bar with me. Our first physical fitness test in October was only two months away.

During the noon meal formation the entire Cadet Wing marched into the dining facility to the beat of drums. Then two of my classmates and I found our assigned seats. Like during Basic Cadet

Training, I was still required to eat at the strict position of attention. I spoke only when spoken to. "Miller, how many days until I graduate?" one of the second-class cadets, or juniors, asked while we waited for our food. That morning I had jotted down on a sticky note the number of days until each of the four classes graduated, in addition to the number of days until Thanksgiving break and until Air Force played Army in football.

"Sir, the answer is six hundred and fifty-six days," I yelled from memory, loud enough to be heard over the other tables training their four degrees. Another upperclassman asked my classmate what was for dinner. My classmates and I also needed to be prepared to recite quotes, or knowledge, out of silver, pocket-sized books called *Contrails*, which had replaced the paper version, *Wingtips*. Each week, an upperclassman would announce new knowledge— Air Force planes' specifications, quotes, and Department of Defense (DOD) regulations—we were expected to memorize.

That afternoon after classes, Jo went to swim practice with the intercollegiate team. With my other classmates who hadn't been recruited for a sport, I lined up in the hallway in my BDU uniform. Thirty upperclassmen joined us for an afternoon beat session.

Dinner followed, and then at 7:00 p.m., I closed the door to our room, finally off limits to the upperclassmen. We did homework until 11:00 p.m., giving ourselves six hours to sleep before doing it all over again.

One morning a few weeks into the academic year, I sat in the back of my military history classroom opening my notebook in preparation for the day's lecture. My professor, a blond, gangly pilot who had graduated from a civilian college's Reserve Officers' Training Corps, turned on a projector from the center of the darkened classroom. At a table one row ahead of me, two sophomores discussed the four degree women in their squadron. "They're so fucking weak," the bigger, taller one complained.

"I'm sick of them breaking every five minutes," the other one agreed. By "breaking" he meant failing to do exercises like push-ups without looking pathetic.

"Fucking dogs," the bigger guy said. All fifteen students, including the only other woman, stopped talking to listen to the loud conversation. I had never heard upperclassmen disparage women so blatantly.

There were other things said about us women, we noticed. A few of my classmates overheard a conversation during which the senior cadets divided four degree women into two categories: dykes or sluts. I was a dyke, they said. Jo was a slut. It seemed they made the distinction based on how girly we acted, whether we wore makeup or not. One of the women shrugged off the comments by saying the same labels were given to women in other parts of the military, too. "You can't win," she had concluded.

Calling us dykes or sluts didn't seem as bad as calling women dogs. Our professor interrupted the men. "Perhaps we shouldn't use that language toward other cadets," he said.

"Perhaps we shouldn't let females become cadets," the bigger cadet said. I twisted my head back to our professor, but he didn't respond. I had become acquainted with him from visiting his office for extra help with assignments. He took interest in my professional well-being, and I sensed he engaged similarly with many students.

"I'm serious," the bigger cadet argued. "They don't deserve to be here. We're supposed to be the best of the best and all that crap."

"And having women here makes that less so?" the professor asked.

"If you dealt with the shit from them that we do on a daily basis, you'd understand."

"Some of my most competent fellow pilots have been women."

"I doubt that. There are so many reasons why that's a load of shit."

"Really? Enlighten me."

The cadet stood and strode to a section of the freshly cleaned white board that wrapped around the darkened room. Picking up a black marker, he began writing a numbered list—as though he was reciting memorized knowledge. As he wrote, he read out loud:

1. They're less intelligent.

Less intelligent? I balked. *That* was bullshit. But no one said anything. I dropped my head and started drawing blue pyramids along the border of my notebook. The cadet continued his sloppy writing:

2. They're physically weak and lack upper-body strength.
3. Their emotion overrides all logic.
4. They can't keep their legs shut.
5. They serve no purpose in the military if they can't go into direct combat.

The cadet popped the cap back on the marker and tossed it in the tray. When I looked up from my blue boxes, my professor glanced toward me and then to the other woman with surprised, apologetic eyes. Would he say something? Anything? After several long seconds, he turned toward the projector. "Let's start class," he said. He clicked open the PowerPoint presentation and began.

The list was crap. While I didn't think that many of the class's other men agreed with the assessment that we were unintelligent, weak, emotional sluts, their silence, and that no one bothered to erase the board, spoke louder than the list itself.

Between classes, I hurried to make it to the women's bathroom on the opposite side of the academic building. There, I sat my books on top of a long, tall plywood box anchored to the wall. The box covered urinals from when the Academy was all male. Women had integrated into the Academy in 1976, seven years before I was born. Not until I realized that plywood boxes hid the urinals did I comprehend how recent twenty-five years was and appreciate women's short history at the institution. Squeezing between other women and the plywood to get to the stalls was a small inconvenience, if that much, but the urinals made me wonder if the Academy didn't want to remove them in case they were needed again someday, as if women's status was more tenuous than I had ever imagined.

When I became a cadet, I hadn't cared about my class's gender breakdown. But the longer I was a cadet, the more I started to count the women around me. Out of thirty-five four degrees in my squadron, there were merely seven women—and that was a greater percentage than most squadrons. In my military history class, there was only one other woman in a class of seventeen. There were four out of twenty-five in chemistry. Two in calculus. One in military strategic studies. Five in engineering mechanics. None at my lunch table. When there weren't other women, I felt as if my performance alone decided if women could rise to the Academy's "cream of the crop" standards. At lunch, if I forgot one of the upperclassmen's drink preferences and accidentally put ice in his water, I was failing for women, not just for myself. During a beat session, if my shaky arms gave out mid-push-up and I allowed the uniform of my country to graze the floor, it reflected poorly on any woman who had ever been or hoped to become a cadet. I had begun to count other women because with them, I felt less pressure to prove the list of women's inferior qualities wrong. I felt the palpable difference in the tension in my shoulders when there were fewer women at my sides.

The burden of performing for the sake of woman-hood created a dynamic in which women were hardest on women. "Upperclass-women," a term that didn't exist, screamed loudest when four degree women failed. If we as four degrees weren't going to meet the standards, the upperclasswomen would prefer for us to just quit and cease to become a case-in-point illustration to the men who thought we were weak, stupid, useless sluts. Upperclassmen of both genders also pushed out the male cadets who couldn't meet standards, but nobody extrapolated the performance of a weak guy into a statement about the ability of men in general.

My squadron's women targeted a sophomore woman who had become notorious among the entire Cadet Wing for sleeping around. The *eDodo*, an underground, online magazine written by graduates that mocked Academy life, nicknamed her the Whore from Four, a reference to our squadron. Their cartoons depicted her knocking on male's doors to beg for sex. She proved everything some men believed about how we women couldn't keep our legs shut, and upperclasswomen shunned her.

The seven of us four degree women in my squadron somehow defied the odds. We didn't turn on one another. One of the women was better at shining boots, and I was better at ironing, so often we swapped tasks. I helped Jo with her math homework, we made our bed in teams so that there were enough of us to pull each corner as tightly as possible, and many nights all seven of us went to the pull-up bar in the dorm stairwell together. Each time I increased the number I could perform, the other women high-fived. Some of the men may not have wanted us at the Academy, and the upperclasswomen resented our mistakes, but at least we could rely on each other.

On a Friday morning three weeks into the academic year, I dressed in my fanciest uniform—my service dress, the dark blue collared jacket. It was Parents' Weekend, and my mom was waiting for me near the Terrazzo. Though Mom and I had traded snail-mail letters and had a phone call over the summer, it would be my first time seeing her since becoming a cadet. I had missed Devoted Mom—her cooking, especially her pancakes and chicken and rice soup, and also her unyielding belief in me. During Parents' Weekend, we could leave base for two whole days. I would get to see Roger, too, who had driven Mom across two states to meet me.

"Mom!" I yelled when I saw her. I ran to her and gave her a long hug.

I hugged Roger next. "Hi, sweetheart," he said. I rested my forehead on his shoulder. I hadn't felt such connection with another human being in months.

Roger, Mom, and I would spend the day together at the Academy, touring and sitting in my classes. Later that night my sister Megan would arrive and the four of us would stay together off base. I wasn't sure if my dad and my other sister, Amy, both living down the highway in Colorado Springs, even knew I was a cadet. I still hadn't spoken to them.

Mom and Roger emboldened me to walk wherever I pleased across the Terrazzo, ignoring upperclassmen. I took my family into Mitchell Hall, and they gasped at the neat rows and columns of four hundred tables, adorned with sparkling silverware, and the two-story windows that faced the foothills. I was in awe, too, for the first time soaking in the grandeur without the limitations of caged eyes.

Later that morning my professor ensured his discussion of multivariable calculus was particularly complex for the parents' sake. Roger called it Greek and winked. I treasured Roger's accolades.

Each luxury that weekend amazed me: the soft hotel bed with sheets and covers I could mess up; home-sewn blue and gray checkered fleece pants Mom had brought; driving in a car; speaking without being spoken to; long, hot baths; being called Lynn rather than Cadet Miller; slouching. I was a human being again.

Mom bought a mountain bike I could use to compete in intramural competitions on the days I didn't have an after-school beat session. We also found a few comforts: lotion, underwear that hadn't been stained with mud, and extra boxes of Twinkies. At the mall, while Megan and Mom browsed a different store, Roger and I assembled a Build-A-Bear, giving it a blue sweater that said "USA" under an American flag on the front. I was eighteen now and a cadet at the US Air Force Academy, and I was supposed to have given up my stuffed animals when I put on combat boots, but I still needed an outlet for the "little-girl me" I hid from everyone but Roger. So when he offered to make the bear with me, it was an answer to my deepest cravings. Before we stitched the bear's belly shut, Roger held its cloth heart and said when he couldn't be there, he hoped the bear would give me strength and comfort. Then we buried the heart deep in the bear's stuffing.

On Sunday we loaded buses with other four degrees and their families for an optional tour of Jack's Valley and its obstacle courses. "So tell us how they'd yell at you," Megan asked. She sat across the bus aisle from Roger and me. Megan was in her second year of medical school, and she said she liked to brag to her friends about her badass little sister who was an Air Force Academy cadet.

"Did I just see you take eight chews? Where the hell do you think you are?" I yelled at Megan before we both erupted into laughter.

Once the bus stopped in Jack's Valley, we walked to the Assault Course under the sign that said Only the Strong Survive. Mom took pictures as Megan, Roger, and I played on the obstacles, swinging on ropes across mud ponds and climbing towers. I pretended to yell at Roger and Megan as if I was an upperclassman, then Roger took his turn. Roger had been Army Special Forces, so he knew all about training underlings. In one of the pictures Mom took, I'm crouched on the ground with my fingers interlaced at the back of my head, and Roger's mouth is open mid-yell, his thumb straight up in the air, his pointer finger outstretched in my direction.

CHAPTER 8

In a 2014 anonymous survey, approximately 20,000 service members
indicated they had been sexually assaulted in the previous year.

—Department of Defense Sexual Assault
Prevention and Response Office, *Annual Report*
on Sexual Assault in the Military, 2014

At 7:00 a.m. on September 11, I happened to be looking up news articles on CNN.com to recite to upperclassmen later at lunch. When I saw the explosion in the giant skyscraper with a caption that said more information would be forthcoming, I figured I'd report on the accident the next day. But then an upperclassman knocked on my open door, told me about the terrorist attack, and warned me I'd need to show an ID to get into the academic building. It was her inability to look me in the eye that first told me something was very wrong. Then on my way to class, the adult officer in charge of our squadron, Major Tate, waved me and a few other four degrees into the TV room. Normally we weren't allowed inside. A dozen upperclassmen stood in a semicircle around the TV, incredulous. The way Major Tate held his hand to his chin scared me even more than CNN's news anchors. More cadets squeezed into the TV room and the voices grew louder, upperclassmen and four degrees speaking to each other as if our hierarchy had disintegrated. Some wondered if we would be evacuated to the fallout shelters underneath the Terrazzo. Others discussed the long-term implications, whether the Air Force would graduate its seniors early to join a war effort.

Fighters flew cover over the Academy for three days, their contrail rings hovering in interlocking circles. The white smoke made me grapple with the possibility of real-world engagement with an enemy of the United States. The nation hadn't been to war since Desert Storm, more than half a lifetime ago for me. I knew that joining the military would force me to make sacrifices, like cutting my hair and moving from base to base, but I wasn't excited about the idea of combat.

We refocused on our cadet jobs because that was the only thing we could do. But every once in a while, when I walked by the newly constructed security fence, I wondered how my time in the Air Force was irrevocably changed after September 11.

Three weeks after 9/11, Roger drove from Kansas City to visit. I would use the semester's one overnight pass to stay with him so that I didn't have to come back until late Saturday. After classes on Friday, I put on blue jeans Mom had sent me. Because of 9/11 and concerns over additional attacks, four degrees were temporarily allowed to wear civilian clothes off base. I ran down the hill behind the cadet area to meet Roger by the athletic facilities dressed like a normal person. I ran into his arms, and we swayed back and forth excitedly, my head only as high as his armpits. I regressed into the girl who had sat on an afghan between him and his wife a few days after I told on Thomas. I was safe. I was cared for. I was loved.

At dinner—my first meal off base since Parents' Weekend—I told Roger about my A in calculus and my struggles in engineering mechanics, an introduction to a long series of engineering courses I'd be required to take over the next four years. Roger told me he was going back to active duty. Back in his twenties, twenty years earlier, he worked with the Army Special Forces. He told me once he raided a Middle Eastern palace and killed the guards by crushing their tracheas with his forearm before they could scream.

I asked what his wife thought. Roger tossed his napkin onto his plate and pushed it to the edge of the table for the waitress. "You know, we aren't on the best terms. She'll be relieved if I'm off to war." Roger had told me that since Ruth had miscarried two years earlier, their marriage had suffered.

That Roger entrusted me with such grown-up topics made me feel less abashed at being such a little girl inside. With Roger, I could be a friend and confidant, while he could also be like a big brother, willing to accept the more vulnerable parts of me.

That night Roger and I shared a room at a hotel off base. I would never have been able to afford my own room on my one hundred dollar monthly stipend. Besides, we had also slept in the same room the previous spring when he and his wife drove me to Colorado, so it didn't feel weird. Roger watched TV, and I took a bath. While the tub filled with steaming water, I studied my reflection in the mirror. My face seemed different, skinnier maybe, and I saw fatigue in the puffiness under my eyes. My short hair still surprised me. I removed the six clips that kept my wispy bangs out of my eyes. I lounged in the bath, soaking my achy muscles in the soapy water until the bubbles disappeared one by one and the water turned tepid. But before I dressed, I shaved my legs, a rarity. As if I didn't remember how to shave, the razor slipped and peeled my thigh like it was a soft peach. A narrow, three inch strip of skin dangled from the razor blade, and blood clouded the water.

I was still dabbing my thigh with tissue when I came out of the bathroom wearing my athletic gear—blue shorts and a white USAFA T-shirt—my most comfortable clothes. Roger asked if I was ready for a movie. I nodded and settled into a stack of pillows propped up on a bed. I wanted to stay up late and enjoy a real blanket and a real friend, but instead, I succumbed to the exhaustion. When I woke up Roger was turning off the movie. I took the pillows out from under my head and went back to sleep. I curled on my right side to avoid the cut on my left. Instead of lying down on the second bed, Roger lay down next to me. I rolled over to face away from him, even though it stung to put pressure on the cut.

I don't know how much time had passed before I woke up again. The realization came to me in pieces: something had startled me awake; something was pressing against me; it was his hand; his hand was down the back of my shorts. Roger's hand was down the back of my shorts, his wrist against my butt, his fingers groping my genitals. This wasn't another nightmare. I was awake, and it wasn't a dream, and *this* was happening. I couldn't move. I couldn't move to make my body mine again. I couldn't breathe, like there was something in my chest that made me incapable of taking in air. "What are you doing?" It wasn't me speaking; I had no control over what came out of my mouth. "What are you doing?" I said again, starting to cry. I didn't feel the wetness that slid down my cheeks against my will. Even my tears didn't belong to me.

"I love you, sweetheart." He removed his hand from my shorts. "I love you so much."

"But why would you do that?" my mouth said.

I wanted to run to the bathroom to get away from Roger, but even that wouldn't be enough. I wanted to get away from myself. What was wrong with me? What the fuck was wrong with me that this was happening to me *again*?

I tried to get up, for a moment still connected to my body by the tiniest of muscle fibers. "Don't leave me," Roger pleaded. I pulled away, but he stopped me. He held me in place with his arm around my chest. I tried to get up again, still crying, but he kept holding me. At first I felt his thick forearm pushing against my chest like a modified headlock, but then it was as if his arm released, even though it stayed firmly against my torso. I didn't feel his arm against me and I didn't feel the phantom touch of his fingers groping me. I didn't feel the sting as my thigh pushed my razor's cut against the bed. I didn't feel the sheets against my legs or the cold air on my arms. I didn't feel my tears.

From the other side of the hotel room, I looked back at my body still held on the bed. I recognized the girl—her pale skin, short brown hair, skinny arms—she was someone whom I had once known. I watched as the girl surrendered to the mammoth forearm wrapped across her chest. She didn't even attempt to wiggle herself free. Roger was behind her, holding and pleading, though I couldn't see his face. I couldn't hear his words, either. All I recognized of him was the arm, the arm that he had once used to crush the trachea of a Middle Eastern palace guard. The rest of him wasn't identifiable.

Eventually the girl stopped crying. He released her enough that she curled her knees into her chest and closed her eyes, though for the rest of the night, Roger didn't move from behind her.

When I woke the next morning, I mostly occupied my body again. I went to the bathroom to dress. Pretending as if nothing had happened was easy. I had a memory of watching myself from across the room, so that meant that whatever happened had to have been a dream, right? I didn't know the word for my experience—"dissociation"—and that trauma victims often reported watching their bodies from a distance as if they were someone else. It had been a dream, but the recollection of Roger's fingers against me felt so vivid, I wasn't sure what to believe. I pushed a finger into my forearm and released, watching my skin turn from white back to pink without the slightest sensation that it was my own body.

I put on my jeans and sweater, straightened my hair with a few quick brushes, and sold myself the lie: "Nothing happened," I said, looking in the mirror. It was a nightmare, just like all those times I had dreamed of Thomas, when I needed to remind myself when I woke that *it* wasn't still happening to me. Once, during Basic Cadet Training, I had even dreamed that Roger touched me just as Thomas had. I had laughed at my own paranoia when I woke. This time was no different. After all, Roger had been the one to rescue me from Thomas's touching. He called me his little sister and would never use me as Thomas had.

I watched myself in the bathroom mirror and repeated "nothing happened," but there existed a part of me that knew better. A part of me knew exactly what Roger had done. That sliver of me that held onto the truth, that still wanted to get the hell away from Roger, protested the idea of spending the day with him horseback riding in the mountains with Jo as we had planned. But I wasn't about to ask to be taken back to the Academy, where I'd face the men who said I was too weak to be a cadet, and the Department of Defense, which planned to send me to war. I was supposed to be getting a break from all that.

On the way to the mountains, I cranked up the volume to the car stereo so I didn't have to hear Roger's voice. The high peaks towering over the ranch where we rode horses were covered with snow, and the aspens' leaves were brilliant golds and yellows, but I didn't exist in that fantasy world, just like I didn't exist in the nightmare of the hotel room. That evening I obliged when Roger pulled me into a good-bye hug, but I didn't squeeze him in return.

I didn't have time or energy to analyze what happened or didn't happen with Roger. The Academy designed its demands to fill eighteen hours a day for even the most competent cadets. I didn't have the luxury of wondering whether male cadets wanted women to be at the Academy, if my five-year post-Academy commitment to the Air Force would one day send me to some country named Afghanistan, or what happened in that hotel. The Academy wanted us, particularly us four degrees, to be windup toy soldiers, going and going and going without thinking. Ever. We weren't supposed to have individual wants, needs, or opinions. The Air Force owned my body, my time, and my priorities. So I caged my eyes, ironed my uniform, ran to class, spouted knowledge, did push-ups, and wrote papers like it was someone else twisting my back's imaginary crank. I did all those things for other people, for upperclassmen and professors. It didn't matter to me how many push-ups I did; I didn't register the fatigue. It didn't matter how loud the upperclassmen were when I attempted to study; I couldn't process their voices anyway. Everything around me—the other cadets, the silvery buildings, the bear with the USA sweater—felt like movie props.

I still didn't allow myself to question four degree rules or become resentful of the push-ups or sleep deprivation. I continued to tell myself it was the price to pay to be a pilot; all I had to do was keep enduring.

My first authentic sensation in those days following the hotel incident with Roger came in late October as I walked to the field house for my first physical fitness test. For the first time in days, I snapped out of my automaton trance. Failing could result in probation and eventually dismissal. The test would have five events: pull-ups, long jump, sit-ups, push-ups, and a six-hundred-yard run. Each of the exercises was matched with a point value based on the curve of average cadet scores. The scores weren't based on the real-world demands of an Air Force officer, but rather percentiles, and I needed to score within a certain ranking of cadets within my own gender.

I waited to start the test on a pull-up bar, worrying that I would panic and choke, but I cranked out six pull-ups without much hesitation. During my last, I paused at the top of the bar, savoring the ease in which I held myself there. I did okay on the long jump, passed the push-ups, and rocked the sit-ups. Finally I circled the track, feeling the toes of my shoes push against the rubbery surface. I easily stayed mid-pack with the other runners. I sensed the accomplishment in the burning and opening of my lungs.

Passing the physical fitness test momentarily gave me the strength to acknowledge the truth: Roger touched me where he shouldn't have. I thought it was equally true that Roger wasn't the perpetrator Thomas had been. He never plotted to hurt me. Just like I wanted to cream the physical fitness test and prove that I was strong enough to be a cadet, I wanted to tell Roger how I felt to prove I wasn't a helpless child. That weekend my squadron of four degrees earned phone privileges because we did well on our weekly knowledge test. So I called Roger from the squadron pay phone.

"Hey, sweetheart," Roger answered. I wished he would stop using that word.

"Hi." My voice fell flat.

"I'm going to get in my truck so that I can talk to you better." That he felt he couldn't talk to me in front of his wife made me that much more determined to speak the truth. "So, how was the fitness test?"

"I passed." I didn't want to elaborate; I needed to change the subject or else I might never. "I want to talk about what happened." Then the words just spilled out, though I hadn't rehearsed them: "Roger, I didn't want that to happen. I didn't want that with Thomas, and I don't want that with you. I just need someone I can trust. What happened? Why did you do that?"

At first there was silence. Then he began to cry. "Lynn, I am so sorry. I never meant to hurt you. I'm so sorry you think I violated that trust." Roger told me he would never hurt me again and that he took his job as my protector seriously, as seriously as protecting our nation. See? He wasn't like Thomas. I just needed to talk to him. This is how an adult handles problems, I told myself. By facing them.

Walking back to my room to write a history paper, I felt a little less afraid of the upperclassmen who threw questions in my face about the specifications of the Air Force inventory. Bring it, I thought, when they dropped me for push-ups.

CHAPTER 9

Over a third of women who were raped
as minors are also raped as adults.

—White House Council on Women and Girls,
Rape and Sexual Assault: A Renewed Call to Action, 2014

The following weekend, in early November, I bought essential study food at the Cadet Store—more Twinkies—and walked by a rack of novels. A book, I realized, was what I needed to fight against the feeling that I was a windup toy soldier. I chose *We Were the Mulvaneys* because it had an orange *O* on the cover, and I trusted Oprah's recommendation. It didn't take long to reach the part of the story when the main character, a teenage cheerleader with an otherwise perfect life, is raped. Jo was studying across the room, and when I sighed, she asked what was wrong. I told her, and she asked if the girl had been drinking.

"Yeah, why?"

"Well, it's just that my dad says that every time he sees a girl who says she's been raped, she was doing something stupid." Her dad, the doctor.

I didn't know how to respond to Jo. Once, when I was ten, I watched a movie with my sisters in which a college-age woman was raped. She had been wearing a short dress that hugged her chest. I said, "What did she expect wearing that?" I didn't know why I said something so victim blaming. Megan, who was sixteen, snapped back at me, "It doesn't matter what she was wearing." Megan had never before been so angry with me. She calmed down and ex-plained it didn't matter what a woman was wearing or doing, she didn't deserve to be raped. What Megan said made sense, but Jo's beliefs seemed too engrained to argue with, and I wouldn't dare contradict her father. His profession made me respect him and wonder if he understood something I didn't.

I never finished *We Were the Mulvaneys*, but those hours in its pages awakened the part of me that wasn't merely a cadet. Despite all those months at the Academy, I had only been driven further away from my goal to become a pilot. What I needed was to fly again. I decided to contact the Aero Club so that I could fly on weekends. The Saturday before Thanksgiving break, I e-mailed the club's point of contact. A senior named Marcus Bowman responded immediately. "There are several tests you have to take before you can check out a plane," he said. "They can be pretty tricky. If you send me your AOL screen name, we can chat about them." My classmates and I often used AOL's instant messaging to coordinate, for instance meeting at the pull-up bar, but I had never before spoken to an upperclassman online. I gave him my username nevertheless.

"Hello, sir," I wrote when his dialogue box popped up on my laptop.

"Ah, drop that sir stuff," he said. "When we're at the airfield, none of that rank stuff matters." Intercollegiate athletes, like Jo on the swim team, never called their teammates sir or ma'am, so the informality made sense. He told me about the tests I'd have to take, suggesting we meet in the library so he could give me study guides.

That night after dinner I met Bowman in the library. He was a lot taller than me and African American, one of the few minorities at the Academy. We walked the halls as we chatted about our backgrounds and interests, about his position on the boxing team. I didn't wonder, like maybe I should have, when he told me he was under investigation but wouldn't say for what. We decided to meet again after Thanksgiving, after I reviewed the practice tests.

For a reason my mom never explained, she booked my tickets home so I would land in Kansas City where Roger lived, four hours away from her house in Saint Louis. Roger picked me up from the airport to drive me across the state. As promised, Roger was a friend again.

His wife showered me with hugs, and we ate at my favorite Midwestern restaurant chain where I devoured my own order of french fries, plus most of theirs. At home I wore flannel pajamas until noon, slept between sheets, and ate the pancakes my mom cooked for me. I didn't do a single push-up. I visited friends and feasted on turkey with my mom and sister Megan.

During one night of my Thanksgiving leave, Roger drove me to meet my former CAP squadron. We met at our old hangout spot, Steak 'n Shake, pushing our usual row of tables together and filling the diner's back section. I sat between Roger and my former CAP commander at one end of the table while my younger, teenage friends sat at the other.

One of the kids asked me what basic training had been like. I told them all about Jack's Valley, beat sessions, and low crawling. I showed off the scars from brush scratching my hands. "Are the upperclassmen really that mean?" he asked. I joked with them in a stern voice, telling them to get their shoulders up, back, and down and to cage their eyes. Their questions reminded me that I had an experience they envied. I had forgotten that being an Academy cadet was a coveted position others respected, no matter what year I was. I felt a bit like a celebrity.

I was so invested in the conversation that I didn't pay attention when my former CAP commander slid an envelope across the table. "I have something for you," George said. I glanced at the envelope addressed to me, tucked it under my plate, and turned back to my friends.

After paying the bill, my friends and I stood up from the table, but George and Roger made no move to follow us. "I'm surprised you didn't immediately tear open that envelope," George observed. I had forgotten about it. The other kids filed out of the restaurant while I paused to open it. The two men looked up at me expectantly from their chairs. George was a lot shorter than Roger and had gray hair, even though he was only in his early forties. He had enlisted in the Army years ago and still said things like "copy that" and "rules of engagement." He loved CAP because he could teach younger kids about the military. "It's good news," he said. Then I remembered the investigation against Thomas.

I finally read the header, "LETTER OF COUNSELING," written in all capital letters. I glanced at the long paragraphs, and a sentence near the bottom of the letter drew my attention: "The Wing IG finds that LtCol Thomas is guilty of the allegation of conduct unbecoming a senior member and violation of the CAP Cadet Protection Policy."

I looked at Roger and George. "He was kicked out!" Roger said. George nodded, grinning. But I didn't feel anything—excited, relieved, or glad. I kept reading. "The Wing IG finds that Cadet Miller is GUILTY of the allegation of conduct unbecoming a cadet member. This indeed was an unfortunate incident that could have been prevented by anyone or all of those involved." GUILTY. In all capital letters. I was guilty, too. The letters were like a hornet's sting to my chest. Could have prevented by anyone, I repeated. Could have been prevented by me. They blamed me. I felt sick to my stomach, like I would throw up all of the spaghetti I just consumed. I looked at the two men, who continued to smile. They agreed with the conclusion. Everyone blamed me as much as they blamed Thomas. If I ever wanted to be allowed back in CAP, I would have to go through cadet-protection training. CAP was punishing me for not being able to stop Thomas. I hated myself for now believing what Thomas did was a crime, when clearly no one else did. I remembered him forcing my head down to his penis as he leaned against the side of the Cessna. What about the other times he held me down? What about the fact that he was fifty-three, a high-ranking officer, my flight instructor, and a father figure?

A more grown-up seventeen-year-old would have figured out how to make Thomas stop. CAP's letter confirmed what I had known since Thomas put his white-ivory gun in my hand: I was as culpable as he was. That's why Roger and my commander were pleased with the investigation. CAP blaming me didn't faze them because they were happy Thomas was being held accountable, too.

I shouldn't have let Roger report Thomas to CAP. I could only be grateful that I no longer needed CAP to advance my career, and that their verdict would have no bearing on my standing as an Air Force Academy cadet. "Yeah, it's great that Thomas was kicked out," I said and forced a smile, but I couldn't look up at them, at the men who saw my guilt.

The Sunday night after Thanksgiving, upperclassmen blared "Jingle Bells" from their dorm rooms. "Are you missing Mommy?" they mocked when sad-faced four degrees returned. "Do you wish it was Christmas already so you can run back to her?" It was tradition for the upperclassmen to make four degrees feel like the month between Thanksgiving and Christmas would last forever. For most of my classmates, going home for the first time since becoming cadets was a reminder of all the comforts they had given up: cell phones, jeans, cars, music, home cooking, and the normal college experience. I don't think anyone was happier to be back than me. My mom had behaved herself over Thanksgiving, not even once slipping from Devoted Mom to Angry Mom, but I needed to be far away from CAP's damning accusation.

The next Saturday night, I ran to the library to meet Bowman again as it started to snow. "Hey," he said when I met him inside the library's double glass doors. He was wearing his running suit as he had the last time, a privilege of upperclassmen.

"Good evening, sir."

"Ah, drop the 'sir' stuff!" he chided.

"Sorry, I forgot," I said, even though I hadn't. It still felt wrong to me. But I acquiesced.

"How was your Thanksgiving?" he asked.

"Fine, I guess," I shrugged. I was trying not to think about the CAP letter that I had hidden in my desk's locked drawer. "Yours?"

"Yeah, it was great to be home and out of this snow and winter bullshit."

"Southern California, right?" He nodded. Bowman was tall enough that I had to look up at him. His shoulders were wide and bulky from years of boxing. "Where do you want to study?" I asked, directing focus on the reason we came.

"Have you ever studied upstairs?" I shook my head. "There's a cool place. I'll show you." I was excited at the idea of finding a new study spot. Other than my dorm room, which was often loud, the only other place I could go was the academic building or the library. I loved finding new nooks with deep chairs, especially if it had a window overlooking the city out on the plains. Plus, somewhere on a floor above there was a section of historic aviation texts I still hadn't found.

We walked past tables of four degrees studying quietly to the circular stairs in the back. My shoes clicked against the marble stairs. He surged ahead and leaned over the railing in the center of the spiral to watch me. Why was he acting like he wanted me to chase after him? It was weird, I thought. On a top landing, he turned—still not waiting—and walked briskly past aisle after aisle of dusty texts, deserted of any other cadets. This upper floor was quiet, other than a humming coming from the heating vents. I followed after him as he rounded a corner to a row of cubicles. He stepped inside one.

"You want to study in here?" I asked. I was hoping for some-place with more of a view, especially since it was night and the city would be lit up.

He didn't answer. Instead he stepped between me and the door. "You know, you are really sexy," he said.

Tightness spread from my chest to my throat. He moved to lean his back against the desk, two feet away, clutching the edge of it in his fists. "Come over here," he said. I didn't move. Even though he was feet away, his eyes and puffy cheeks felt so near to my face already. I didn't realize I had been scooting backward until I bumped against the fabric wall behind me. He reached out and grabbed my hips, pulling me into him. He leaned his face into mine to kiss me, but I pushed away. "Ah, what's the matter? Are you scared? Don't worry, no one comes up here. We won't get caught." I heard the implication in his statement: no one comes up here. No one was there, in the back corner of a top floor of the library on a Saturday night, to save me.

"I don't want to kiss you," I said, as if stating my needs mat-tered to him.

"It's just a kiss. What's the big deal?"

"I said I don't want to."

"It's okay. Come here. Trust me."

He pulled me into him again and kissed me on the mouth. His lips felt thick, wet, suffocating. I couldn't stand to look at him; instead, I kept my eyes squeezed shut. When his lips pulled away from mine, I wanted to scream. But there wasn't any air in my lungs. I gasped for a breath, but it didn't matter anyway; no one was around. Even if he wasn't three years older, one hundred pounds heavier, and far more trained in hand-to-hand combat as a boxer, I wouldn't have believed in my own strength to defend myself. Thomas's message to me, that I was a feeble girl, and my cadre's branding of me as weak, still remained at the core of my self-image. But the defense mechanism I had developed with Thomas remained, too, and my mind abandoned my body yet again.

I watched from above as he kissed me. I saw the top of my head, my messy hair in pins. I didn't feel his lips prying their way into my mouth or his tongue against mine. I didn't feel his hand squeeze my hip or his palm flat against the back of my head. I saw the square cubicle and the two bodies pushed against each other inside of it as if I weren't one of them.

I didn't know how I came to be flat on the floor or how many minutes had passed. My blue polyester pants and my underwear were around my ankles, my butt bare against the nylon carpet. He kneeled over me, his penis jetting out of his running pants like a blade. His wide boxer shoulders hovered a foot above my chest. My body started squirming. "Shh . . . shh . . . it's okay. It'll feel so good." He sounded playful, as if we were two kids roughhousing. For one desperate moment, I came back into my body. I tried to roll out from under him, but he jammed his knee into my thigh and his forearm into my shoulder, pinning me to the ground, my head crushed hard against the nubby carpet.

I left myself again. I didn't look back at my body, whose only defense was to play dead like a bunny in a raptor's talons. I have no memory of what happened next. My mind's ability to split away from my physical body was a gift. Dissociation was a way of protecting myself from experiencing the trauma, a way of denying for the next minutes, hours, and weeks that anything bad had happened in the cubicle in the back corner on a top floor of the library on a Saturday night.

I didn't hear if he said anything else to me, and I didn't feel where his fingers made contact with my skin, if he grabbed my breasts, or if he fingered me like Thomas used to. I didn't feel his penis tearing me open, thrusting into me again and again, stealing what was left of my virginity. I didn't feel his semen come inside me. I didn't have to look at him as he eyed my nearly lifeless body, or see the satisfaction in his face at rendering me helpless. I didn't have the memories to replay the details of his conquest over and over in my mind as he surely did. I don't know if he took five minutes or an hour. If he helped me put my clothes back on, or if he said anything as he opened the door of the cubicle to let me out. I only remember the long, slow walk back to my dorm room.

By the time I left the library, the other four degrees had already left their tables on the first floor. Outside, the sky was so dark I couldn't see the mountains behind the chapel. The overhead lights cast an eerie orange glow. Snow blew horizontally and clung to my parka. Within seconds, the cold started freezing my nose and fingertips. I had gloves in my pockets, though I didn't bother to put them on. I wrapped my arms around my parka, hugging myself. It was late enough that there weren't any other cadets on the Terrazzo. I choose a straight line between the library and my section of the dorm, ignoring four degree rules. I didn't stay on the white marble strips. I didn't run. I hid the patch on my parka that said "05," my class year, with my arms curled in front of my body. My hood covered my short hair, hiding the physical marking of a four-degree woman. The wind hollered as it whipped between buildings, and I had to lean into it to keep from falling over. Snow pellets battered my cheeks. I walked with my eyes mostly shut to keep them from stinging.

My dorm room was dark and empty. Jo was still gone with the swim team. Without turning on the lights, I peeled off my uniform, throwing it carelessly in a heap in the corner. I wanted more than anything to have warm sweats. Or my old pair of checkered blue and gray fleece pants with the drawstring I could cinch against my abs. I put on my dirty USAFA jogging suit that crinkled and bunched as I dropped my body onto the mattress. I couldn't face my body by showering, even though I felt as dirty as the jogging suit. I didn't feel sore or bruised, and I needed it to stay that way. Surely looking at myself would change that.

I didn't explicitly consider the letter from CAP, and wonder if the Academy would blame me for following Bowman up the stairs, just as CAP had blamed me for not stopping Thomas. I didn't let my brain think that far. It didn't cross my mind that I should tell someone. I didn't remember the briefings at the beginning of the semester during which a victim advocate passed around wallet-sized cards with a rape crisis hotline number. The card was probably tucked away in a Rubbermaid bin in the storage cabinets over my closet.

I certainly couldn't have imagined that someday I would tell, that someday I would stop hiding and would be surrounded by support. For now I was alone. I curled into a ball facing the wall and willed myself into a dreamless sleep.

CHAPTER 10

Just take whatever comes your way and shut up about it.
—Advice from a sophomore, in William L. Smallwood,
The Air Force Academy Candidate Book, 3rd ed.

I don't have a single memory of the days following the event in the library. Sometime in the next week, I know I reported to an administrative office in my service dress for my yearbook picture. A woman, a civilian with long blond hair and carefully crafted makeup, pointed toward a black stool. I sat and waited while she tinkered with her camera. "You have such a pretty complexion," the woman commented. What? Was she making fun of me? The single attribute that contributed the most to me being unattractive was my acne and its scars. She could have said anything else and perhaps I would have believed her. But she couldn't be serious. Once, when I was about eight, my mom and I were shopping in Dillard's on one of her angry days when a woman at the check-out counter said to me, "You have such beautiful, long eyelashes!" Startled, I didn't even smile, let alone thank her. It was the only time in my childhood, after the age of four, when my baby blond hair turned a boring brown, that I remembered someone saying something nice about my physical appearance. I wondered if she had given me the compliment because she saw the sadness in my eyes, and it was the only thing she could think to say. Maybe this woman on the other side of the camera understood Academy culture and knew that as a four degree woman, I wasn't likely to hear anything kind. Or maybe just like the woman in Dillard's, she saw something in my eyes.

Later that day in an AOL chat, Roger said I sounded sad. I'm not sure what I wrote to give him that impression, but he offered to come see me the next weekend. I mentioned the plans to Jo. We were both at our desks studying, our backs to one another. "You're seeing Roger again?"

"Yeah. Why?"

"The relationship is sort of weird, that's all. I don't understand you two." I didn't respond, but what I thought was: you wouldn't understand because you have two stable parents and weren't sexually abused before coming here.

The Saturday after the event in the library, I met Roger at the field house. This time our hug wasn't the enthusiastic back and forth swaying kind.

First we stopped at Jeff's house. Jeff was the man who had dropped me off on my first day, and his was also my assigned sponsor family, a home away from home. I had seen Jeff and his wife a few times over the semester, using their basement as a quiet place to study. Technically the kind of pass I was using to see Roger was only supposed to be used to visit my sponsors.

After visiting with them, Roger continued driving south. A while later he pulled up to a pink building with a bell tower, the Broadmoor, Colorado's most famous hotel. "How about a fancy dinner at the Broadmoor?" Roger had constructed the sentence as a question, though it wasn't.

A giant wreath with a red ribbon and white lights hung from the building. Red ribbons also decorated old-fashioned lampposts, and garland was strung from a fence. "Look over there," Roger said. We had parked near a lake that reflected the white lights. He pointed again at an old red carriage with two horses.

"We're going to ride in it?" I asked. Roger nodded exuberantly, as if keeping this secret had been killing him. The driver helped me step into the high carriage, and Roger sat down next to me as we covered our legs with a wool blanket. The horses' hooves clicked against the asphalt. They took us around the surrounding rich neighborhoods, past mansions also decorated for the holidays. Some still had post-9/11 American flags hanging.

After the carriage returned us, Roger said there was something he wanted to give me. I felt queasy again, but I couldn't pinpoint why. Roger linked arms with me and led me to the lake. My toes were cold and I was hungry, but at least the twinkling lights reflected in the dark water were beautiful, I told myself.

"I have your Christmas present for you, but, I didn't think it was the kind of thing I wanted to give you in front of your mom." He pulled his hand out of his pocket and held a jewelry box, opening it to reveal a sparkling gold band with three shiny diamonds nestled together. "Sweetheart, I want you to know how much I love you. It doesn't matter what kind of relationship with me you want, I am always going to be here for you. This ring has three diamonds, representing our past, present, and future together."

"It's beautiful," I said, though not meaning it. I didn't like flashy jewelry. Why did he still not know that about me? And why was he giving me a ring anyway?

Roger took the ring out of the box and grabbed my left hand. My fingers were skinny, but the band was even tinier, so he had to squish it on my ring finger. I studied the cut of the three diamonds. It was big enough to steal attention from the pink skin of my left hand. My left hand, I realized. Roger put a diamond ring on my wedding ring finger. The placement contradicted everything he had said about not caring what kind of relationship I wanted with him.

At dinner I ordered prime rib despite the price tag. Or maybe because of the price tag. I didn't care about jewelry, but I liked food, especially great meat, and ordering the most expensive item I could felt like punishing Roger for making me confused again. For most of our meal, Roger and I made fun of the extravagance of the restaurant. Like the server who filled my water every time I took a sip. Or the waiter who gave me a look when I asked for a straw, like it was an offense to their prestige. For a moment—a passing moment—I laughed along with Roger at the waitstaff's expense, forgetting the ring. But then Roger looked at his gold watch, and his tone changed from playful to serious: "It's only eight. How about you come back to my hotel with me?" Again, he formed a sentence as a question, though it clearly wasn't.

I finished cutting a bite of prime rib, ignoring him. I probably looked like I was thinking about his proposition, weighing it, but I wasn't. Something stronger than conscious thought was taking over me—self-preservation. I didn't consciously recognize what I was about to do. I put down my utensils, looked at him directly in the eyes, and smiled. "Of course," I said. My tone had changed, too. It was determination in my voice, determination not to be his victim. Then I did the unthinkable. I slid my foot out from underneath my chair until it found his, and I rubbed my shoe against him.

The previous winter, during the middle of the months that Thomas molested me, I went through a phase in which I initiated sexual contact. I didn't understand why at the time. I couldn't explain then that initiating, that getting to say when and where and what, made me feel more in control. If I willingly sucked Thomas, sometimes he wouldn't touch me at all. In forcing him to climax, he forgot about my body. I could keep on my clothes that way, and it was over quicker. So I took the same form of twisted control from Roger as we finished our dinner. I played footsie and sucked suggestively on my straw; all the while, Roger giggled like he was twelve years old. I didn't care what the waiter thought as I blatantly flirted with this older man. Let him think I'm a creepy slut, I thought. It was probably true. That's what Jo believed, anyway.

In Roger's hotel room, I unbuckled his cowboy-wannabe belt and unzipped his too-tight jeans. He leaned against the headboard and interlaced his hands behind his head, ecstatic. When I first saw it, I stared at his hard penis, enormous like it belonged on a bull. "I'm sort of well endowed," Roger said. "I've never once failed to please a woman." Looking at Roger's body, a flash of a memory from the weekend prior paralyzed me. Bowman, erect and hovering over me. But then I pulled myself together to do what I needed in order to protect my body for once, to save it from the bull penis. I touched, and I kissed, and I rubbed. I put a smile on my face like I was happy about it, too, like it was an honor to jerk him off. Distracted, Roger never gained the presence of mind to violate me on his terms. He didn't make me kiss him on the mouth and he didn't have the time to touch or grope, probing me with fingers like he had in the hotel two months earlier. Pretending to love him felt far less painful than allowing him to rip me open.

After he exploded semen all over my hand, Roger pulled me into him and held me next to him, my cheek pressed against his chest, and that's when, finally, blessedly, my mind left my body. I don't remember when he put his clothes back on or leaving the hotel. Twenty minutes passed between taps, my curfew, and Roger dropping me off. I wasn't in my body, so I have no idea why we were so late. Three upperclassmen waited for me at the staff desk in the corner of our L-shaped squadron. The main hallway lights had been turned off already and only the nightlights illuminated their angry faces. "Cadet Miller, you need to call your sponsor dad immediately," one of them barked. He handed me the phone. When I was late they called Jeff because I had listed him on the sign-out form.

Jeff first asked if I was okay. The question was out of concern, but his tone was angry. I said I was fine, and he unleashed a what-the-hell-were-you-thinking lecture that felt worse, more condemning, than anything the upperclassmen could have said. Being late for taps should have resulted in punishment—like months of confinement—but instead, the upperclassmen took back the phone and told me to go to my room. Maybe Jeff, versed in Academy manipulation, said something to convince the upperclassmen to give me a reprieve. I wished Jeff hadn't protected me. I believed I deserved the lecture, and I would have deserved the punishment, too. I was a piece of shit, far worse than Jeff even knew.

I woke Monday morning to a burning in my crotch. Peeing made it worse, like I was urinating into an open wound. Whatever happened in the library caused this reaction. I considered going to the Cadet Clinic, but knew better than to mar my military medical records, which would follow me in my career forever. I could call Jeff's wife, who maybe could take me to a civilian clinic. Except I didn't have any more passes to leave the Academy; I didn't have her e-mail, only Jeff's, and I couldn't use a phone to call her; and besides, how would I explain myself? The thoughts were a flash, a passing musing immediately drowned out with other demands. Finals began in only four days. I didn't have the luxury of falling to pieces. The difficulty of the last year had only tunneled my vision more dramatically, and becoming a pilot felt even more vital now than ever. It was all I had left to lose. That's what I thought, anyway. I buried my fears about what was wrong with my body, just as I buried Roger's ring at the bottom of a desk drawer under pencils and erasers.

Where does repressed pain and rage go in a body? Does the
wound of daughter turn to something else if left unattended?
—Lidia Yuknavitch, *The Chronology of Water*

Three weeks after Civil Air Patrol effectively kicked me out, two
weeks after I met Bowman in the library, and one week after Roger
took me to the Broadmoor, I hunched over a textbook at my desk.
I still had an hour to get to my chemistry final by the time I finished
the last bits of memorizing. I stood from my chair to put on my
uniform, but before my legs fully stretched, a sudden wall of pain
exploded from my neck and head. It felt like something had crushed
into my skull. I crumpled back to my chair and rested my forehead
against my arm, propped up on my desk's cool surface. The pain
made it difficult to get air into my lungs. I had to focus to take deep
breaths that reached my diaphragm. I stood again, hoping that the
odd pain would disappear as abruptly as it began, but the throbbing
worsened. I balanced with a hand against my desk.

"You okay?" Jo asked.

"It's just a weird headache. I've probably been studying too hard."

As I ran along the Terrazzo edge, and each of my feet alternated
slamming against the marble tiles, pain rattled in my head. My weak
and shaky legs threatened to give out.

A hundred kids packed the chemistry classroom. My pulse
pounded so loudly in my temples, I couldn't focus my eyes. The
words blurred. I flipped through the pages, hoping in vain to understand at least one question. I closed my eyes and rubbed the sides
of my head. Over my heartbeat, I heard the minute hand advancing

on the round clock mounted on the front wall and pencils scribbling against paper. I started to feel afraid, not for what was happening to my body, but that I wouldn't be able to complete my test. I slowed my quick breathing and opened my eyes, blinking to readjust to the fluorescent lights. I read the first question twice before I understood what it was asking. Then my stomach clenched like I would vomit. Taking advantage of my professor's prior approval, I ran down the hall and around two corners to reach a toilet just in time. Afterward I cupped my hands under the sink to sip water, which eased the burning in my throat left from the bile. I saturated a paper towel in cold water to press against my hot forehead. Holding it there to my head, I felt dizzy, and I leaned against the wall in order to stay upright.

I puked twice more before I reached the back page of my test. I knew many of my calculations weren't correct, but I at least wanted to write something in each blank, hoping for enough partial credit to pass. Only two hours into the test and well before my classmates surrendered theirs, I handed the barely completed packet to my professor.

I ran straight to my room, escaping any corrections from upperclassmen, and put on my running suit to lie down. I closed my eyes, but my headache kept me from sleeping. That night I skipped the study group for my military strategic studies test I would have the following morning, and I didn't review any of my notes. For the first time in my perfect academic career, I went to bed without studying.

I woke the next morning to my stomach clenching and bile rising in my throat. I ran to the bathroom, at attention and eyes caged. Once I was done puking, I turned around to pee. That's when I noticed sore lumps on either side of my groin in the shape and size of hard-boiled eggs. I didn't know what to make of them. I pulled up my pants and slid to the floor, turning my back to the stall's tile wall, holding my head in my hands. I couldn't believe I didn't feel any better. The only silver lining I could find was that today's test would cover concepts, not numerical calculations. I hoped that with the headache that made my brain foggy it would be easier to write an essay than it had been to finish yesterday's chemistry calculations. Stay positive and look ahead, I reminded myself.

"You okay in there?" I recognized the voice belonging to one of the seniors, a woman who always smiled. Unlike most upperclassmen, she exuded a calm energy.

"Yes, ma'am," I answered. I pulled myself to my feet and unlocked the door. I walked by her to wash my hands.

"You don't look so good," she said, studying my face.

"It's just a headache," I said in the strongest voice I could find. I tried to straighten my posture and smile. Even though she was one of the nicest upperclassmen, letting her see how sick I was would be letting an enemy in on a weakness. Besides, I knew she couldn't do anything to help. It was Saturday, and the cadet clinic wouldn't reopen until Monday. Even then, I wouldn't want to visit them. I had heard of women losing their PQ—pilot-qualified—status after one migraine. Going to an Air Force doctor with a headache and vomiting would have been career suicide. I didn't have a choice but to pull myself together and take my test. Otherwise, everything I had survived would be for nothing.

"No, really, you look awful," she insisted. "Come with me." She put a hand on my shoulder and led me down the hall. With each step, my body felt lighter. My headache began to feel more distant, as if it was afflicting somebody else, and I wasn't in control of my feet that walked alongside the woman. I only felt connected by the touch of her calm hand on my shoulder.

We arrived at Major Tate's office in the corner of our L-shaped squadron. "She says it's just a headache, but she was puking in the bathroom," the upperclassman explained to our commander. "And look at her. She looks like she's about to pass out."

My commander told me I had to go to the ER. I argued it was just a headache and I had a final, but he countered that he would talk to my professor. "You're going."

"What if it's a migraine?" I asked. I didn't need to explain my fear; everyone knew migraines could impact a PQ status.

"If you don't use that word with them, they likely won't either." I didn't have a choice but to obey.

On autopilot, trying desperately not to panic at my commander's verdict, I walked back to my room to find my wallet and to
tell Jo that our commander was driving me to the hospital across
base. She offered to come with me, and I appreciated the gesture,
not wanting to be alone in an emergency room. Yet, as we trailed
behind Major Tate to his Jeep, Jo's presence didn't comfort me. We
shared a dream of becoming pilots, but inhabited vastly different
worlds. In hers there was a competitive intercollegiate swim team
to distract her from four degree training, and attentive parents to
whom she could turn for advice and comfort. And in her world,
rape only occurred when women were drinking, so it was their
fault. She made that much clear during our discussion of *We Were
the Mulvaneys.*

Major Tate dropped off Jo and me, and I checked in at the
front desk with my military ID. I was floating again as the nurse led
me through the swinging doors and to the emergency room bay.
I lay down on a stiff gurney covered with a white sheet, and the
nurse clicked the railings into place at my sides, locking me onto the
stretcher. She yanked the curtain closed, and Jo sat a few feet away
to continue studying. Instead of the pain continuing to worsen, as
it had over the previous eighteen hours, it began to ease up. In its
place my brain felt more groggy and blurred. It was easier to close
my eyes and lose awareness of what was happening around me.

I wasn't sure how much time had passed before a doctor opened
my curtain and stepped next to my bed. "How many times have you
vomited?" he asked.

"Four, maybe?" I couldn't remember. Speaking was getting
harder.

"Well, you don't have a fever," he said. He used a light to look
into my eyes and he pushed on my throat. Then he asked me to
touch my chin to my chest.

"I can't," I said as I bent it halfway. "My neck feels tight."

The doctor positioned one hand on my shoulder and the other
on the back of my head. He pushed my head forward and pain
shot down my back, but my neck didn't bend anymore. "You're
tightening all your muscles. You need to relax," he instructed. He
thrust the back of my head forward again, but still it didn't obey.

When I was little and sick, my mom, fearful of meningitis, had sometimes woken me up in the middle of the night to make sure I could bend my neck. That memory made me feel melodramatic, but my inability to bend my neck was as real as the fact that I was in an emergency room.

I slept through most of a technician's clumsy struggles to insert an IV. Blood spurted all over the medical chart. It was hard to pinpoint what sensation came from where: burning, aching, throbbing, numbness, heaviness, lightness—all were true of various parts of my body. I closed my eyes again.

I only regained enough consciousness to register pieces of what happened next: a horde of hands rolling me to my side; Jo declaring she hated needles as she fled the curtained sick bay; the doctor tugging my shirt up to my sports bra; someone's hand gripping mine tightly. "You can squeeze as hard as you want," a nurse said. I didn't understand that the doctor was prepping me for a spinal tap, a lumbar puncture, to test for white blood cells in my spinal fluid indicating whether I had an infection—meningitis. One of the doctors that hovered over me squished my knees into my chest until I lay in a tight fetal position. Burning spread across my lower back. The nurse's hand squeezed mine, as if she was experiencing the discomfort I was too disoriented to fully register. She saw what I couldn't: the long, thick needle that penetrated my spinal canal and the murky, yellow fluid pouring into vials. The nurse's touch anchored me, just as my upperclassman's hand on my shoulder had earlier that morning. Without either, my mind might have drifted away from my body and never returned.

"I would admit her no matter how the LP comes back," one of the men advised. By the time I processed the words, wondering what he meant by "LP," the team had all gone, and I was alone with the curtain fully closed around my gurney that still locked me in place.

"Cadet Miller," the doctor called. I opened my eyes. Jo was studying in the chair again, her neck bent over her math book. Beyond my feet, the doctor's head emerged from behind the blue curtain.

He held it like he was in the shower and wanted to hide his body from the person on the other side to whom he spoke. I couldn't focus my eyes enough to make out his face clearly. "You have meningitis," the doctor said. "We're admitting you." Then he disappeared. I didn't react or begin to wonder what the diagnosis meant for my career or my health. I couldn't think of anything beyond the crushing pain.

Someone wheeled my gurney out of the emergency room and into a dark hallway. Ceiling tiles whirled overhead, and a man's voice said we were going to intensive care. Obviously I didn't hear him correctly, I thought. I had been in the hospital more times than I could count as a kid, but the only time I had visited the ICU was when my grandpa was dying. I hadn't been in the ICU when I was a baby and allergies kept me from gaining weight, or any of the half-dozen times I'd had pneumonia. I'd had a tonsillectomy and a grotesque spider bite that required lancing, twigs impaled into my thigh, knee surgeries, and a broken arm. When I was nine I had surgery to repair a hole in my eardrum, but during the operation my lungs collapsed and I had to be resuscitated. A priest gave me my last rites, but I didn't visit the intensive care unit even then.

A sliding glass door separated my room from the rest of the ICU bay. A nurse, an older woman with short curly hair, wore a mask across her face and leaned over me. At some point I must have been moved from the gurney to a cushiony bed with blankets. "Are you hurting, honey?" She said each word loudly and distinctly, her harsh syllables only worsened my head's pounding. I nodded slightly, careful not to anger the pain. She pushed a syringe with clear fluid into my IV tubing, and a dizzying lightness sent me back to sleep.

Later that night a tall man wearing a white, collared sweater and jeans, and no mask, walked into my darkened room. He pulled a chair next to my bed. When I strained to look over at him, for the first time I noticed the tangle of wires and tubes crisscrossing my body. "I'm Dr. Creech," he said. I recognized his round wire-rim glasses and boyish smile. On my first day as a cadet, he was the doctor, an Air Force captain, who had chuckled and told me to "be positive, too" when I reported my blood type.

"Hi," I whispered. I didn't want to speak loudly, just like I didn't want to move for fear of aggravating the pain.

"What did they tell you in the ER about meningitis?" His voice was soft and slow and didn't irritate the headache.

"Nothing." All I knew of meningitis was that it killed people and terrified my mother.

"It's an infection in the spinal fluid and the lining around the brain," he said. "It could be from bacteria, but I think yours is probably from a virus." He explained more, but I didn't understand. "Do you have any questions?" he asked.

"Will I still be PQ?" I didn't think of asking anything about my prognosis other than if the Air Force would still rate me as pilot-qualified.

"Most likely," he said. "Chances are you will make a full recovery." Dr. Creech stood over my bed and clicked on a tiny black flashlight he shone into my eyes. I winced as it burned my retinas. My eyes watered. "I know, I'm sorry," he consoled. He listened to my heart and lungs through my white USAFA T-shirt. "Can you roll over on your side for me?" I tried to find the energy to shift my weight, but Dr. Creech supported my back to help and then straightened out the tubes and wires. He listened to me take deep breaths before sitting back down in the chair I now faced.

"Are you sexually active?"

"No," I whispered on impulse. I gave the answer before I could have even considered being more honest. I didn't weigh what he meant by "sexually active"—if he referred to intercourse or touching, too; if he meant consensual sex or if forced counted. I didn't wonder if what Bowman did to me in the library, whatever that was, met his criteria. I just stated "no." I couldn't possibly admit, to him and to myself, the complicated mess opened by the question. I also didn't think to tell Dr. Creech about the egg-size swelling in my groin, or about the burning sore on my crotch I had five days earlier, a week after the night in the library. The sore took three days to go away, but that now felt like a lifetime ago.

"Where are you from?" Dr. Creech asked.

"Missouri."

"Who did you live with there?"

"My mom." That my dad, whom I hadn't seen in more than three years, lived twenty minutes away was added to my unacknowledged truths.

"I'll give her a call. I'll check on you in the morning. Get some rest." He left. I wanted to yell after Dr. Creech not to call my mom. It would probably be like that time I was nine and had woken up from anesthesia after the priest administered my last rites. She had cried over my hospital bed, and I had been the one to comfort her, not the other way around.

The nurse came in a few minutes later and handed me a phone to connect me with my crying mother. "I'm fine, Mom," I said in my strongest voice.

Each time I woke throughout the night, I opened my eyes to the same pain and darkness. The only hint of light came from the glass doors, filtered through the curtain, and orange lights from machines behind me. The clock on the wall was too dark to read and gave no hint of the passing of time. I had no way of knowing if I had slept for seconds or minutes or hours. Or if time was moving at all.

The only change between wakings was my body growing colder and colder. My core felt chilled, as if I was freezing from the inside out. Shivering, I reached for the tangled mess of blankets around my legs in an unsuccessful attempt to straighten them over my torso. No matter how hard I tried, I couldn't find an end to pull it higher. My throbbing headache felt so monstrous, I was sure my head had doubled in size. The rest of me felt tiny compared to it, like a toddler with a disproportionate skull. I spat up stomach acid into the pink basin tucked just inside my bed's railings. My mouth tasted sour and my tongue dry and sticky.

Finally a woman in blue scrubs slid open my door. "Blanket," I whispered. But she didn't help me straighten my covers. Instead something tugged and beeped in my ear.

"One hundred and four. No wonder," she said. "Your body needs to cool down. We can't give you a blanket."

The pieces all hit me at once. I was in the intensive care unit. With meningitis. And a 104-degree fever. I was so weak I couldn't get up, and I was in such intense pain I wouldn't want to anyway. The nurses were afraid to come near me without a mask. I had been foolish for worrying about my final exam when I should have been worried about my life. The memory I had been shoving away for the last two weeks came roaring back. My head against the library carpet. Marcus Bowman jamming a knee into my thigh. His forearm across my shoulder while he yanked his penis out of his pants. The *event* in the library wasn't just an event, but a rape. He *raped* me. How could I have possibly told myself he couldn't hurt me, as if I lived in some kind of "sticks and stones" nursery rhyme? His violation against my body was as real as the infection that now invaded my nervous system. He did this to me. I didn't know how, but I knew that much was true. And not only could it keep me from graduating, it could even take my life.

But I had followed him up the library stairs. I hadn't found the strength to scream. Afterward I hadn't had the courage to admit what happened to anyone, including myself. I believed I did this to myself, too.

In the middle of the night, in the ICU bay, I emerged in a pit at the bottom of a long, dark, spiral slide and looked up to begin to see what had happened to me in the last year: Thomas shoving his penis in my mouth repeatedly; CAP blaming me; upperclassmen telling me I was weak and pathetic; Roger betraying me; Bowman raping me; the Broadmoor and Roger; now the ICU. There was no way out of this pit. I had let myself become a rapist's target. I deserved this infection that raged in my spinal fluid.

But I wanted help, too.

I rolled slightly to my side and reached for the phone built into the bed's railings. The numbers lit up when I held the receiver in front of my face, but my fingers were shaky, plus they were getting puffy from my IV, and I struggled to dial. I propped the phone on top of my cheek while it rang. Mom took several minutes to answer, probably because she needed to wake up and then put in her hearing aids.

"Hello?" she answered in a groggy voice.

"Mommy?"

She didn't say anything. I opened my mouth to explain why I was calling at whatever hour it was. "I'm . . ." I started, but couldn't finish my sentence. I'm what? Hurting? Lonely? Terrified? How could I possibly convey to her the weight I felt, the compilation of a year of unacknowledged trauma compounded by the fear of dying, alone, in a darkened ICU bay.

"What?" she said. Her "what" wasn't part of a soft, "What is it, sweetie?" but rather a "what the hell do you want?" Angry Mom, not Devoted Mom, had answered the phone. I wasn't three years old anymore, having meningitis didn't exempt me from her fits of anger, and she would blame me for following Bowman up the stairs like I believed everyone else would.

"I have to get up in two hours to drive to see you, Lynn," she said. She said my name with a firm *L* and a harsh *n*. "I have to meet Roger in Kansas City by ten."

"Roger's coming?"

"How else do you think I would get to Colorado? Do you expect me to drive all that way on my own?"

"I'm sorry," I whispered, and put the phone back in its cradle.

PART III

Dark Ages

CHAPTER 12

*Half the women in the military have been sexually assaulted in their
pasts, most often as children, so if you add that to the one-third
who are sexually attacked in the service, a high percentage will be
experiencing abuse for the second, third, or umpteenth time.*

—Helen Benedict, *The Lonely Soldier:*
The Private War of Women Serving in Iraq

At the end of Christmas leave, I labored four flights of stairs to my
dorm room. I had been sick with meningitis for more than two
weeks, and my headache persisted in squeezing my skull. My body
was shaky, and I clung to the metal railings.

Dr. Creech and the neurologist had released me from the ICU
after five days. Roger and Mom took turns staying with me, their
presence suffocating, the small hospital room growing stagnant with
body odor. After each rotation with Roger sitting in the recliner by
my bed, I wished he would disappear, only to be more disturbed
when my mother took his place. By the time I recovered enough to
take a brief shower, I insisted to Dr. Creech that I preferred to re-
cuperate at home on Christmas leave, and they released me. At least
there I could shut my bedroom door. When Roger drove Mom
and me back to Missouri, he stopped for the night in a tiny Kansas
town. The three of us shared the hotel room where Roger slept
on the floor, though that didn't prevent his hands from finding my
body in the middle of the night. I turned on the light to stop him,
sure he wouldn't take a risk with my mother in the room. Roger
did stop, but in the morning, my mother scolded me for ruining her
sleep without asking why I had switched on the lamp. They were

the same problems, only with different details. Except this time, I wasn't surprised. I even understood why Angry Mom called me a selfish bitch for wanting to fly back to Colorado at the end of leave rather than accept Roger's invitation to drive me. Though she didn't say it, I understood she felt afraid to drop me off at an airport, by myself, while I remained so ill, and she also felt she couldn't drive me on her own. She would rather entrust me with this man, despite my protests, than deal with her own feelings of fear and powerlessness.

Standing at the top of the stairs on my first day back, I turned to look out the floor-to-ceiling window, even though I was supposed to cage my eyes straight ahead. Four stories below, Roger waved a childish wave, flapping his fingers against his palm. Roger resembled my mother. He would never put my needs first, only his agenda. And his agenda, the entire year I had known him, was to have sex with me. It was the reason he recognized that Thomas was molesting me when not a single other person did. It was the reason he wrote card after card to me when I was in Basic Cadet Training. It was the reason he visited me in the ICU and then drove me back to the Academy. I didn't feel aggrieved by him, just as I didn't feel aggrieved by my mother. My disgust was only with myself. I had played footsie with a man specifically because I hadn't wanted to have sex with him. How fucked up was that? How fucked up was I?

I thought my helplessness and weakness was the reason bad things kept happening—not because those around me consciously chose to violate me. When Thomas put a gun in my hand, I didn't use it to stop him. I followed Bowman up the marble staircase to the isolated upper floor of the library, even though my gut told me he was a creep. I let Roger visit me even after he violated me by touching me while I slept. I had trusted each of them more than I had trusted my own intuition. And that's how I had lived my life: following what others told me to do, then compartmentalizing what happened and steeling myself to move on. I had told myself that if I just survived each day, I would eventually graduate, become a pilot, and everything would be okay. I would be okay.

Getting meningitis had shown me that surviving each day wasn't enough. Meningitis could have taken my career. Or worse: it could have killed me. I couldn't afford to be a victim anymore. I needed to help myself. Not that I understood *how* to help myself, just that I needed to figure it out, and quickly.

I continued to stare out the windows where Roger waited on the cement sidewalk below. RescueGuy, his e-mail proclaimed. I had thought he saved me from Thomas, but he couldn't rescue me. I had to rescue myself. I took one last look at Roger and swore to myself I would never see him again. I turned from the window and marched at attention to my room.

Exhausted from lugging my backpack up the stairs, I rested on top of my bed. Jo hadn't returned yet, and I left the lights off. My drapes were open, but it was too cloudy outside for the sunshine to bring in much light. Upperclassmen called these months after Christmas the Dark Ages, warning us that frequent storms would hide the foothills. The sun would set behind the mountains as early as 5:00 p.m., and the bitter cold and wind that tore through the Terrazzo would make runs miserable. For us four degrees, the Dark Ages would be even more difficult. We still had two and a half months until Recognition, the three-day, two-night beat session in March that would mark the end of hazes. After Recognition upperclassmen wouldn't yell or beat us anymore, we'd be able to walk around like normal people and earn luxuries like cell phones and wearing jeans. Recognition would be the pinnacle of our training, but the two and a half months until that goal felt unconquerable.

My first stop on my I-need-to-help-myself campaign was to follow up with Dr. Creech the next morning. While the rest of my squadron shuffled dorm rooms and bought new textbooks, I went to the Cadet Clinic.

"Look at you all dressed up!" Dr. Creech said. He was wearing his green flight suit with gold captain bars on the shoulders and his round wire-rim glasses. I was sitting on top of the flimsy white paper rolled over the exam table, wearing my blues uniform, looking far more put together than I had in the ICU. That I was sitting up, completely unsupported, was a change from when he had seen me. "How are you feeling?" Dr. Creech asked, genuine with concern.

"I still feel pretty bad," I understated. It would have been more accurate to say, "I'm still really fucking sick." My head still throbbed so badly that I had to hide my head under my pillow the night before when the upperclassmen filled the hallways with their yelling. I threw up at least a few times every day. I felt weak from eating so little. I had zero chances of magically regaining the strength to survive a beat session.

"It might be a few more days before you feel your energy come back," Dr. Creech said. He listened to my heart and lungs before adding, "Let's give it two more weeks. Come back and see me then if you still don't feel well."

I left the clinic with a prescription for more Percocet and a Form 18 medical excuse. A Form 18 was an exemption from strenuous four degree training and beat sessions. I folded the slip of paper into a tiny square that I would keep in my pocket in case an upperclassman dropped me for push-ups.

That afternoon everyone in the squadron shuffled roommates. I was to move down the hall to a room I would share with Charlie. I carried about two small loads before Charlie realized the difficulty I was having. She's the one who was able to push my trunk, crammed with my heaviest textbooks and field gear. During Jack's Valley, Charlie and I had bunked next to each other. Not only was she one of the physically stronger and most intelligent of the four degrees, she had two things most of our classmates lacked: a sense of humor and the balance to keep up with the hectic demands without "spazzing." Spazzes worried constantly, rarely slept, and stressed out their roommates. For instance, one of the four degree women was notorious for vacuuming in the middle of the night. Charlie, a Zen Californian, was the opposite.

Charlie helped me organize, too. We had less than twelve hours to perfectly arrange everything, and in the "collaborate to graduate" culture, she worked on my closet, which required standing, while I unpacked the stuff for my desk, which allowed me to sit. Every few minutes, I rested my pounding head against the desk's cool surface.

Finally settled in my new room, I dealt with Roger, my second stop on my self-help campaign. I opened my laptop and read three messages from him. The last said, "Poor Rogie doesn't have any good e-mails," followed by a frown emoticon. He didn't ask me how I was feeling. For the first time, I felt angry at him. It was a twinge, but oh-so-real anger, directed squarely on his shoulders. Not mine.

"What's going on?" Charlie asked. She had probably seen my face because she was standing next to me, scrubbing the ledge of our window. Upperclassmen who didn't have white-glove room inspections had lived in this room before us.

"One of my friends is being selfish," I said.

"Roger?" she asked. I started to ask her how she knew of Roger, but then thought better of it. If Jo gossiped with the other women, I didn't want to know. "Just block him from AOL," she said. I didn't need to explain before she gave this advice. She gleaned enough about the relationship from whatever Jo said. So I blocked his instant messaging AOL account. Then I blocked my mom from AOL instant messaging, too. I would eventually answer her e-mails–she was my mother, after all—but I wasn't going to talk to her on demand.

Next, I addressed another relationship that probably made me the subject of further gossip. I imagined the other four degrees saying, "Lynn's dad lives down the highway and he doesn't even know she's a cadet." I wrote to him using the e-mail my sister gave me. I didn't ask for a response, I only said I was a cadet and wanted him to know.

Meanwhile, a kid from my fall semester calculus class messaged me on AOL. Erick asked me if I was okay, worried because I hadn't shown up to our final exam. I told him about the meningitis, and he bombarded me with questions, asking how I was feeling and if I was going to be able to make up finals. Erick fit the typical cadet stereotype: smart, attractive, with short brown hair and brown eyes, totally built. A few months earlier, he had asked me to get pizza with him in the student center during his birthday weekend—both of our squadrons had earned that privilege—but I turned him down. I didn't need any boy drama. But I didn't turn him down on AOL when he became one of only a few people that day to express concern.

—————

My self-help campaign ended after those first two days. The reality of the tremendous effort required to function despite my headache became a moment-by-moment battle in a losing war. In the morning Charlie helped tidy my side of our room, but there wasn't anything she could do to help me dress or brush my teeth. Putting on my belt required dexterity to weave the end through the buckle and then strength to pull it tight and latch it.

On the way to class, I walked alongside my classmates running the white marble strips. "How come you're walking?" upperclassmen asked. I would say, "Sir, the answer is I have a Form 18." Speaking in a loud, confident voice drained my energy. Then there was the problem of climbing the two flights of stairs to my English class. Four degrees weren't allowed to take the elevator. By the time I sat down in class, my head pounded with my pulse, drowning my instructor's words. Plus, I was so drowsy. I missed most of what she said. The same was true after differential equations, chemistry, behavioral sciences, physics, and computer science.

At lunch, one thousand four degrees shouting inside Mitchell Hall made me want to get the fuck out of there. It was so loud, so overpowering, so crippling to my sore head. At least these upperclassmen at my table, who were from my squadron, knew I was recovering from meningitis, unlike the cadets who saw me walking on the Terrazzo, so they didn't tell me I was pathetic when I struggled to regurgitate quotes alongside my classmates.

By the time I returned to my room in the afternoon, each step was a feat. I collapsed on my bed, and I didn't move until the next morning. I didn't go to dinner, and I was so dehydrated that I didn't need to pee. Charlie was adept at accepting sacrifices, and while I slept she considerately used a small desk lamp rather than the overhead fluorescents and studied late into the night. She wanted to go to the DOD's medical school and couldn't afford less than perfect grades.

I waited exactly fourteen days to return to Dr. Creech. When I told him about my continuing symptoms, he shook his head and studied his shoes. I hadn't completed my final exams, was behind in my new classes, and was wearing out the upperclassmen's patience. It was like I was trying to pass as a cadet when I had the worst flu of my life.

Dr. Creech guided me to his office across the hall where he called someone. After he hung up he explained, "Dr. Powell, the neurologist who oversaw your care while you were in the hospital, thinks you have a post-infectious headache syndrome. That means that the symptoms you have are residual from the infection."

I left Dr. Creech's office with another Form 18, more Percocet, and Pamelor, an antidepressant sometimes used for pain. "Just keep hanging in there, one day at a time," Dr. Creech said encouragingly. Dr. Creech didn't understand that I was in too much pain to live day by day; I could only survive minute by minute.

The next afternoon, I took my engineering mechanics final exam from the previous semester, despite not having studied. None of the words made coherent sentences on the first page. So I flipped to the second, the third, and the fourth pages without finding a single question that felt easy. When I finally understood enough to begin working a problem, my mind couldn't keep track of the numbers. I left my professor's office knowing I failed. I failed my calculus final as well, even though it was math, the subject that always showed me consistency and logic. Most of my grades dropped a letter grade because of my final exams. I had never earned a B on my report card before, let alone a C.

After I finished my last final exam a few days later, I felt dizzy, weak, and panicked walking down the academic building's stairs. The steps blurred, so I had to feel for each with my toe before putting down my weight. My headache felt so strong it was like someone pushing on my head from above, threatening to crumple me onto the stairs. Instead of trying to walk all the way back to my dorm room, I went to the library to e-mail Dr. Creech. Thankfully he answered immediately and told me to come down to the clinic.

In a back corner of the clinic treatment room, a technician started an IV. I didn't feel the needle's pinch. She pulled a blue curtain around my gurney to shade me from the overhead lights. Dr. Creech leaned over the gurney's railing, holding the IV line in one hand and a syringe in the other. He pushed the fluid in the IV. "What are you giving me?" I asked. By the time I finished the sentence, my body felt lighter and my brain buzzed.

"It's a combination of meds to help your nausea and headache. Try to get some sleep, okay?" My eyes were already half closed, but Dr. Creech put a hand to my arm. "You're breaking my heart."

After that first afternoon in the treatment room, I went back to the clinic two or three times a week for the same help. The narcotics didn't erase the pain, but they made me care less about the headache, my grades, and letting down my classmates. The intravenous medicine Dr. Creech gave me helped a little with the nausea and incessant vomiting. But mostly closing my eyes and resting for a couple of hours was what I needed. I slept more peacefully in the clinic than I did at night, when the pain made me startle every few minutes.

Sometimes a woman named Molly came to the treatment room at the same time I did. Once, as she rested on the gurney next to me, I asked her why she was there. "I have to get antibiotics every eight hours because the doctor botched the surgery to repair my thumb. You'd think my broken back would be a bigger hassle than my stupid thumb, wouldn't you?"

"How did you get injured?"

"Midget tossing." Her two word answer explained everything to me. Midget tossing was banned, but that didn't stop most squadrons from continuing the tradition on Saturday nights while our commanding officers were home. Upperclassmen ordered four degrees to drag their bare mattresses into the hallways and place them back to back, creating padding along the floors and walls. Whoever threw their "midgets"—the shortest four degrees—the furthest, won. Helmet optional. As a five-foot-two four degree female, Molly had three strikes against her. She had no choice but to be thrown. Six of the men raised her into a horizontal position over their heads. They took a running start before hurling her like a javelin. Molly landed in a heap against the padded wall. The cadets laughed and high-fived. True to her cadet training, Molly stood up and walked to her room, despite the crippling pain shooting through her back. Several hours later Molly asked for a ride to the ER and discovered her back and thumb were broken. The administrators supposedly cracked down on "midget tossing," angering the upperclassmen who in turn blamed Molly for ruining their fun.

Molly and I had more in common than the IVs dripping saline into our veins; we both understood what it was like to be a broken four degree woman. We both put up a daily struggle pretending to be less incapacitated than we were.

At the end of January, Dr. Creech sent me to meet with the neurologist, Dr. Powell. I didn't recognize him from when I was in the ICU, but then again, a lot probably happened in the ICU without my being aware. Dr. Powell was a lieutenant colonel. I sat down on the opposite side of his office desk, crowded with stacks of books and journals. His eyes were focused on the star on my uniform, an achievement pin for receiving a GPA above 3.0 the previous semester. I had barely earned it after failing half my finals. I didn't understand why Dr. Powell was staring at my star so intently.

"It takes time for these things," Dr. Powell said.

"Sir, I'm not sure what you mean."

"Meningitis. It takes time to heal. You can't expect to be one hundred percent right away." I wondered if he knew just how much difficulty I was having. He hadn't asked. I asked how long healing would take. "Hard to say." He was looking out the window now, at the snow in the parking lot creating a traffic jam. "Maybe two or as much as five months."

His prognosis was a kick to my ribs. I couldn't stand another day, let alone another five months. I could flunk out of the Academy in less than five months. I could lose my dream of becoming a pilot in less than five months. I could be back in my mother's house in less than five months. "Two to five months?" I repeated without bothering to add a "sir." Dr. Powell continued to look out the window. "Is there anything you can do to help make me better? I'm not sure I can maintain my duties as a cadet for that long, sir." I thought that was the reason I was here, so that he could help me. Dr. Powell hadn't done any kind of exam or asked me any questions.

"I suppose we could put you on some medicine that might reduce your nervous system's inflammation, though I'm not sure it will help. As far as your cadet duties, if you cannot handle them, there are services at the counseling center to help you adjust." I didn't respond to his accusation that my struggles as a cadet were psychological. Our meeting lasted less than five minutes.

My dad e-mailed me back after two weeks and asked to take me out to dinner. I felt torn about accepting his offer. I hadn't left the Academy in over a month, but I wasn't sure I could afford to spend the energy. Plus, the only way I could get to the restaurant was if he drove me, and I wasn't sure I wanted to be in a car with him. My mom had told me that he crashed his car into an overpass once when he was drunk. Like all of her stories, I wasn't sure if it was true or not. After debating for two days I decided I might regret it if I turned down his one invitation to see me.

I waited for Dad in front of the field house in the dark. A pair of headlights approached and stopped in a far corner of the parking lot. A door slammed, but another minute passed before its occupant reached me. My dad was blond, balding, and tall. We hugged clumsily before getting in his car. Once we were driving, I clung to my seat belt in the dark and silence. I didn't know what to say, and apparently neither did he. The awkwardness continued in the restaurant. We finally talked about his dog, and I asked about my sister. Dad said she was living in the mountains with her husband, a man older than Dad whom I hadn't met.

Before he dropped me off I asked if we could stay in touch. I had asked him the same thing when I was fifteen, but this time was different. I wouldn't be waiting by my e-mail for him to make contact. If I decided I wanted to see him again, I would e-mail. If not, I wouldn't. It wasn't my mother's or my father's choice. It was my choice.

On February 1 upperclassmen e-mailed a document called "Rules of Engagement for Forty Days." We had exactly forty days remaining until Recognition, so upperclassmen were intensifying the rules. Whenever we passed any of the ninety or so upperclassmen, we would be required to greet them with their rank; first, middle, and last names; squadron position; major; and hometown. For seniors we would also have to recite the job they would assume in the Air Force upon graduation. Beat sessions would become even more frequent. We could be required to recite the specifications of every plane in the Air Force inventory in alphabetical order, including the manufacturer, alpha numeric designation, nickname, primary function, and crew positions of all thirty-seven aircraft. Walking down halls was prohibited; only lunging was acceptable. Bath robes were banned; we could only wear rain coats to the shower. Before leaving the squadron we had to complete a series of push-ups and pull-ups. The most strict of rules was the proclamation that we were never, ever, under any circumstances to be alone. If Charlie needed to pee, I would need to go with her. If I needed to vomit, she'd have to run with me to the bathroom. We had to coordinate our academic schedules so we never returned alone from the academic building.

Forty Days began on a Saturday. The yelling in the hallway exploded at 10:00 p.m. Charlie and I were both in our room, wearing athletic gear, trying to study. "What's my hometown?" one of the upperclassmen yelled among a cacophony of other shouts. Out the peephole, a swarm of upperclassmen surrounded three of our classmates who had been trying to use the bathroom. Charlie looked up from her biology text, frustrated. If the yelling continued, we would both need to join them. Technically I had been on a Form 18 since the beginning of January. But sometimes I needed to give my classmates a show of support and the upperclassmen a demonstration of my work ethic to stay in their good graces. My performance was pathetic, but as long as I tried every once in a while, it kept them from harassing me. "You're recovering from meningitis," one of the upperclassmen said once. He was one of the tougher trainers, and his compassion shocked me. It seemed every other time misfortune fell upon a four degree—illness, injury, or punishment—upperclassmen blamed that individual's weakness. I didn't want to lose his good faith.

Out in the hallway, my classmates did push-ups while they tried to guess the hometowns and majors of each of the upperclassmen yelling at them.

"Sir, the answer is aeronautical engineering."

"No!"

"Sir, the answer is engineering mechanics."

"No!"

"Sir, the answer is behavioral sciences."

"No! Do you even know my hometown?"

"Sir, the answer is Miami, Florida."

"No!"

"We have to go out there," I said. Charlie hesitated to agree. She was struggling to keep her As in all six classes, and even at 10:00 p.m. on a Saturday night, she couldn't give up study time. Charlie and I hurried to put on our BDU uniforms. Before walking out the door, we both glanced at an Excel spreadsheet we had compiled, memorizing a few more majors and hometowns.

Within fifteen minutes, our entire squadron of thirty-five four degrees was in the hallway with more than fifty upperclassmen. Two of the guys who did push-ups next to me kept their bodies near enough to me that I could slightly lean against their arms, giving a little extra support so I didn't fall to the floor as often, though my head pounded with the exertion and the yelling. The impromptu beat session lasted an hour. From then on we limited our trips to the bathroom. Many of the men kept juice bottles in their rooms to use as urinals. Like many of the women, Charlie and I often peed in our dorm room sink, which, at the time, didn't seem at all bizarre. It was just another way of surviving.

CHAPTER 13

*More than half of the service members sexually
assaulted in the military every year are men.*

—Department of Defense Sexual Assault
Prevention and Response Office, *Annual Report
on Sexual Assault in the Military*, 2014

One Friday morning in early February, I woke to a burning between my legs. When I rolled over it felt like a wound being ripped
open. Charlie and I put on our uniforms and walked at attention
to the bathroom, passing only a few upperclassmen along the way.
Inside a women's room stall, peeing exacerbated the searing pain.
This sore was just like the one I had before getting meningitis. Less
than a week after it appeared, I was in the ICU. In the bathroom
stall, I cradled my throbbing forehead in my palms. The need to tell
Dr. Creech about the sore came to me as a fact, not a possibility
with which I could wrestle. It was like a connect-the-dot puzzle: I
linked the last point, and the picture of what had caused my meningitis infection became obvious. I had done research online about
viral meningitis, and knew that herpes could sometimes cross the
blood-brain barrier from where it lived in the nerves of a person's
back. From there it could infect the spinal fluid, or even the brain,
especially when the patient was under considerable stress. Herpes
could also be the cause of the sore between my legs. The vaginal
sore could be the clue Dr. Creech was missing. Maybe if he knew,
he could make me well again.

Telling Dr. Creech I thought I had herpes would open up the
question as to how I contracted the virus, and that I lied to him

in the ICU when he asked if I was sexually active. But I thought of my declaration at the top flight of stairs my first day back after Christmas to start helping myself. Holding true to that might make the difference between getting well and continuing to be sick, between graduating and being kicked out. Dr. Creech might blame me just as CAP had. The Academy might punish me for having sex with an upperclassman, fraternization, and kick me out just as CAP had. The choice was lose-lose: seek treatment by admitting I had been raped and face possible punishment, or keep silent while my health drained away. Either option could cost my dream of becoming a pilot.

I waited for Dr. Creech on a sheetless gurney in the treatment room. Dr. Creech seemed hurried like the other doctors when he leaned over me, clutching the railings at my side. "What is it you needed to talk to me about?" His tone felt like an equal mix of impatience and concern.

I hesitated. "It's about how I got sick." I glanced to the patients at my side, my best this-is-private gesture. He understood and led me to his office.

"Something happened last semester right before I got sick. He was a senior and he said he would help me study. I have a sore and I think I have herpes." I stared at my shoes.

When I looked up Dr. Creech wheeled around in his desk chair to sit a few feet from me. He looked me straight in the eyes, so directly it momentarily brought me back. "I'm sorry," he said. He understood exactly what I meant without needing me to be more specific. I searched his face for disapproval but couldn't find any. He didn't think I was lying. "If you were my daughter," he added, still looking directly into my eyes, "I would kill him." Dr. Creech's anger wasn't at me. He was mad at my rapist. He didn't blame me. He didn't think I was weak or a slut. At least there was one person in the world who didn't judge me. A tight spot in my chest immediately loosened. I breathed in deeply, deep into my diaphragm. "There's someone I want you to talk to," he said. He turned to his desk and reached for a stack of yellow Post-It notes. "Juana is the Academy victim advocate, and a very dear friend. She was a nurse here when

I was a cadet. When she retired from active duty, she chose to stay to help cadets like you."

I immediately dismissed the idea of speaking to someone else. I needed action, not talking. Nevertheless, I stuffed the Post-It in my pocket.

"The sore you told me about," Dr. Creech said, turning his attention back to my medical needs. "You have it right now?" I nodded, painfully aware of what would happen next. "Okay," he said softly. "Let's head to an examination room so that I can take a look." My body tightened—my stomach, my chest, my jaw, my crossed legs. But there wasn't a choice, for me or for him.

After I undressed, Dr. Creech and a medical tech, a woman, came into the exam room. The sheet covered my hips and thighs, my socked feet hanging off the far edge. The woman opened up sterile packaging on a tray next to my feet while Dr. Creech stood next to my abdomen. He looked up at the ceiling where a cartoon had been taped. "What's it say?" he asked.

"Does this tail make my butt look big?" I read. Above the caption, an elephant turned to look at a bow tied around her tail.

"I don't get it," Dr. Creech said, pretending not to understand.

"Girls always think their pants make them look fat," I explained.

"I'll have to remember that when my girls get older."

"How old are they?"

"Four and six." The thought of his two daughters—young, beautiful, protected—made me ache with jealousy.

I slid to the edge of the table, and Dr. Creech held my toes to guide my feet to the stirrups. He held one hand to my left toe slightly longer than needed, a brief gesture of warmth. "Okay, let your knees fall," he said. I let an inch of air open between my knee caps. "A little more." His voice sounded as hesitant as my knees. I widened them only slightly further, taking deep breaths that radiated down my arms and legs, calming me. "You'll feel my fingers now," he said, but still I flinched. Despite the shock of his touch, and the memories it conjured of Thomas, Dr. Creech's cautiousness made me feel respected, even when the medical tech handed him something that looked like a razor blade, which he used to scrape the sore for a sample. Despite the acuteness of the stinging pain that shot through my pelvis, Dr. Creech's gentleness was something I had never known. The examination was a confusing mix of violation and comfort.

After I dressed I met Dr. Creech back in his office. "Do you think it's herpes?" I asked.

He nodded. "But we can't say for sure until the test comes back in a few days."

Even though my awareness of the pieces of information had been building for two months, it was too much to process: I probably had a sexually transmitted disease, Bowman gave it to me, and he was the reason I became so sick, and was still so sick.

Dr. Creech told me he had spoken with Dr. Powell, who wanted to try a drug called DHE, often used for migraines. I'd need to go into the hospital to get it in an IV. My desire to fight against a second hospitalization lasted only a few seconds. I went back to my dorm room to pack a backpack full of textbooks and comfortable athletic gear, and Major Tate drove me back across base to be readmitted. I left a note for Charlie and an e-mail to Erick telling them where I'd be, though without a car, neither would be able to visit.

A young nurse, a woman whose silver jewelry dressed up her blue scrubs, led me to a room at the end of the hallway, in the opposite direction of the ICU. At least I wasn't as sick as I had been. At least now I could walk unassisted. I sunk into the cushiony mattress in my new room. "It's so soft," I said to the nurse.

She laughed. "Every cadet says that." I pulled back the pink knit blanket and white sheet. Covers, such a simple luxury.

Dr. Powell, the neurologist, came in after the medication began to drip in my IV. "So you still aren't well?" he said. It felt like an accusation, not a question.

"No, sir."

He flipped through my chart, avoiding my eyes. "Well, hopefully the DHE will help," he said. He turned from the room before I could answer. He had stayed less than two minutes and had hardly looked in my direction.

Once I was alone in my room, the quietness shocked me. I didn't hear upperclassmen or four degrees barking. Being alone had exacerbated my fear in the ICU, but it didn't now. I needed this silence. The memories of Dr. Creech's compassion that morning kept me company, the way he said he was sorry for what had happened and held my toes. Besides, I didn't feel like I was dying like I had in the ICU. I wasn't panicked with fear. I was more hopeful than I had been in two months. I was proud of myself for telling Dr. Creech the truth, for helping myself. I would feel better soon, and with enough time to salvage my grades and finish the semester. I would be a pilot.

When my phone rang, the noise rattled off the bare walls. I didn't know who would be calling. "Oh my God! You're in the hospital again," Roger said before I said hello. His voice was high and whiny. Roger continued a monologue about how awful my repeated hospitalization was without asking me how I felt.

"How did you find me?" I hadn't spoken to him in five weeks.

"The nurses gave me your room number," he said. Of course the nurses wouldn't have any idea why I wouldn't want to speak to someone who identified himself as my big brother, but that still didn't explain how he knew I was in the hospital. I didn't then know that Roger had created an alternative AOL username, one that I hadn't blocked, so he could monitor when I was online, or in this case, wasn't. I mentally screamed "fuck you!" at the nurses' naïveté, and an even louder "fuck you" at Roger for being a stalker. I wanted to yell that he was a fucking asshole to be so self-centered. I wanted to yell at him for letting his dick ruin our relationship. If he were a better man, he would have kept his promise to protect me like I was a little sister. If he were a better man, I would have someone other than my doctor to comfort me. What happened between us wasn't my doing. I understood that now. He was the one who put his hand down my pants in the middle of the night in October, and again the night doctors released me from the ICU.

Despite the hateful words careening through my mind, I said in a calm tone, "I can't talk right now." I may have been strong enough to keep the promise to myself about ridding him from my life, but I didn't yet have the courage to voice this new anger.

Before Roger could reply, I hung up. He called again, and again, each time the ring bouncing off the walls so there was no gap at all between each, just a continuous stream of annoying, headache-aggravating noise.

The next morning a nurse bounced into my room carrying a stuffed bear that held a Hershey's chocolate-filled basket in its paws. I offered her a smile, but as soon as she left I threw it against the empty recliner in the far corner, hard enough to send the chocolates flying.

Despite the medication, my headache didn't improve over the next two days. Instead I felt worse. My headache throbbed too loudly, making me more nauseated and dizzy. That's how the last two months had gone: one better day followed by days of worse pain and malaise. By Sunday night the hand my IV drained into puffed up like an inflated latex glove. The nurses pulled the line and tried in vain to start a new one. Nurses and doctors, even an anesthesiologist had a try, as if starting an IV were a contest. Six people crouched over me, all wrapping tourniquets around my arms and poking me with needle after needle. My body fought against them. Each time they inserted an IV into my skin, I wished they would fail. I was fed up with being penetrated against my will. If I could keep myself from allowing an IV into my vein, even though its intentions were to help me, I could gain a small sense of control over my body. I didn't mind the pain of the needles—I was so split from my feelings that I hardly registered it—and the frustrations of the nurses only awarded me a sense of satisfaction. Fuck them, I thought. After two hours they gave up and let me sleep. Cotton balls and strips of clear tape covered my arms, but finally my room was dark and quiet again.

The next morning Dr. Powell returned. "Looks like the DHE didn't work," he said. Just like his previous visit, he didn't make eye contact. "I'll start your discharge paperwork." He left as soon as he finished his sentence, leaving me no time to argue. Weren't doctors supposed to release patients because they were better, not worse? What about my disclosure to Dr. Creech? Why didn't the probability that I was infected with herpes give them a better course of action than a migraine drug? I was furious at him for releasing me, for giving up trying to help me.

Back in my dorm room, I forced myself to catch up on homework. First rounds of exams approached, but I hadn't come anywhere close to completing all the reading. Plus, I hadn't a clue what I had missed of my professor's lectures.

"Feel any better?" Erick asked on AOL.

"Only worse," I answered before shutting down my laptop.

That night Erick snuck into my dorm. He climbed on top of my bed and spooned against my back. His warmth and pressure comforted me like I had never before been comforted by a man. Maybe cuddling didn't bother me because Erick had no power over me. I liked his concern and friendship, but I didn't need him in order to become a pilot. He wasn't decades older than me, and I never looked up to him like he was a father or a big brother.

Yet I was concerned for him. He wore a white tank top and athletic shorts so that he could pass as an upperclassman, but it was risky. If he were caught leaving his squadron as a four degree and entering a woman's room, he would be severely punished. Kicked out, even.

"What if they catch you?" I whispered.

"They won't," he said. He stayed a couple of hours before creeping back to his room on the other side of the dorm.

The next afternoon, after I sat through hours of classes without absorbing a word my professors spoke, Erick asked if I wanted to meet him down the hill at the athletic facilities, one of the few places where four degrees could talk. We walked the halls of the gymnasium, passing the water polo pool and the weight rooms, and after an hour or so, ended at the hockey rink, where we stopped. "Something happened to me last semester," I told Erick. I still couldn't say the *r* word. "I think I got herpes, and that's what gave me meningitis."

"How is that even possible?" Erick asked. He meant how herpes could give me meningitis. I shrugged. "I'm sorry that happened to you," he said, and then he kissed me. My confession hadn't caused him to turn away from me. It did the opposite. Confused, I kissed him back. The kiss felt sloppy and suffocating, but not like a violation.

A few days later we walked the athletic facilities again. This time, Erick said, "I really want to make love to you." I didn't see a reason not to have sex. I didn't compare it to what happened two months earlier in the library. Somehow I considered the notion of having sex with Erick without ever admitting to myself I had been raped and that I had already had intercourse. Erick would be my first, but I didn't focus on that point, either. To consider myself a virgin would have required me to recognize one's virginity was something to lose, something about which I should care.

As a member of the intercollegiate swim team, Erick knew where we could go to be alone. I followed behind him through the indoor pool's double doors, the smell of chlorine intensifying. Beyond the bleachers, high ceilings made room for broad, tall walls painted with falcon imagery and American flags larger than I was. I looked up at the diving platform five meters over my head and down into the deep blue water of the Olympic-size pool. Like most places at the Academy, it made me feel miniscule.

Neither of us spoke as I trailed after Erick, and I didn't have any second thoughts. Erick led me down a rickety, spiral staircase to the swim team's supposed hangout. I clung to the center pole as I circled downward, dizzy from my temples' throbbing and from having not eaten. At the bottom, in the darkish, unused utility room, four or five bare mattresses haphazardly covered the cement floor. The air smelled rank with sweat. The control room had a blue glow from the panoramic window that opened to the depths of the pool beneath its surface. Through it, a dozen set of legs kicked furiously back and forth across the length. All the hours I had spent swimming in the pool, I had never known the window was hidden underneath the surface. My eyes drifted from the window to plump breasts and bare legs on the covers of porn magazines scattered across the room. Used condoms, which I had never before seen, littered the floor and mattresses. Erick didn't seem fazed by any of it, so I decided not to be, either. I didn't care that the room felt sleazy; I was sleazy. A series of men had repeatedly branded me a piece of meat and infected me. It wasn't possible to become any more debased.

"Are you sure you want to?" Erick asked. He looked at me and paused like he wanted a genuine answer. That I had a choice made me want to that much more. Besides, Erick and I fucking would be a normal thing for eighteen-year-olds, as evident by the semen-filled condoms at my feet. I wanted desperately to be normal.

I didn't want Erick to see me naked, and I didn't let him take off my shirt. He took the time to put on a condom in case I did have herpes, otherwise the sex was rushed and awkward. The pain reminded me of one of my high school friends describing sex as being skewered by a telephone pole. I turned my head away from Erick's eyes to the panoramic window to the swimmers' legs and torsos. Despite knowing they couldn't see me, I felt like the one on display. Like the world knew I was there, in the dark, underground poolroom among the used mattresses, porn, and condoms, like another piece of trash. I mentally split away from my body more and more until I couldn't feel anything. I didn't regret my decision, but I didn't want to experience it, either. Erick fucked an empty shell of my body.

I may not have ever been able to say "no" successfully, but at least now I could say "yes." Thomas, Roger, and Bowman may have easily made me their objects, but I could take it all back now by fucking on my own volition. Finally I was in charge.

Each day after my hospitalization, my headache grew worse. By Friday morning a week later, I went back to the clinic. Dr. Creech was on vacation, so I saw a different doctor who glanced at the computer and confirmed that I had herpes. My stomach clenched so violently that I thought I would vomit all of my organs onto the floor in front of her.

"I guess we can try more meds to help you feel better today," she offered, and led me to the treatment room.

I rested on a gurney for hours. My lips felt cracked and my mouth dry. Clear tape covered the fleshy part of my forearm where an IV forced saline, cold and foreign, into my blood. Various stages of blue, purple, and green bruises covered the rest of my arms, marks from all the earlier needles. Everything, except my headache, felt fuzzy from the painkillers. My headache wasn't fuzzy but stabbing. And squeezing. Squeezing so violent I matched it pound for pound in fists around the cold railings.

Another doctor, a woman, guided a cadet to the bed next to me. A blue curtain separated us. The patient cried from her bed while she waited for the doctor to come back with a white cotton blanket. "You're going to feel better soon," the doctor said.

"What if it isn't just a migraine? What if it is something more serious?" The mention of a headache yanked my attention away from my own. She didn't need to explain her fear. Word of the case of meningitis—*my* meningitis—had spread across the Cadet Wing, and even two months later, the collective consciousness of the meningitis scare had lingered to the point that this girl worried I had somehow infected her. She didn't know who I was or that I occupied the gurney next to hers. She didn't understand that I didn't have that kind of contagious meningitis, the bacterial kind we had all been vaccinated against; she didn't understand that the kind I contracted came from a virus. Herpes. Bugs from my rapist's semen that penetrated their way through my body's helpless defenses to the fluid and tissue around my brain. The reality of that fact I now knew for sure sunk into my chest.

After the doctor left I heard dialing on a cell phone, one of the many rights of an upperclassman. "Mommy, will you pray for me?" she asked, crying again. What it would be like to say that word, "Mommy," to someone in whose voice I found comfort. I clenched the cold, unmoving railing next to me and counted the things this girl had that I didn't: a blanket, a cell phone, a mother, tears, faith, and a migraine.

When my IV bag emptied and my doctor finally returned, I told her I was ready to go back to my room. The reality was that I couldn't conjure tears to express how sick I felt. I had never expressed my pain that outwardly. Even if I did, no one either cared enough or knew enough to do anything for me. Even if I had a cell phone, I didn't have anyone to call who could make it better. I had just been discharged from the hospital days earlier because the doctors' attempts at fixing me hadn't worked. I didn't think there was anything left they could do, so I asked the doctor to please unhook me from the IV. She did.

Just in case an upperclassman asked me the reason I was on the Terrazzo in athletic gear and not running, I kept a Form 18 medical excuse in my hand as I staggered back to my room. Each step took a conscious effort to force my legs to move. My body felt wobbly. Heavy. Back in my room, I fell once again onto my bed. It was the middle of the afternoon, so I didn't dare unfold the stiff blanket at the foot that had to be kept in a perfect pattern. I still didn't have anything in which to wrap myself. I curled into a ball in the corner of the bed, on top of the silver wool, facing the wall.

When I woke up hours later, music blared down the hall. My walls vibrated with the bass. Charlie had propped open the door, and my classmates were all in the hallway. I didn't understand. Four degrees weren't allowed to stand in the middle of the hall and talk. Then I remembered it was 100s Night; one hundred days remained until the seniors graduated. To celebrate, they all went out to drink. In exchange for being allowed to roam freely among the halls, four degrees were given the task of "decorating" the seniors' rooms before they returned. My classmates schemed to cover one room's floor with water-filled Dixie cups. The seniors would have to pick up, but not spill, enough cups to make a path to their bed after they came back drunk. Per tradition, the men went to a porn shop to find the most offensive pictures of burly men penetrating busty women to hang in the room of the girls they considered the biggest "bitches." The two women my classmates had chosen to target were known for being strict and unfriendly to the four degrees, though plenty of the men treated us the exact same way.

I was supposed to be helping my classmates, and I wanted to be talking and walking freely like them. The night was a celebration for four degrees, too: only one hundred days remained until we became upperclassmen. But I couldn't make my body move.

The next time I woke up, Erick was shaking my arm. "Baby, open your eyes," he insisted. I didn't understand why he was next to me. Then I remembered again: 100s Night. For those few hours only, four degrees could walk into other squadrons. I'm sure he wanted for me to wake up to enjoy the freedom with him. My eyes closed again, and everything went dark. "Baby, open your eyes just for a second."

"Are you okay?" Charlie's voice asked somewhere behind Erick. Erick shook me again, but I couldn't answer them.

CHAPTER 14

Less than five percent of all sexual assaults are
put forward for prosecution, and less than a third
of those cases result in imprisonment.

—*The Invisible War*

After 100s Night I didn't regain consciousness until midmorning the next day, Saturday. I wasn't sure why I had been out for so long when I hadn't taken any extra drugs. By Monday I pulled myself together enough to appear in classes, though the professors' words were incoherent. I couldn't focus on anything they said, but not just because of the sheer pain. I couldn't follow logic from one sentence to the next. I didn't understand what was happening to me.

As I neared the third month after contracting meningitis and remained hopelessly ill, I needed to help myself more than ever. I remembered my declaration months earlier to save myself. But I didn't know how. I didn't know how to stop ignoring my body. I didn't realize I could have refused to get up off the gurney in the clinic the previous Friday afternoon. Or that I could have returned to the emergency room. Beneath my robotic behavior of reporting to class and attempting to remain a four degree, beneath my conscious thoughts I was terrified of being kicked out. If I stopped appearing in class, I could lose everything. I could end up back in my mother's house. I wouldn't be a pilot.

During Recognition a few weeks later, I watched from the bleachers as upperclassmen beat my classmates on the indoor track's faux grass. They ran through tire obstacles, did 2,005 consecutive

jumping jacks in reverence to our class year, and did push-up after fucking push-up. Over my camouflage BDU blouse, I wore a
reflective yellow armband, bright like the color of a highlighter,
marking me as a "broken" cadet. My scarlet letter. Surprisingly my
upperclassmen didn't give me a hard time for not having the medical
clearance needed to participate, but I held the shame nevertheless.

For three days the upperclassmen beat my classmates until they
could hardly stand, but I couldn't help them. All I could do was as-
sist with reciting knowledge when they were so drained they forgot
the quotes we had been memorizing all year.

On the third day of Recognition, I stood at attention with
Charlie as upperclassmen trashed our room in the most violent of
room inspections. At least I could support Charlie with my presence
while the upperclassmen flipped our mattresses and pushed books
from our desks, yelling at us for our poor room standards, which of
course wasn't true.

That afternoon I rode in a van with other broken four degrees,
like Molly with her broken back, as our classmates ran in the snow
to a rock formation where the seniors had painted rocks with our
class color—silver—for us to find and haul back to our squadron.
Charlie and I returned from the "Run to the Rock" and found our
rooms immaculate, recovered from the mattress-flipping room inspection that morning. Our freshly ironed service dress hung ready
for us. The upperclassmen had cleaned for us. We were joining their
ranks and were no longer underlings to train. Their job molding us
into warriors was complete.

The thirty-five of us four degrees waited in the television room,
unsure what would happen. An upperclassman called my classmates'
names one by one and directed them out the door. During my turn,
I walked down the center of our squadron's hallway. The lights had
been dimmed, so all I saw of the upperclassmen on either side of me
were their shadows. As I passed them, most saluted me. I didn't then
know that upperclassmen only saluted those whom they respected,
and that receiving so many demonstrations of approval was rare. At
the end of the hallway, I reached Major Tate, the adult officer over
our squadron. "Congratulations, Lynn," he said. It was the first time
one of my superiors said my first name. He shook my hand.

I joined my classmates in a square formation. We stood at attention with our back to the door. When our final classmates had arrived, a mass of footsteps approached from behind. Our training officer said in his usual harsh tone, "Upperclassmen, fall out and make corrections." My heart beat faster at hearing the phrase that often began beat sessions. "There are no more corrections to make," the upperclassmen responded in unison.

"About face," said our training officer. We turned around to face the upperclassmen waiting to award our Prop and Wings. Giving a four degree the small, metal insignia was another sign of respect, and upperclassmen usually picked out a handful of four degrees to award them to. One by one, upperclassmen congratulated me with my first name and pinned a pair of Prop and Wings on my service dress. My collar filled with the shiny insignia. I received even more than Charlie, our squadron's strongest woman. I didn't understand why they respected me despite my not having done a single push-up with my classmates in three days. Now I realize they saw strength in me even when I wasn't allowed to do the exercises. They saw how I persevered despite how sick I was.

Recognition was supposed to signal the end of our transformations from worthless basic cadets into competent soldiers, whole cadets and whole people. But I was still broken. I was finally allowed to have blue jeans, a cell phone, a fuzzy bathrobe, and blue fleece sheets with white clouds, but, even though those items gave me comfort, they didn't resolve my headache or my shame. Charlie and I now chatted on our way to class, strolling across the Terrazzo in diagonals, ignoring the white marble strips, never running. I no longer kept my eyes caged, but often I felt too lazy to put on my glasses, which often ended up buried in my book bag, despite my worsening vision since developing meningitis. I walked across the Terrazzo blind to the sky, the mountains, and the friends whom I passed.

A few weeks after Recognition, I made an appointment to see the victims' advocate only because every time I saw Dr. Creech he pestered me about it. Juana's office was in the counseling center in the other dorm across the Terrazzo. On the way down the stairs, I passed a life-size painting of Lance Sijan, for whom this building was named. Sijan was a 1965 Academy graduate whose plane crashed over Vietnam. For forty-six days he survived in the jungle with little food or water, evading the Viet Cong despite a fractured skull, leg, and hand. Eventually the Vietnamese captured Sijan, and he suc-cumbed to his wounds several months later. We had all memorized this story, and his biography rested on each cadet bookshelf. In his portrait Sijan wore his green zip-up flight suit, his yellow helmet resting between a hand and his hip. His eyes were dark in a shadow, but they were like the Mona Lisa's, following me as I crept past him. Sijan made my plight seem tiny in comparison. If he survived in the Vietnamese jungle for forty-six days despite being broken, then what was I doing visiting a victims' advocate to talk about my problems? My feet slowed, knowing it was wrong of me to wallow. Yet for a reason I couldn't identify—maybe because somewhere I hoped to find help—I inched toward the counseling center.

In Juana's office jars of chocolate candies and jelly beans sat next to Kleenex. A giant quilt with handprints and words of thanks hung on one of the walls. Opposite the quilt there was a poster of a woman in an A-line dress and high heels standing in front of the "Bring Me Men" ramp. I recognized the picture from when the first class of women entered the Academy in 1976.

"So, what has happened to you?" Juana asked. She was a short woman with hair just like my mom's—dark, short, and curly—but she spoke with a Brooklyn accent. I mumbled something about my flight instructor molesting me before I arrived at the Academy. I didn't want to tell her at first about the upperclassman in case she blamed me and decided to report me for fraternization. As I spoke, I couldn't feel my palms squished between my thighs, even though my legs crushed them hard enough to leave indentations from the seams of my pants. Juana didn't fill the silence after my story with trite sympathy, nor did she express a smidgeon of judgment. I glanced at the quilt on her wall and saw the words of gratitude from other women. Clearly I wasn't the first to make a confession to Juana. So then I told her about the library, herpes, and the ICU.

"How are you feeling now?" she asked.

"Not well," I said, minimizing, as always.

"And Dr. Creech is still working with you?" I nodded. "He's a really great doctor and such a sweetie pie." I hadn't ever heard someone at the Academy use that expression, "sweetie pie." "What does he say?" I shrugged. He didn't know how to make me better, but neither did the neurologist, the doctor who should have had the answers. "There's got to be something they can do to help you."

I liked Juana's matter-of-fact tone. She didn't want me to wallow, but she encouraged me to confront my current situation: I was barely surviving, and though I had pulled myself together enough to pass my classes so far, something needed to change.

Back in my dorm room, I researched herpetic meningitis on the Internet. I found a journal that explained that, even though herpes didn't respond to antibiotics, it did to a specific antiviral drug. But when left untreated, herpetic meningitis may not resolve on its own. I understood then I still had an active meningitis infection. I was never "post-infectious," as the neurologist made it seem. I debated what to do. If I did nothing, I might worsen. If I tried to convince the neurologist how sick I was so that I could have a second spinal tap to confirm the lingering infection, he might send my case to a medical review board, which might decide to expel me. The only reason Molly hadn't been kicked out was because she had parents who had the clout to petition on her behalf. The Academy had recognized the inappropriateness of "midget tossing," and she was granted permission to remain a cadet despite no longer being medically qualified to serve in the Air Force after graduation. I doubted the Academy would show me that sort of mercy.

A few days later I shuffled to the bathroom, where the only thing I could vomit was stomach acid. Then I inched back to my room to make myself look presentable for class. I hadn't showered in two days and was wearing USAFA sweatpants with slippers, my hair in a messy ponytail. My hair had barely grown out to be long enough to pull back, and my bangs often fell into my face. "Still feeling sick, Lynn?" Major Tate asked as he passed me in the hall.

"Yes, sir," I said. I no longer needed to add that word "sir" when speaking to upperclassmen, but customs and courtesies would always apply to the active duty officers who oversaw us.

Major Tate led me into his office, where he asked what I thought was wrong. Trusting him was a conscious choice.

"Sir, I think I still have meningitis," I said.

"What do you mean?"

"I would need a second spinal tap to be sure, but I've researched the kind of meningitis I have, and I know it lingers more than other types, and the neurologist doesn't believe how sick I am. He won't do anything to help me."

"What do you mean, what type of meningitis do you have?"

My eyes drifted to the healthy cadets walking briskly to their classes on the Terrazzo below. Major Tate continued to wait. He wasn't like Dr. Creech, whom I had first trusted; Major Tate's voice was deep and firm unlike Dr. Creech's slow, calm words. Major Tate would never express sympathy as outwardly as Dr. Creech, but he had never spoken disparagingly to us women, either.

"I was raped," I said. It was the first time I said that word. "He gave me herpes, and it went into my spinal fluid." The confession hung in the office, but at least it occupied someplace other than just my chest.

Major Tate didn't respond at first. He held his closed fist to his mouth. "I can't tell you who, but there are other girls in this squadron dealing with the same thing." Major Tate didn't call me a liar. Or weak, insisting I should have been able to stop it, like CAP did. I wondered who these other women were. There were about twenty women in my squadron, and I couldn't imagine a single one of them letting themselves be made a victim. "I'll talk to them at the clinic. They'll take care of you."

Major Tate called whomever he had to, and I received an e-mail with an appointment for the very next day.

For my second spinal tap, I didn't have the benefit of IV drugs as I did for the first, which I hardly remembered. Dr. Powell thrust a blue gown in my direction, led me to his procedure room, and left. When he returned he warned, "This is going to burn a little," and it did far more than a little. The medicine that would numb my skin

torched across my back. I twisted my arms around each other and
squeezed my own hand. I wished I had a nurse to hold my hand as
I did in the ER.

After I put my clothes back on, I met Dr. Powell next door in
his office. "There were a few white blood cells in your spinal fluid,"
Dr. Powell said. I still had meningitis. I still had fucking meningitis.

I had learned online that spinal fluid shouldn't have any white
blood cells in it. They meant I had a continuing infection. For the
past four months, I had attempted, and mostly succeeded, to function
as a four degree with an active meningitis infection. Why hadn't I
made someone treat me earlier? What the hell had I done to myself?

Yet again, my anger wasn't directed toward the neurologist
who overlooked my care, but at myself. A normal person would
have screamed in someone's face to get the help they needed. But
I couldn't stand up for myself. I didn't consider why I hadn't demanded more attention—that I would have risked disenrollment
and had nowhere else safe to live or any other ambitions for myself.
I didn't think of Molly, who had also tried to minimize her injury
when she returned to her dorm room despite her broken back. I
didn't think how the Academy had trained me to act exactly as I had.

"So what are we going to do about it?" I asked.

"I suppose if we wanted to be aggressive we could give you IV
medicine for the infection."

He supposed. He still didn't understand what the past four
months were like for me. "Yes, sir. I think we should do that." I
kept my response polite despite my rage, which was starting to flip
toward him.

"Well, let's think on it. I'll talk to Dr. Creech and we'll decide
what we should do in the next few days. Go ahead and go back
to class."

Class. He wanted me to go back to class. With meningitis. But
I was a four degree, and he was a lieutenant colonel. There was no
arguing.

I didn't go back to class as ordered. Instead I sought the one person who had seen my illness more than any other. At the front desk
of the Cadet Clinic, I said to the sergeant, "I need to see Dr. Creech.
Immediately." The sergeant didn't argue as she would have with

any other cadet who hadn't spent the semester with IVs shoved in their arms. Instead she led me to my usual gurney in the back corner of the treatment room, and even gave me a white cotton blanket when I asked for it.

"So?" Dr. Creech asked as he found me. He walked up next to my bed and clenched the railings with both hands, leaning over my legs.

"Still white blood cells," I answered.

He dropped his head. His dark, short hair shook side to side. "What does Dr. Powell want to do?"

"He told me to go back to class." My tone of voice gave away my anger.

"I'll go talk to him," Dr. Creech said.

When he came back he told me I could return to the hospital. I would be there for eight days while they treated me with the antiviral IV medication. He left again to write up the paperwork, but as he walked around the end of my bed, he paused. He grasped my socked foot. He held it in his hand for a minute, looking down. "I wish we could have done this for you sooner," he whispered.

I didn't bring my textbooks with me to the hospital this time; I finally respected my body's need for rest. I only packed athletic gear plus toiletries, my CD player, and my teddy bear, the one with the blue USA sweater I had made with Roger, but I tried not to let it remind me of him. The bear was all I had. I had cuddled with it night after night.

One of the nurses, whom I knew well from my last hospitalization, was waiting for me at the nurses' station. "I put you in your same room," she said as she walked me to the end of the hall to the quiet room with a recliner and a great view of the city. This time I didn't mind the IV. With it, relief would come.

I didn't call my mother, but I called my dad, and he even came to visit. My sister Amy came, too. I hadn't seen her in more than four years. She brought flowers planted in a little pink wooden box that I kept on my nightstand. Losing my sisters due to their estrangements with our mother was one of my most painful child-hood experiences. But now I had them back. Both of them.

On the second to last day of my hospitalization, a Sunday, Dr. Creech came to visit midmorning. It was nearly May and the sky outside was a deep blue, unblemished by clouds. I had been resting with my blankets covering me up to my nose, staring out at the city below, feeling more at peace than I had in months, or maybe ever. I would be well soon. I was about to finish my four degree year. I was a year closer to graduating and becoming a pilot. Dr. Creech took a seat in the recliner a few feet from my bed. I sat up from my covers. I told him I still had my headache, but it wasn't quite as bad, just a dull throb rather than a pounding. I hadn't thrown up in two days. "Good," he said. But then he looked out the window, hesitating. Something was wrong.

"What is it?"

He turned back at me. "We have decided to have a medical review board for you."

"We?" I said, shocked. I could tell there was no "we" who had made the decision. It was Dr. Powell.

"Don't worry, don't worry." He explained he would meet with a panel, including Dr. Powell, and a few of the commanders over-seeing the Cadet Wing, and they would most likely give me a med-ical leave of absence. "They won't kick you out, but you need time to recover." After everything I had survived, now they wanted to send my case to a review board. I had fought through four degree training and classes and had passed them all, but now they wanted to send me home for however many months.

"Get some rest. I'll update you when it happens," Dr. Creech said, and he left my room.

Just that quickly I squashed the shreds of anger and grief that had begun to surface, and I returned to automaton mode. I called my mom to tell her I might have to go on leave and I wanted to stay in Colorado. Dialing from my hospital phone, I prepared myself for her tears and my guilt that I was putting my own needs above hers. But the tears and blame didn't come. Instead of flipping into Angry Mom, she offered to send me money so I could rent an apartment.

I wasn't in the space to wonder why she wasn't mad about me not coming home.

As I waited for the medical board and my commanders to make their decisions, I began studying for finals. My grades were the lowest I ever had in my life—B's and a few C's—but I was grateful to be passing. For once I had a smidgeon of self-forgiveness.

That Friday evening Charlie and I walked to the student center to get pizza for dinner, a luxury earned after Recognition. Walking back to our rooms, I wasn't paying attention to whom we passed until all at once, I felt someone's eyes. I looked up to see Marcus Bowman. My rapist. I matched his stare. His hands curled into fists. My own hands felt fragile around the pizza box. Just as we passed, Bowman began laughing. Laughing at *me*. Charlie continued to chatter, oblivious. Sometime in the previous weeks, Charlie had told me that Bowman had also raped one of her friends in another squadron. He had also been arrested over Christmas break—at the same time I was in the ICU—for sodomizing a teenager, a girl with cerebral palsy who needed a wheel chair. I didn't remember when Charlie had given me that information, probably because at the time I couldn't make sense of it. Then I understood fully for the first time. Bowman sought me out specifically to be one of his many victims, just as Thomas had. Now what I didn't understand was why he was still walking across the Terrazzo, a free cadet.

The day before final exams began, I studied from my chemistry text in my dorm room. My headache persisted, but it had softened since being treated with the antiviral medication, and I could now more easily read and understand the words and equations. Major Tate knocked on my door frame and informed me that his commander's decision was to make me leave immediately, before finals, on a seven-month medical absence. Slowly I realized the implication. Returning in January meant I would have to redo the entire spring semester. Beat sessions, Recognition, everything. I would walk at attention, memorize knowledge, do push-up after blasted push-up, and cage my eyes. I was being punished with being made to redo half of my four degree year while my rapist was walking freely across the Terrazzo.

"So I'm what? Un-Recognized?" I had never heard of such a thing.

Major Tate said, "Well, at least you can bring up your grade point average that way. Plus, you can come back to this squadron, so it won't be as hard to fit back in." Major Tate's words were an honest attempt to comfort me, I could tell. It wasn't in his character, just as it wasn't in the Air Force culture, to let me feel sorry for myself.

In the next few days, I narrowed my focus to each small task on my to-do list. Robot mode. At personnel a sergeant cut up my military ID and issued me a temporary one that would expire in the event I didn't return. I signed paperwork acknowledging my status as a cadet on leave. Mom sent me a check to buy a used car—from where she got the money I wasn't sure—and Erick taught me to drive the SUV I purchased from a graduating senior, a stick shift. Charlie came with me to sign the lease on my new apartment across the highway. They both helped me pack my car. The last time I walked across the Terrazzo, I kept my vision focused on the pebbly stone at my feet. I couldn't stand to look at the silvery buildings or the chapel spires, knowing I wouldn't be welcome back for seven months, and even then I would no longer have the right to allow my eyes to gaze.

CHAPTER 15

The world is a dangerous place, not because of those who do evil,
but because of those who look on and do nothing.

—Albert Einstein

I assembled puzzles to pass time in my new apartment. I used a fold-ing table, the only piece of furniture I owned other than a twin bed I had borrowed from Jeff. I hunched over the pieces, organizing them by shape and color patterns. At first the puzzles I chose came with 100 pieces. To delay the crushing disappointment of finishing them and not having my life back, I migrated to bigger and more complex patterns. Eventually I found a puzzle of 1,026 similarly shaped pieces to form a space shuttle. The picture was comprised of white and orange photomosaics, tiny images of astronauts and space vehicles. Surely I would be a cadet again before I could ever complete it.

When staring at the tiny pictures too long made my head throb, I stood on the patio balcony. My apartment was in a brand new building untouched by previous occupants, and the walls were a pristine off-white. The light pink carpet felt cushiony under my socked feet, but I didn't appreciate the newness. The only opin-ion I held about my apartment was disappointment that it faced away from the mountains and the Academy. Instead it overlooked a brown, vacant field. I leaned against the cement balcony, listening to the buzz of a twin-engine airplane from the airfield where my classmates were learning to fly gliders. The noise filled me with a strange combination of envy and annoyance. I should be up there, flying. Instead I was alone in my apartment, the noise only aggravat-ing the pulsing of my temples. Since being treated for meningitis, I felt less fatigued, less under siege. My muscles strengthened. But my head still hurt every moment of every day. Dr. Creech said that I was probably too sick for too long, and that it would take time for my headache to fade. The erasure of the physical pain was just one more thing—in addition to my return to the Academy—for which I was waiting.

In July, after Erick finished a training exercise in which he survived in the woods by killing and eating bunnies, evading capture by up-perclassmen dubbed "enemy" forces, he asked me to take a road trip with him. We planned a drive to a Florida beach, visiting my mom in Missouri on the way and his parents in Texas on the return.

Erick drove my Explorer most of the way to Saint Louis. I covered my eyes with a blanket to keep the piercing rays from exacerbating my headache. We ate gas station beef jerky and listened to Nickelback and Alien Ant Farm while the wind from the open window blew my shoulder-length hair into knots. We talked about both family and the Air Force. Erick wasn't like most cadets in that he didn't want to be a pilot; he wanted something more on the ground, perhaps Special Forces. He was a combination of tough but sweet and didn't hesitate to mention his cat back home that he missed.

At Mom's house Erick carried my duffel to the basement where we'd sleep. Since I had left a year earlier, Mom had moved again, this time to be closer to the inner-city elementary school where she now taught special education. I was proud of her for achieving her dream career after years of suffering through fast food and cleaning jobs. She worked hard to overcome her hearing disability, so I tried not to mind that I didn't have a bedroom in the tiny house. Instead most of my things were in boxes, and my bedroom furniture was assembled in the corner of the basement, sectioned off by two-by-four studs instead of real walls. Fresh sawdust scattered the cement floor around the studs. "Don't worry, we'll get dry wall up soon and you'll have a room again," Mom said. She said "we," but I didn't notice the plural pronoun. I didn't wonder who might have put the studs into place. I threw my bag on top of my comforter next to a half dozen of my old stuffed animals arranged around my pillows. Erick put his bag on the couch on the other side of the basement where he'd sleep. My mom wouldn't say anything if we shared a bed, but I only had a twin, and not sleeping well would result in a monstrous headache.

The next morning my sister Megan drove from her medical school a few hours away. The four of us, including Mom, played in the Saint Louis Science Center. Together we assembled a ten-foot-tall arch, a replica of the steel iconic version. Mom held the wedges in place so they formed a column, her short black curly hair pressed against the yellow plastic. Megan supported the other column with her lean arms. As Erick and I stacked the columns higher and higher, they swayed and teetered, and we moved faster and faster to complete it before it collapsed. "That one," Megan pointed, and I reached for the next wedge near my heel while Erick stabilized the highest pieces. Mom laughed at our intensity. Finally Erick reached to put the last, skinniest wedge in place at the top. Mom and Megan released their arms and the arch stood, fully supported as each of its legs leaned into the other. "Woo-hoo!" we cheered and high-fived, as if assembling the mini-arch was a remarkable accomplishment.

"Your mom isn't that bad," Erick said later when we were back in the basement. "My family never has fun like that." His dad was a geeky type, absorbed in books, and his mom remarkably quiet. They didn't play board games or go camping like mine. I remembered playing with a Playskool jumbo jet when I was about four years old. Mom made propeller noises as she pushed the plane through the air in loop de loops, and I giggled so hard my belly hurt. Despite the difficulty with Mom, we always had good times to counterbalance the bad. Erick's envy made me feel a stab of guilt for being so hard on her, for not wanting to live with her again.

Later that afternoon we drank lemonade on the back patio. The air was even more humid than it was hot, and we all clung to our cold glasses. "We had an open house last weekend," Mom said casually.

She was talking about the real estate business she had recently started on the side.

"Who is 'we'?" I finally asked.

"Oh, I have a real estate partner."

"Who is it?" Megan asked.

"Oh, no one. Just a friend." Mom giggled girlishly. Megan and I let the vagueness slide. Mom was living alone for the first time in her life and seemed happy. If there was a man in her life, what concern was it of mine?

"I went to the Muny the other night," Mom said next. The Muny was the Saint Louis outdoor theater.

"Who took you?" Megan asked, knowing that Mom did not magically grow the fortitude to see a play on her own. "Oh, no one." She giggled again, holding her hand over her mouth like she was trying to contain her excitement.

After we finished our lemonade, Megan came with me to fill my car with gas. Erick and I planned to leave in the morning. "She's clearly seeing someone," Megan reflected as I drove. She had her elbow propped up against the window, her palm crushed against her forehead. Megan had the same skin tone as me—darker than our dad's fair skin, far lighter than our mom's olive tone.

"But why is she acting so weird? Why doesn't she just come out with it?" I asked. I could no longer ignore the way my mother said "we," the fresh studs in the basement, or my stomach's growing knot. As I held the gas pump in place, it hit me, the reason for the nausea I'd felt when I plopped into bed after first getting home: the stuffed animals that lined my pillow were all the ones Arthur Thomas had given me.

"What's wrong?" Megan asked as I sat back in the driver's seat. Her forehead was wrinkled, her eyes staring into mine intently. "What's that look for?"

"It's nothing. For a second I thought maybe it's Arthur Thomas she's seeing. I'm being paranoid." I knew his wife had finally divorced him, but still.

"You're right. That can't be it," she said after a pause that lasted a beat too long. I had told Laura about the abuse ages ago, and she knew our mom walked in on him touching me. So she understood the improbability of my fear.

Back at Mom's house, I did what my mom would have done to uncover the truth. While Megan, Erick, and Mom drank a second round of lemonades outside, I snuck onto Mom's computer to read her e-mail. I read one from Mom's high school friend Joyce, who was giving Mom directions to a resort where they would vacation together. My mother's original e-mail to Joyce was attached at the bottom. In the last line, Mom made a joke about whether she should give the security guards at the resort her current name or if she should tell them Arthur and Donna Thomas. I was stunned: my mom was making a joke about her last name becoming Thomas. She was dating Arthur Thomas. My mother was dating my rapist. I knew her well enough to know that if she was dating him, she'd marry him. She was only ever romantically involved with one man during my whole childhood, and she had exchanged rings with him after knowing him for four months. My mother didn't date. She married. That's why she was joking about her last name. My limbs felt weak, like double clicking the print icon to document the proof required nearly more force than I had. I stood on my wobbly legs.

"Megan, it's him," I said when I found her in the kitchen. I showed her the e-mail. As she studied it she looked as shocked as I felt.

"I'm going to confront her," she said, like the protective big sister she was.

I took back the evidence and folded it in my palm. My legs raced down the stairs to my pseudo-bedroom. I looked around at the stuffed animals I had thrown from my bed and the fresh sawdust under the new two-by-fours. *He* had been here. *He* had been the one to arrange the stuffed animals and was building walls for my room. Two mushed words ran through my head on repeat: helpyourself, helpyourself, helpyourself. . . . My mind was still reeling, but my hands knew what to do. They started piling the things I couldn't live without into a mass on my bed. My photo albums. A scrapbook Megan had given me. Some picture frames. A few stuffed animals, not the ones from Thomas. There was no time to sort through boxes for anything else, any other pieces of me that I needed to protect and save. I pulled the pile into my arms to run to the car, the picture frames threatening to fall from under my elbow and shatter on the concrete. Erick, confused, came with me. "We're leaving. I'll explain later," I announced. That was when I first consciously thought, I'm leaving Mom. I'm leaving Mom forever.

Back in the house, I overheard my sister's argument with my mom. "I don't know what you are talking about!" Mom shouted.

"We know, Mom, okay? We know you're seeing Arthur Thomas." I kept still on the other side of the kitchen wall, listening to my mother defend herself. Erick, beginning to understand something bad was happening, crept by the argument to get our bags while I continued to listen. After several minutes Mom stopped denying the accusation. Instead she cried. I pushed my shoulder into the plain wall, listening to my mother break down.

"What do you want me to do, Megan? Do you want me to just die lonely, huh? You girls can just go and leave me here all by myself, and you don't think I have the right to date anybody?" Mom probably didn't know the full extent of what Thomas had done to me, only what she saw in the basement and whatever sense she made from my declaration that I didn't want to see him again.

"You know what that man did to her!" Megan screamed. I had never before heard my sister yell so fiercely. I admired her bravery. Mom didn't answer. So that was it. Mom didn't deny that Thomas molested me, but she wanted him anyway. She wanted him more than she wanted me. What was wrong with me that I was so unlovable?

While I waited for their screaming to end, I found my pet love bird in his cage in the living room. Mom had bought the love bird for me when I was in the seventh grade and my stepdad moved us to the country, away from my friends. I had named him Neptune after my favorite planet. I stuck my fingers between the bars of the cage and reached to pat the soft green feathers on his forehead, wishing he could come back to Colorado with me. He chirped happily, oblivious. For years Neptune lived in my bedroom with me. I had cleaned his cage, fed him, covered him with a cream towel at night to remind him to sleep, and talked with him when I was lonely. And now I was leaving him behind. I withdrew my touch slowly. Abandoning him felt cruel. Abandoning *her* felt cruel, too, leaving the person who had sacrificed money and energy she didn't have to provide every possible advantage to me, who taught me to read and multiply, who convinced me I could do anything in my career. But that's exactly what I decided to do. It was the third time I was putting my needs above my mother's. The first was when I left her to go to the Academy. The second was when I didn't come home on medical leave, though I hadn't understood then why Mom hadn't been upset. Now I planned the most selfish act of all: complete desertion.

My mother's eyes had dried by the time we gathered outside to say good-bye. Despite the yelling a few minutes earlier, despite my leaving a day early and the chasm that had opened between us, Megan, Mom, and I smiled at each other. I learned how to play pretend from my mother, and that afternoon we said good-bye on the lawn, we gave our best performances. Megan, who also prepared to leave, said bye first. I wasn't sure if Megan had made up her mind to never see Mom again as I had. Megan had already been in a back and forth relationship with our mom for years. As I watched them hug, I tried to keep from sneezing because of the freshly cut grass under our feet. I was allergic to it, and besides, it was yet another reminder of a man's recent presence. I had read once that the smell emitted from newly cut grass was a defense mechanism, a signal of the plant's anguish at being severed. I held my fist to my nose in a vain attempt at preventing myself from inhaling the pollen.

When I hugged Mom I pretended it wouldn't be the last time. "Love you," I said. I did love her, and maybe I thought bringing peace into our final minute together was the only gift I could give her. Or maybe I avoided direct confrontation with her because that's the only thing I knew how to do well. I wasn't like Megan.

"Love you, too," Mom said. "Drive safely." Drive safely, the last motherly advice I would ever receive.

I put on Metallica and jacked up the volume as we sped away. Though I don't remember when I told him, Erick knew what Arthur Thomas did to me, and he, more than anyone else, lived with the consequences. We had sex often, but I rarely kissed him because it reminded me too much of suffocating with Thomas's dick rammed in my mouth. Sometimes I had panic attacks in the middle of sex. So Erick understood, at least a little, the violation of my mom's engagement to him. He had no experience with a family who played games together, but he had no experience with this sort of betrayal, either. We didn't talk as I sped across state lines.

On a Panama City beach, I lay motionless on my towel. Children laughed nearby as they played, but I couldn't make sense of the noise. The voices of their parents sounded foreign, as if they were speaking Chinese. I felt heavy and sluggish, and the sunscreen in my backpack lying in the sand next to me felt too difficult and too far away to find and apply. Anything other than the compulsory task of breathing in and out several times each minute required too much will. I ignored my skin as it burned.

But that night I did something other than breathing and keeping myself alive. In a military hotel, Erick and I fucked hard, hard enough to drive away the faint twinges of my grief, rage, and guilt. We fucked again in his parents' house in Austin, and then in a vacant field in Nowhere, Texas, where the weeds were taller than our heads. We fucked until the only pain I felt was the stinging of the sunburn's blisters on my back bursting open and oozing onto my Air Force–issue blanket, my punishment for being a despicable daughter.

Back in Colorado Springs, an envelope from Mom waited for me in my mailbox. Inside, a blank piece of paper hid a check for five thousand dollars. Money to live on until I returned to the Academy, I realized. She had been sending me one thousand dollars every month, but this way we could avoid future contact. I had never said to my mom that I didn't plan on seeing her again, but she anticipated it. Both of us had always known the fate of our relationship. I didn't think about how my mother had found that much money to send me on her teacher's salary. Only much later would I allow myself to realize from where the funds had come all summer—from Arthur Thomas. The money I used to buy macaroni for dinner and to pay rent came from the man who molested me. Was it denial, or was it self-preservation, that allowed me to mindlessly deposit the check? While still sitting in the bank's parking lot, I reached for my cell phone and deleted the entry for Mom.

CHAPTER 16

Shame cannot survive empathy.

—Dr. Brené Brown, "Shame Is Lethal"

A few days after my road trip with Erick, I met with my therapist in the Counseling Center. Juana, the victim advocate, had referred me to Dr. Miles the previous April, just after my third hospitalization. He was a civilian, a behavioral sciences professor who also did psychotherapy. When I went on leave the Counseling Center gave me special permission to come back for therapy, even though I wasn't a cadet in good standing. "How was your trip home?" Dr. Miles asked at the start of our session. Unlike most of the military officers, he was short and small, a competitive runner. He had short curly hair and clunky glasses.

"It sucked," I said. Typical teenage words but oh so understated, as usual. I wasn't looking at Dr. Miles but rather at the closed oak door. I knew the door was for my own privacy, but it felt like a threat. My only other memories of being alone with an older man were the times I was molested and raped. A stray hiccup escaped my chest and interrupted the silence.

"You hiccup when you're nervous, don't you?" Dr. Miles spoke slowly and carefully, in a gentle tone, unlike the barking that came from nearly everyone else. I nodded. I had recently developed the strange tic. "How come you are anxious? What happened at home?"

"I found out my mom's dating the man who molested me. They'll probably marry."

If Dr. Miles reacted, I didn't notice. I was still looking at the oak door. "I don't understand," he said. "Were they together when

168

he molested you?" I shook my head. Since beginning therapy three months earlier, I had only shared protected pieces of my story, usually extracted by Dr. Miles after long intervals of awkward silence. In fact I still hadn't told anyone the whole truth, not Charlie, not Juana, not my sister Megan, not Erick. I could tell Dr. Miles didn't understand what had happened to me when, and by whom.

I told him everything. I started with my mom, and how I believed she broke my arm and ripped a ligament in my thumb when I was a toddler, and the yelling and tears and name calling. Then I told him about sitting on the tarmac's asphalt with Thomas's arm around my shoulders and his declaration to love me like a father. I told him my mom saw him molest me and turned her back on me. I told him about Roger and the Broadmoor and the ring, and then Bowman, and how I didn't fight him and I didn't tell anyone and that it was my fault I ended up in the ICU. It all came out as involuntarily as my hiccups. He didn't interrupt me, not even when my sixty minutes was up. I talked for three hours.

Only when my throat was raw and I stopped speaking did Dr. Miles ask questions. He took me back to the beginning of the story, to my mother. He asked about what she would say when she became angry, her impulsivity, her fear of losing her children even when we were small, her inability to maintain friendships, and how she saw the world in black and white without room for ambiguity. "It sounds like your mom possibly has borderline personality disorder," he said. "People who are borderline usually struggle to maintain relationships because they've suffered extreme childhood trauma. Do you think that perhaps your mom chose to be with Thomas to push you away, because she was so afraid you would abandon her one day anyway?" When I considered the situation with my nineteen-year-old brain, and not my splintered, little-girl heart, Dr. Miles's suggestion felt exactly true. I knew my mom loved me. I knew my mom would never want me to leave her. How many times growing up did I hear her cry, "Someday you're going to leave me and I'll be all alone?" My mom had brought about her own worst fear. I nodded. Dr. Miles said, "You weren't selfish in deciding not to see her again. Just because she made the choice to date your molester out of fear and her own trauma doesn't mean you have a responsibility to stay in the relationship. You did what you needed to do to protect yourself." To protect myself. I had never before been able to shield myself from those who hurt me.

When I left his office it was after 5:00 p.m. and the other staff had all gone home. Just outside the Counseling Center, I stepped into a single-person bathroom. The lights were off but the room was bright, the frosted windows barely filtering the glaring sun. I locked the door, unzipped my hoodie, and threw it to the ground. My mom did this to me, I thought. She contributed to all these things happening to me every bit as much as I did. I was parentless. Why did it feel worse to feel wronged than it did to feel guilty?

I slid down against the linoleum onto the floor that smelled of bleach. The cold tile relieved my sweaty, burnt skin. For the first time since I became a cadet, I cried. At first my tears were silent, but then panicked sobbing came from my chest. My mom did this to me, mymomdidthistome, mymomdidthistome, mymom-didthistome. . . . I bawled so hard I retched a banana into the toilet that I had eaten hours ago. My throat burned as much as my skin but I continued to sob, now cradling my own legs in my arms, rocking myself.

I didn't return to my empty apartment. Instead I drove to Major Tate's house. Even though he wasn't my commander anymore, he called me often to check in and gave me an open invitation to his house. That was common, for professors and commanders to act like second sponsor families. Since getting meningitis I rarely spoke with Jeff. I was ashamed and didn't want him to see what a mess I was. The Tates already knew I was a wreck. Nancy, Major Tate's wife and an Italian, made pasta that night. Eating real food was a relief. When I first moved into my apartment, I wasn't even sure how to boil spaghetti or brown hamburger. Living with Devoted Mom, I was so spoiled that I hadn't ever cooked a meal. Sitting next to the Tate's four-year-old daughter was a relief, too. While I devoured the rigatoni, she chatted relentlessly about the games she had played at school. Entering her fantasy world was the respite I needed.

But it was only that, a temporary break. That night a scream woke me up. The sound came from my throat, but I didn't recognize it as my own. I opened my eyes to endless darkness squeezing at me. My heart thumped. I couldn't control my breathing, and my chest heaved for air as if I had been sprinting. I curled into the tiniest ball I could to protect myself from whatever was out there in the darkness. Someone was about to hurt me. I couldn't be sure it was a man. It could be a woman, or maybe not even a human at all. My blankets, sweatpants, and underwear weren't enough to help shield me. I kept my eyes open wide to watch. I had to protect myself, unlike all those other times.

My eyes adjusted to the darkness, and I realized I was still at Major Tate's house, sleeping in his daughter's playroom. "Lynn?" Nancy called. She sat near where I laid on the futon. It was too dark to see her clearly, but I could feel her there in the space next to me.

"Yeah, I had a nightmare," I said.

"Try to go back to sleep," she whispered, and she stayed there, right next to me.

The next morning while her daughter was at school, Nancy and I walked with their two huskies. We hiked over pine needles as we cut west through the forest just beyond the cluster of base houses. Nancy's short red curls bounced as we walked. As the dogs tugged on their leashes, I told her about the visit to my mom and the nightmares I had nearly every night. I told her about my flashbacks, too, how sometimes out of nowhere I felt I was being molested or raped all over again. I remembered Thomas the most, probably because the abuse happened so many times with him, and because those memories were the strongest. I still didn't remember exactly what happened in the library; I only knew that from it, I contracted herpes. I also told her about my relationship with Erick.

"You have no business having sex right now," Nancy said. When I didn't respond, Nancy talked about sex and what a healthy relationship ought to look like. She said sex could be wonderful. Until then, I didn't know that being penetrated could be anything other than something to endure—that a woman could find it plea-surable. I wondered if she was right, if I shouldn't be sleeping with Erick, but I doubted that I would ever be capable of the intimacy Nancy talked about. I wasn't even sure I wanted that type of con-nection with a sex partner. I resented that I was a sexual being at all. It seemed sex was the reason those men had hurt me so badly, and when I had sex with Erick, I felt as corrupt as my rapists. "The longer you stay with Erick, the harder you are making it on your-self," Nancy said. "You need to deal with your trauma before you continue in a relationship."

The conversation was the first time in my adolescence that I talked with an adult about sex. I believed what she said about its virtues when it was part of a healthy relationship. Yet I didn't break up with Erick. There was safety in staying with him. Erick hadn't abandoned me like so many other people had. Plus, he abided by my unspoken rules when we slept together. He didn't try to make out or grope, which all reminded me too much of being molested. I didn't even have to take my shirt off if I didn't want to, and I usually didn't. Erick stayed in our relationship because he loved me, but I stayed with him because I was still too timid to stand on my own.

On a Tuesday evening in September, I drove to the Academy's Counseling Center, not to meet with Dr. Miles, but because Juana had asked me to. She wanted to form a survivor's group for those of us with whom she worked. I hesitated on each of the stairs lead-ing down to the Counseling Center. I wasn't sure why I agreed to come. I was done talking about what had happened to me. I didn't want to say the words, "I'm Lynn, I've been raped," as if I were at some type of twelve-step meeting. I was dressed casually—in jeans, Erick's faded gray Hard Rock Cafe T-shirt, and with a ponytail. Walking across campus dressed like a civilian made me feel like I went to a normal college. I could pretend the Air Force didn't own me and my body. I could just as easily pretend that I didn't need the other women about whom Juana had told me. Then I remembered the panic attacks, the nightmares, the difficulty I had focusing my attention, and my anxiety when I thought about returning to my cadet status, and I continued walking.

On the other side of the doors, three women sat in the waiting room chairs wearing various combinations of blues uniforms, US-AFA athletic gear, jeans, and T-shirts. They could be any one of the other few hundred women cadets at the Academy. We exchanged half smiles. "Come on in, Lynn," Juana said. I felt comforted by Juana's matter-of-fact, no-theatrics tone, just like I felt comforted by Nancy Tate. Juana had been working at the Academy for as long as I had been alive. The only reason she didn't retire, she said, was because she worried about what would happen to her clients without a victim advocate who understood the Academy culture.

While we waited for the others, two of the women compared notes on an engineering class they shared. My toe tapped repeatedly against the carpet. When a woman I recognized from my former squadron, Trish, walked through the door in gray USAFA sweatpants and T-shirt, her blond hair spilling over her shoulders, our eyes locked. She paused before her next step. "Hi, Lynn," she offered after a long second. I said hi back. In that one moment, I understood her. The crankiness she had oozed as a sophomore toward all of us four degrees in Squadron Four. The red eyes with which she left Major Tate's office after long closed-door meetings. Her nickname: the Whore from Four. I saw reflected in Trish's brown eyes my own fear, anxiety, and shame.

When eight of us filled the chairs, Juana stood. "Well, ladies, I'll be in my office if you need anything. Let me know when you are done." She wouldn't stay to moderate our conversations. She only wanted us to have the opportunity to share our experiences.

We remained silent. I squished myself further back into the blue cloth chair. Each of us waited for the other to speak first. "Let's break open those jelly beans," one of the women said. We erupted in nervous laughter. She reached for the bubble dispenser Juana had left for us on the middle table, passing it around. As the other women started with the basics of introductions—names, years, squadrons, hometowns—the blues, greens, reds, and blacks of the candy stuck against my sweaty palm.

The introductions became more serious. A squadron mate raped Mandy at a party. An upperclassman raped Lesley on a picnic table at a field-training exercise. A friend and classmate raped Reagan in his car. A classmate raped Jen in an academic classroom after hours. Another four degree raped Lindsey on several occasions in the underground control room next to the pool littered by mattresses, condoms, and porn. A training officer, a senior, raped Lori after he gave her a date rape drug.

When it was my turn, telling the truth wasn't nearly as hard as it had been that first time with Dr. Creech or the second time with Major Tate, but I still paused. "I was raped by a senior in the library who had said he would help me study," I said finally. "In high school I was molested by a man my mom is probably going to marry," I added before my shame could make me filter. "I've been assaulted more than once." The air exhaled from my lungs.

"Me, too," Reagan said. Really? I thought. This woman, a senior with beautiful long black hair and muscular shoulders, had also been assaulted more than once. She looked tough and courageous, but it had happened to her, too. I couldn't see how she would possibly be to blame for her multiple attacks as I thought I was.

Next, Trish shared her story. She was the only one in our group who hadn't been raped by a cadet. When she was fourteen, her stepdad, an Army sergeant, started having sex with her. She didn't tell anyone until she became a cadet. Hers was the only perpetrator who faced a conviction: her stepdad was serving a year in military prison. "My mom stayed married to him," she said. "She took his side." Then it was my turn to answer "me, too." Trish looked as relieved as I felt. I couldn't believe another girl had also experienced the complete rejection of her mother choosing her perpetrator over her. She didn't deserve her mother's betrayal. I didn't deserve my mother's betrayal, either.

Trish said, "I had sex with a lot of guys last year. Like, maybe two dozen? I don't remember." Only now did I understand how cruel those Whore from Four cartoons had been.

I didn't look at Trish, or Reagan, or any of the other women and judge them for what their perpetrators did to them. I didn't look at them and think of how weak they were for letting themselves be victims.

That first night we mostly talked about how we were surviving as cadets. The other women talked about how hard it was to study between panic attacks. Many of them also had medical problems. We talked about what it was like to see our rapists in class or at lunch or in formation.

When I told the women I had been raped by Marcus Bowman, they recognized the name. He had been sentenced to fourteen months in prison for sodomizing the teenager with cerebral palsy, and he had been discharged from the Air Force without a diploma. I also found out that before me, two other cadets had said Bowman raped them. Including those two, myself, the civilian, and another woman in my class who said he raped her four months after me, five of us eventually accused Bowman. The other women in our group shared rapists, too. Going around our circle, and talking about other survivors we knew, we listed a handful of the same perpetrators.

Each Tuesday six to ten of us met at 6:00 p.m. in the Counseling Center. Each Tuesday we listened to each other's struggles. Lindsey was plagued with daily panic attacks. Lori had such a hard time concentrating that she was failing her classes. Trish struggled with the stigma of her vicious nickname. Jen went into the hospital repeatedly with ovarian cysts. Lesley fought a disenrollment for psychological diagnosis, a supposed personality disorder. Reagan faced the shame of having been raped by two men. Mandy struggled to push charges against her perpetrator after investigators lost her rape kit, the results of the medical exam, and the DNA testing she did immediately following the assault.

Though all of our individual stories were unique, the same topics recurred: doctors at the clinic who treated us as hysterical rape victims whenever we asked for medical care, commanders who threw out cases against perpetrators for lack of evidence, anger that all of our lives were left in shambles while the rapists—all except Marcus Bowman—thrived as cadets. Fewer than twelve of us met together during any given week, but between all of the women we knew and heard of, we mentally collected dozens and dozens of the same accounts.

Juana asked us if we would be open for male victims to join us, too. It initially surprised me to hear that men were raped. Juana insisted that there were many male victims, far more than we would guess. Of course they could come, we had insisted, but none ever did. I could only guess how much harder it would be for a man to admit that he had been raped, how much more shame our culture could stack upon him.

After weeks of spending increasingly more time with the Tates, Nancy asked if I wanted to move in with her sister. That September, halfway through my medical leave, I moved out of my bare apartment. Then I had people to share dinners with. On my worst headache days, I curled into a ball on the couch, surrounded by the family's cats.

The list of people who supported me became longer than I ever could have imagined: Juana, Dr. Miles, the Tates, the women in my survivors' group, Charlie, my sisters. Each day in their company, and without my mother's influence, I liked myself a tad more. Sometimes I even looked at myself in the mirror. I made jokes. I thought of myself less as a weak girl who couldn't defend herself but instead as someone who had survived too many violations.

No longer quite so desperate for connection with others, I decided to break up with Erick over Thanksgiving—eleven months after we started dating and a month before I returned to the Academy. Besides Nancy's continuing insistence that I begin to make healthier choices for myself, once I came back as a cadet, I wouldn't be allowed to have a relationship with Erick, Charlie, or any of my old classmates. They'd be upperclassmen, and even a casual conversation could be grounds for reprimands, even disenrollment.

I found Erick in his dorm, and his happiness to see me made me feel guilty. I sat in his roommate's swivel chair several feet away from him. "Erick, I can't date you anymore," I blurted. He couldn't hide his shock. His shoulders slumped and his eyes bulged. I regurgitated Nancy's chorus: "I have so many things that I need to deal with,

I have no business dating anyone right now." I told him more of
the psychobabble, about how I was probably having sex because of
unresolved trauma and I needed to heal from that first. He slouched
back in his chair, silent. Seeing him so sad made me feel bad. I had
been with him for the better part of a year. He had stayed with me
while I was in and out of the hospital, crippled in pain, and rejected
by my mother. That was more than I ever could have expected for
a teenager. Yet I ended our relationship as abruptly as it had once
begun. "I'm sorry," I said, and feeling cowardly, I left.

On New Year's Day I packed my uniforms and school supplies
neatly in my issued trunk and a few Rubbermaid bins, planning to
leave everything at Major Tate's house. As a four degree again, I had
to relinquish my car, cell phone, jeans, slippers, pajamas, Erick's gray
Hard Rock Cafe T-shirt, which I still hadn't returned, my journal,
the mass of stuffed animals I slept with, and each of the relationships
I had gained in the previous months.

I wouldn't be allowed to have painkillers, either, though I packed
them anyway. My headache didn't feel quite as intense as often,
though it still hadn't gone away. One of the physicians I saw while
on leave, a lieutenant colonel and chief of the Cadet Clinic, told me
that I needed to overcome my "psychological issues" if I wanted to
get well. Dr. Powell, the neurologist, wrote in my medical records
that my "adjustment disorder" was to blame—and not the infection
that he left untreated for four months. A civilian neurologist I visited
told me that I appeared to be in far less pain than I reported. No one
could fix my headache. Whether I returned to the Academy or not,
I would remain in pain.

I still vomited often. Sometimes I puked because my headache
was awful, other times for no apparent reason. But I knew my body
at least well enough to know that I carried most of my stress in
my stomach. I didn't blame my psychological issues for my chronic
pain, but I did blame them for my stomach problems.

Anticipating that my headache would worsen back at the Academy, I hid narcotics to take with me. I disassembled tampons from
their applicators, wrapping the pills in cotton and shoving them back

inside the hollow plastic tubes. I hot glued the plastic packaging back into place, though the extra precaution probably wasn't necessary. A box of Playtex was the only place upperclassmen would be afraid to search when looking for contraband. At least I would have the pills to help me survive the next several months.

PART IV

Warrior Spirit

CHAPTER 17

Pledges endure verbal and physical abuse as a condition for membership. . . . By yielding himself to the group this way, the pledge gains a new self, complete with a set of goals, values, concerns, visions, and ready-made discourses.

—Peggy Reeves Sanday, *Fraternity Gang Rape*

On the morning of January 2, 2003, I put on my blue cadet uniform for the first time in seven months. Once Nancy helped me unload my trunk and Rubbermaid bins from her Jeep, she hugged me good-bye. I rested my chin on her shoulder. Unlike so many other moments when others tried to comfort me, I felt her arms wrapped tightly around my back, powerful and supportive. I didn't feel numb to it and I didn't want to let go, but her arms fell from me.

I wouldn't be allowed to speak to Nancy or anyone else who had grown to love me. Without a cell phone, the only way I could reach my sisters would be via e-mail. Charlie, Erick, and the women of my survivor's group were upperclassmen again, tasked with the mission of molding me into a warrior. Even worse, one of the higher commanders, Colonel Watkins, or Uncle Petey, as the cadets called him, also forbade me from speaking to the Tates. Uncle Petey was the same man who decided I would come back as a four degree. He had also declared that I would be moving from Major Tate's unit to Squadron Thirty-Six across the Terrazzo. One of the women in my survivor's group had explained, "He didn't think you'd actually come back, and now he's trying to make your life as hard as possible. Thirty-Six is by far one of the most hostile to women. Uncle Petey is screwing you over." My friend was trying to explain that the four degrees in my new squadron, the only people who I would be allowed to speak to for the next three months, had already been bred for seven months into a misogynistic culture far worse than anything I had experienced in my old squadron.

As Nancy ended our hug, she looked at me firmly in the eyes. "You're going to be fine."

Nancy's Jeep faded in the distance. I took two deep breaths. If I was going to succeed, I had to be strong. And I had to succeed. I was nineteen and had no parents, no money, and no other hopes for myself other than becoming an Air Force pilot. Besides, quitting on my ambition would be letting all the people who had hurt me win. I took one last breath, shutting out my self-doubt, my headache, and the memory of Nancy's comforting shoulder.

The shined laminate floor of my new squadron reflected an image of my blue trunk as I pushed it. My uniform still had "05" patches, my obsolete class year, and as I passed a cluster of upperclassmen chatting in the turn of our L-shaped squadron, they stared. "Who are you?" one asked.

I stopped pushing my trunk and came to the position of attention. "Sir, the answer is a new four degree in your squadron."

"Oh, yeah, the girl coming back from medical leave. How long did you stay last year?"

"Sir, the answer is until May."

"Oh my God! You were Recognized?"

"Dude, did you hear that?" another shouted to his friends down the hall. No one had ever heard of a cadet becoming un-Recognized. To my knowledge, I was the first cadet in history to walk at attention after being pinned with Prop and Wings.

In my new dorm room I would share with a woman named Melissa, I unpacked my trunk, folding and hanging my uniforms. I would have to replace my class patches with new ones that said "06" rather than "05." My blanket with silver trim would need to be returned for one with red trim, my new class color. As my only act of defiance, I pinned my old Prop and Wings on my bulletin board.

———

On the first Friday night, I assembled in the hallway with my new classmates for a "Stairway to Heaven" beat session. The seniors blared punk music and turned down the lights. They ushered us into the bottom landing of the six-floor stairwell at the end of our squadron. In the dark we did push-ups, crunches, up-downs, arm raises, jumping jacks. Each time an upperclassman declared us worthy, we moved up a level. Each time they labeled us pathetic, we moved down. Within only a few minutes of push-ups, my arms shook. Sweat dripped from my forehead. The laminate tile became slick under my fingertips. I had tried to get in better shape before returning, but however many hours I spent at the YMCA couldn't compare to my new classmates' thousands and thousands of push-ups. I told myself to just get through one second at a time. Just one second.

Standing around us, the upperclassmen wore camouflage, BDU pants and blouses, the sleeves rolled up over their muscular biceps. Several folded their arms across their chests. That was the first difference I noticed between my old squadron, Four, and my new squadron, Thirty-Six. In Four upperclassmen always did exercises with us, per the rules. Major Tate would have otherwise accused the upperclassmen of demonstrating poor leadership. But in Thirty-Six the upperclassmen didn't bother.

After two hours, when I had only made it up three stories, the upperclassmen turned the music off and the lights on. All of the four degrees filled the hall, the sounds of our chests begging for air. I stood at attention next to the other three women. In my old unit there had been seven women out of thirty-six four degrees, but by chance in this squadron there were only four out of thirty-five, including me.

"You are so fucking pathetic!" a senior yelled into the face of the woman standing next to me. Pathetic. So many months had passed since I heard that word. "I'm sick of watching your Terrazzo ass stick up in the air during push-ups." "Terrazzo ass," an expression I never heard said directly to someone specifically, referred to the seemingly fat asses of the women cadets. I felt the woman's arms tense at my sides.

After that first beat session, I noticed that the three women often skipped dinner. After not eating at the lunch table, the women snacked on tuna and fruit they kept in their backpacks. Melissa did crunches on our carpet for hours while she studied with a book in one hand. Back in Four, none of us ever worried about our weight.

In Four, reciting quotes and the Air Force inventory mattered just as much as push-ups. In the stairwell of Thirty-six, they didn't give a damn about the B-52 specifications or the words Patten used to motivate his troops.

Another difference: no one seemed to mind that one of our classmates used the e-mail list to send crude jokes and porn to all of the four degrees. After one particularly long afternoon of back-to-back classes, I returned to my dorm and found a video of a horse penetrating a woman, the woman's arms and legs sprawled over a table. The image lodged in my mind as I tried to study chemistry equations. That night I had a nightmare that I was the one being rammed by the horse. Later I asked the three women what they thought of the porn. "It's just Jesse. It's just the way he is," one of them commented. The other two remained silent, and all three looked at me like I was being ridiculous, as if it was foolish of me to worry about a stupid e-mail when we had six academic classes to keep up with between energy-sapping beat sessions.

I saw myself in their myopic perspective. Or, at least the old me. The old me would never have realized that name calling, like Terrazzo ass, and porn should be unacceptable. Why was it that I finally understood how wrong it was? Was it the influence of my survivor's group? They had become increasingly outraged at the bias against women. Or was it living with the Tates, listening to them discuss honor and integrity. Or maybe being away from the Academy for seven months and reading books and watching TV, reminding me that there was a world outside of the military. Or perhaps it was because I liked myself a little more. If someone said I had a Terrazzo ass, I would be pissed. And I thought my classmates should be, too.

On February 1 Melissa and I were standing at attention for a Saturday morning room inspection when an upperclassman told us to turn on our laptop's TV connection. I hadn't been allowed to watch TV since September 11. The space shuttle *Columbia* had just exploded, killing all seven astronauts aboard. *Columbia* had been the same shuttle I had watched launch at the age of fourteen, but now its shattered pieces were scattered all over the southwest US desert. On top of the usual stressors of the winter months and the sadness brought about by the shuttle accident, the United States was preparing to invade Iraq. The administrators assembled projectors on each corner of Mitchell Hall so that we could watch Fox News as we ate breakfast; otherwise, we had little contact with this outside news.

The weekend after the shuttle accident, Melissa attended a ski club trip to the mountains. She was still tipsy when she returned Sunday night. Her thin, straight hair was messy from being in a beanie. "I got really drunk," she admitted. "The upperclassmen had to carry me back to my room last night." She had no idea she could have easily been raped, and then she would be expelled for underage drinking and fraternization, but most likely the rapist would not. I could name a few women who experienced that very thing. I had a sense even then that the harassment I witnessed in our squadron made the environment more dangerous for sexual violence. Much later I would read studies that showed that in units where harassment is tolerated, the rates of sexual assault were often far higher. I warned Melissa, even confiding I had been raped. She shrugged off my cautions.

Everyone seemed to be misbehaving, so I defied the rules that said I couldn't fraternize. Attending a survivor's group was hardly criminal, so I snuck out of my squadron wearing my USAFA running suit, which didn't give away my rank, and left my hair down. The four degree women who had only been cadets for seven months all had butchered hair, but mine was already fully grown out. As long as I didn't pass any cadets from my own squadron, upperclassmen wouldn't know I was a four degree.

Back in the Counseling Center lobby, I filled my hands with jelly beans and told the other women about my new squadron. "I know it feels like a long time, but you only have a few months," Lindsey comforted. Lindsey was from Southern California and wore flip-flops on the weekends, even in the winter. She prided herself on taking bad things in stride, even though she had panic attacks nearly every day. Lindsey had chosen the Academy because she wanted to fly, though her parents could have afforded an expensive aviation school. She was certainly smart enough for any of them, too. "In no time you'll hang out on the weekends with the rest of us," she said.

Since the beginning of the semester, our network of survivors had shrunk dramatically; six of the women had discharged. A few had been kicked out: one for a psychological diagnosis, another for crimes she had supposedly committed the night she was raped, such as fraternization and underage drinking. A few of them had left on their own free will because the burden of continuing on as cadets was too great after their rapes.

The few hours with the other women, talking freely, eating candy, and receiving their comfort, recharged me.

One afternoon while I was dressing for a beat session, I received a strange e-mail addressed to the women of the Air Force Academy. "If you are ever raped, don't report it," the message said. "You'll be kicked out. Go off base to a civilian hospital for a rape kit to preserve the evidence. Don't tell your commander." There were several more long paragraphs addressing the Academy's gender inequity and how we need to be careful not be become a sexual assault victim. The e-mail had been sent with a fictitious name, though all of us remaining in the survivor's network knew intuitively who was behind it: the women in our group who had recently discharged.

Perhaps the e-mail never would have amounted to much if they hadn't sent it to media outlets and dozens of congressmen as well. Perhaps even then it wouldn't have mattered, except that one journalist—John Ferrugia of Denver's CBS-affiliated news channel— investigated the allegations. The story made its way to the national media, and the women appeared on ABC's *20/20*.

Melissa and I both watched from our laptops. I could barely identify each of the six women on the grainy feed. But I recognized Kira immediately. She had been raped by Marcus Bowman four months after me. "They knew he was a serial rapist and they did nothing to protect us women," Kira stated, and she was correct.

Two other cadets had accused Bowman before he raped me, and they weren't silent like I had been. Yet he remained a cadet in good standing, even the point of contact for the Aero Club, which meant that he was the cadet Kira and other women reached out to when they wanted to join the club. Why was he left in that position of trust? The broadcast continued, and one by one the women told their stories. Our door was propped open, and from the hallway I began to hear doors slam, followed by shouts.

"Those fucking whores!" someone yelled. Words like "bitches" and "sluts" echoed down the hallway, too. "Those dykes are trying to ruin us!"

On Monday morning reporters and cameras lined the chapel wall. Their shutters clicked as we ran to class. During the noon meal formation, when I should have kept my eyes caged on the buzz cut of the guy in front of me, I stole a glance up at the reporters. I wondered if they watched me and the other women speckled through each squadron and theorized about who among us were victims. If, with one look, they saw the "victim" tattoo on my forehead.

At lunch that day the cadets' anger was visceral. Mitchell Hall remained loud, full of voices that were normally quiet as cadets ate. I only understood a few conversations at the tables around me, but the word "liar" came up repeatedly. The collective fear was clear: that the women on TV, the women with whom I had once shared a sacred survivor's group, would destroy the Air Force Academy.

The four degree across the table declared, "Sir, I think a woman who gets herself raped isn't strong enough to defend herself, let alone the country, and shouldn't be in the military."

The senior at the head of the table answered, "Couldn't agree more," as if he were commenting on the beautiful weather.

I felt their condemnation in the way each of the nine men at my table glared at me, though I remained silent, staring at the black and white eagle at the top of my white round plate. I understood then that Melissa had told our classmates about my rape allegation. Each of the men at my table knew, and probably the entire squadron. Hearing those words, "not strong enough to defend herself," out of my classmate's lips turned everything I had feared about myself for the past thirteen months on its head. All that time I had believed I should have been strong enough to save myself on that library floor. But something about hearing the asshole across the table speak that fear as gospel led me to question everything about it. Why were they talking about me, and my friends, when they should be talking about the rapists who made the choice to commit these crimes against us? Why weren't they the ones on trial? I maintained the frozen position of attention, but inside I fumed. I had two choices: I could remain quiet, or I could defend myself. I wanted to be courageous, like Megan had been when she confronted our mom, or even like the women on *20/20*, but I knew better. I still had one full month before I would be Recognized, and until then, I needed my classmates' support. I couldn't contend with the other cadet's anger, and I would only make things worse for myself. So I remained silent.

Within two weeks of the *20/20* broadcast, the secretary of the Air Force, an obese man Juana referred to as Jabba the Hutt, spoke to the upper two classes in the auditorium, calling the rapists "bums" and promised to eradicate the problem.

"Bums? Really?" Lindsey shouted in our next Tuesday group. "'Bum' doesn't quite cover it."

Next, General Zayne Spencer, the commandant of cadets, took his turn denouncing sexual assault. I listened in the back of the main student auditorium. "Clearly we have a problem here at USAFA." He strode casually across the stage, carrying the microphone loosely in his hand. "I have three sisters and three daughters. I would be distraught if this ever happened to any of them." He paused to let his words settle for dramatic effect. I dug my forehead into my palm and sank down in my chair. Listening to the rhetoric being sold as sincerity disgusted me. A few months earlier he had said the exact opposite to one of the women in our group. Mandy had been raped at a squadron party. She had been a virgin, and her rape left streaks of blood all over the bathroom. One of her male friends had helped her clean up the blood, but later, when investigators interviewed him and her squadron mates, they all lied. Suddenly there was no blood, and no one could recall her running from the party crying. Then her rape kit went missing, and Zayne refused to prosecute the perpetrator. As was true with any military commander, Commandant Zayne Spencer had the final authority on whether to prosecute a rapist. Investigators and lawyers, those with the professional background to understand a criminal case, only gave suggestions. So Mandy was at the mercy of Zayne's decision. When he met with Mandy, he said that he knew none of his three sisters or three daughters would ever be raped because they behaved appropriately. They were proper ladies, he stressed, who would never drink at a party like she had.

Zayne was a 1978 Air Force Academy graduate. He had been a third-year cadet when women integrated into the service academies, and the class after him nicknamed themselves the "Last Class with Balls." The rumor was that those 1979 graduates hid "LCWB" into their class ring design, and recently they started a web page for their class with the initials. I wondered if Zayne's resentment lingered, too.

Zayne continued his speech from the stage. "Cadets, what would you think if I decided to go drinking in a bar tonight, and then afterward, I walked down the back alley with a one hundred dollar bill sticking out of my pocket? Wouldn't you expect that I would get mugged?" News article after article quoted Zayne's comparison. At least the media understood he was a misogynistic ass who shouldn't be in charge of four thousand young people, let alone make decisions about prosecuting rapists.

The news of rape at the Air Force Academy was plastered across newspapers around the country. *The Today Show, Good Morning America, Larry King Live* all interviewed the women. Whenever a new interview aired on TV or an article ran in the paper, the male cadets became enraged. "Those whores should shut the fuck up," said one at breakfast. "God damn liars," another one said. After the media attention began, the voices of the men who believed women shouldn't be cadets grew louder. "See? This is what happens when you let women in," they argued. Always the attention was on the victims, and not once did I hear a cadet say that a rapist shouldn't be in the military.

CHAPTER 18

In 2014, 62 percent of victims who reported a
sexual assault in the military faced retaliation.
—Protect Our Defenders,
Military Sexual Assault Fact Sheet, 2014

At the end of February my squadron of four degrees assembled for a briefing after lunch with our human relations representative. The senior woman was tasked with a monthly discussion on issues like prejudice, sexual harassment, mental health issues, and alcohol. The Academy designed the HR program in the 1990s after a handful of complaints about harassment, but they were just briefings, words given by a cadet our own age, not our commanders. I suspected they didn't make a real impact. Jesse, the guy who liked to send porn, appeared to be napping. Other men held their heads in their hands. That sort of rude behavior wasn't otherwise allowed, but while the senior woman spoke to us about harassment, there wasn't anyone there to stop them. "It isn't okay to target a classmate because of their gender, religion, or skin color," the HR representative said. Please, I thought. Cadets made judgments like those every day. If a cadet wasn't white, Christian, straight, and a man, they were wrong. I knew that ever since upperclassmen called me a heathen for not going to church and a "fe-male" for being a woman. Plus, cadets made constant "gay jokes."

There weren't any cadets I knew of who were open about their sexuality if they didn't identify as straight, but given this was the era of "don't ask, don't tell," they didn't have a choice but to hide. I wondered if they found each other and connected in a similar way, just as rape victims formed an underground network.

Before we left the HR briefing, the senior offered to speak confidentially if we ever needed to talk about harassment, and I wondered if telling her about the porn would make me feel better.

"You coming?" Melissa asked as everyone stood. She and I both had class next on the same floor, and we normally walked there together. My relationship with Melissa was a lot like my relationship with my first roommate, Jo. We weren't friends as Charlie and I had been. Melissa resented me because she had to move out of the room she shared with the two other women so that'd I'd have a roommate. And me lecturing her about drinking didn't help our relationship, either, but in the "collaborate to graduate" culture, we did everything together. I shook my head no, and after everyone had left, I told the upperclassmen about the porn, describing the woman and the horse and many of the other e-mails. "That's disgusting!" she said. "I'll take care of it." I was relieved for once that I had spoken up for myself.

Two days later I formed up with my classmates for an afternoon beat session. I found a group of four degrees with whom I could stand. All seven of the four degrees I stood next to, including Melissa, wordlessly walked at attention to a different section of the wall. Confused, I went with them. Then they moved again, splitting into groups to join other walls of four degrees. Now each of the groups took up the entire section of wall, leaving me no space to join them. Metallica blared from down the hall, and the upperclassmen filed out of the rooms. I pushed myself against an empty wall, in violation of the most cardinal of rules: never be alone. Six upperclassmen stormed toward me. Out of the corner of my caged eyes, they were a herd of camouflage BDUs and blue berets.

Over the music, one screamed, "What the hell did you do, Miller?" He was inches from my face, his blue eyes digging into mine. "Your disloyalty could have cost you your life. Do you think your classmates are going to save a stupid bitch like you if you are shot down in Afghanistan?" Then I understood. My squadron had discovered that I told the HR representative about the porn. Later

I would learn she had spoken with our commander, Thirty-Six's version of Major Tate. The commander had reprimanded Jesse with a verbal warning, but when Jesse asked, he had also disclosed that it was I who had complained. I had never had a direct conversation with our commander. Sometimes after class he played basketball with the men, but he was in our dorm on so few occasions, when he did come in, cadets formed a long line outside his office to wait to see him. He didn't have a clue if upperclassmen were training four de-grees properly, playing midget tossing, or discussing women's "Ter-razzo asses." The upperclassmen continued to yell at close range. I pushed my back into the wall, squeezing away from the men's faces. To them I had "pimped" Jesse, meaning I put my needs above his. Despite our Honor Code, loyalty was more worthy than integrity.

"Down!" one of them yelled, and they made room for me to drop to my hands and toes while the other four degrees were led down the hallway to be beat somewhere else. Somewhere together. But I was alone with the fury of these men. The men kneeled so close to my body, I was surrounded by their heat and stale breath. "Down!" I dipped into a push-up. I supported my body inches from the floor with my elbows bent. "Up!" I finished the push-up. "Get your back straight!" "Your arms are shaking already, Miller!" "How are you going to survive in the Air Force all on your own?" All six of the men screamed over each other. The music and shouts were deafening. The heat sweltering. "Down!" I dipped again. "Up!" I chose a divot in the linoleum to draw my attention away from the men. I couldn't let them see my fear or my anger that they were punishing me instead of the porn-sending pervert. They would un-doubtedly break me physically, but if they broke me mentally they would win. I'm sure they hoped I would cry. They didn't know that would never happen. These men had no idea they couldn't hurt me anymore than I had already been wounded. Fuck them. They didn't know a thing about suffering. I was stronger than any one of them. "Down!" one yelled, and I dipped. "Up!" They kept screaming.

"Fucking whore!" one yelled. Through the music and shouts, I understood that one distinct word: "whore." The message was clear: I was a bitch to turn in Jesse, but a whore for claiming to be raped. Fuck you, I thought when I pushed myself higher off the floor. "Up!" They yelled again, and another mental "fuck you" sent a burst of strength to my triceps.

Melissa and I didn't talk to each other that night, and the next afternoon the upperclassmen separated me out again. And again the day after that. I had always had my classmates' support, but not anymore. I wasn't allowed to call anyone or e-mail the Tates. I couldn't visit the women of my survivor's group in their dorms. But at least now I had a belief in myself that my actions had been correct. I didn't have any shame, only strength.

The next Tuesday in the Counseling Center, Lindsey, the flip-flop-loving Californian, suggested I seek advice from her therapist. Since returning from medical leave, I had stopped meeting with Dr. Miles. He had become a full-time professor and was no longer in practice. "You can't survive another three weeks before Recognition if you don't do something," Lindsey said. She was right. I hadn't broken mentally so far, but I couldn't be a singular target for much longer. When I met with her therapist, she stressed, "What they are doing to you is criminal." She was squeezing a coffee mug, her fingertips pressed against the plastic. "This is exactly why we are making national headlines right now. How in the world could someone ever report being raped, when it isn't even okay to report harassment?" She advised me to go to OSI—Office of Special Investigations, the Air Force equivalent of the FBI. I hesitated but then thought of Megan and the women on *20/20*. Truly, why couldn't I be like them? I decided this was another notch in my self-help quest and willed myself forward.

Because I didn't have a phone, the therapist called OSI for me. The next afternoon, the OSI commander met with both of us. Telling him about the porn and the upperclassmen's punishments was easy; I wasn't ashamed. It was Jesse and the upperclassmen who should be mortified for being pigs.

The next Saturday morning we had room inspections, followed by a wing-wide parade. It was a bitterly cold March day, and by the time Squadron Thirty-Six paraded by the general stand and saluted, my fingers were numb. Afterward I planned to go back to my room to study for the weekend. The upperclassmen in our squadron would go drink in Colorado Springs bars. Instead our commander told us to report to a lecture hall. "What the fuck are we doing here?" one of the upperclassmen bitched as we all found seats. Our commander refused to answer. Eight men in suits came through the front doors.

"Stop talking!" one of the men corrected us. Another agent introduced the men and explained that they were OSI agents, there to investigate our squadron, and that they would interview us individually. Then he called four names, and they led the cadets out of the lecture hall.

"What the fuck!" an upperclassman moaned as soon as the OSI agents had left.

One by one, cadets followed the men out of the lecture hall. While we waited, most of the cadets slept with their heads down on the table. A few talked, though none to me. While I waited for more than an hour and a half, fatigue weighed on me. I was exhausted by my private beat sessions, by repeatedly blocking out the upperclassmen's insults, by studying with a constant headache, by waking up before sunrise, and by putting forward my toughest self. I was depleted, and I felt the weariness in my eyes and muscles.

Two agents led me to an office attached to the lecture hall. "We interviewed you near last because we didn't want to draw suspicion that you reported the squadron," one of them explained. "It will be a while before we decide what charges, if any, will be filed. But in the meantime, they have all been warned that if they continue to harass you, they will be singularly punished." The other one promised that they wouldn't mess with me anymore.

The OSI agents were right, in a way. The upperclassmen stopped screaming at me for pimping Jesse. Instead they ignored me. Melissa didn't speak to me, and though my classmates now allowed me to form up before a beat session with them, no one acknowledged my presence. I did push-ups, jumping jacks, and flutter kicks while the upperclassmen pretended I didn't exist. For several days the only people I spoke to were a few kids in my academic classes, those who hadn't heard rumors about why I had been un-Recognized, about my rape allegation, or about how I pimped my classmate.

That weekend another woman in our survivor's group discharged. She was a sophomore, the same year I would have been, and thus could leave on her own free will. Cadets didn't become committed to the DOD until the first day of their third year. Lori chose to leave while she still could; her symptoms of post-traumatic stress disorder (PTSD) made it too difficult for her to remain a cadet. Her mom drove from Virginia to help her move back home.

Despite everything, I didn't think of leaving as Lori was. My devotion to the Academy reflected more than my longing to be a pilot, more than my determination and stubbornness. I couldn't have named it then, but now I understand that the longer I was a cadet, the less there was any other part of me. I couldn't have left the Academy because I didn't have the strength to withstand the disruption of my identity. Air Force Academy cadet was all I saw myself as.

Before Lori left I snuck out to go to the movies with her and Lindsey, defying all rules and risking expulsion. The two upperclasswomen dressed me in a pair of their jeans, a sweater, and a scarf, and Lori's mom drove us to the theater thirty minutes away, rather than to the one upperclassmen usually went to across the highway. The knit scarf hid half of my face, and Lori and Lindsey linked arms with me. The three of us ran giggling from the car straight into the theater. The buttery popcorn and two very good friends at my sides reminded me that there was a normal world outside Academy gates where people weren't punished for being disgusted by porn. My tenure as a four degree wouldn't last forever.

And it didn't last forever. Finally my second Recognition came in mid-March. For three days upperclassmen beat us. With only a few hours of sleep each night and constant exercise, my forehead throbbed and my whole scalp pulsed. I puked and puked and puked. I vomited water and yellow bile over the snow where we did push-ups.

On the last night of Recognition, upperclassmen broke their promise. They singled me out along with porn-sender Jesse, taking us to a far, dark corner of the Terrazzo where they beat just the two of us. With the tall, lanky redhead at my side, we did push-up after push-up. To my relief he was every bit as exhausted as I was, and we both struggled to keep our uniforms from grazing the stone beneath us. Jesse hated me, I knew it, but we did push-ups next to each other, bumping arms nevertheless. The upperclassmen's message was clear: it didn't matter what had happened between us, we were on the same team. It contradicted their threats earlier that my classmates would someday let me die in Afghanistan if the opportunity arose. Being beat alongside Jesse reminded me that I would spend my entire career crossing paths with my former fellow cadets, and whether they had once hazed or harassed me, I would have to disregard my feelings about them. That I had to accept Jesse pissed me off, but at least no one was threatening to let me die in combat. Apparently these upperclassmen had decided that this animosity had to end.

At the end of Recognition, I skipped the celebratory dinner where my classmates would devour colossal shrimp and mountainous banana splits. I didn't care about being "Recognized" by these upperclassmen. Screw them if they thought I would rejoice being granted the freedom to uncage my eyes and walk like a normal person. Those were rights I earned a year earlier, as evident by the Prop and Wings plastering my bulletin board, given to me by my former upperclassmen with whom I shared mutual respect. And unlike my classmates, the end of Recognition didn't end my suffering. The three days of beatings had erupted my headache's full fury, from which it would take days of rest to recover. I slept on the bleach-scrubbed tile floor of the bathroom that night, still vomiting. "Are you okay?" Melissa asked when she found me there. I wanted to ask her why she was suddenly talking to me again, but thought better of it. I nodded my response and turned away from her.

In April the Department of Defense officially responded to the sexual assault crisis with an "Agenda for Change." Officers over each squadron would be required to complete a master's degree in counseling. Women's dorm rooms would be rearranged to be clustered together around our bathrooms. The Cadet Punishment System would be integrated with the Uniform Code of Military Justice, the set of laws that govern all military personnel; that way, what would be seen as a crime under civilian laws or UCMJ, such as giving alcohol to minors or an assault, would no longer be lumped in with minor misdoings such as tardiness. A crime would be called a crime, not just an "infraction" of cadet rules.

I didn't think any of these changes would help. According to an anonymous Department of Defense survey, one in five male cadets didn't believe women belonged at the institution. Why would clustering women's rooms around bathrooms change that?

A few of the changes even hurt us survivors: cadets were now required to keep their doors open whenever any nonresident visited, regardless of gender. Lindsey and I now had to whisper in her room so that those in the hallway couldn't hear us. We would no longer have the Counseling Center as a safe space, either; Juana was ordered to stop letting us in after hours. Instead the Agenda for Change specified a new therapy group that would include formal counseling and constant supervision. Clearly the Academy didn't trust us to speak to one another, almost like they blamed our survivor's group more than they blamed perpetrators. "I feel less safe now than before all this started," Lindsey confessed. I agreed.

While most of the cadets were home on spring break, I watched while a work crew removed the "Bring Me Men" lettering hanging over the Terrazzo ramp. They used scaffolding and giant crowbars to unceremoniously pry off the letters, the opening line of Sam Walter Foss's poem, which had been on the wall since the early 1960s. The Terrazzo stone had faded around the letters so that the message remained anyway. Academy patriots and many cadets became irate. The class of 1979, the "Last Class with Balls," took out a full-page advertisement in the Colorado Springs newspaper, the *Gazette*, blasting the Academy for pandering to women. Perhaps the most visible changes were the replacement of key leadership. The three top officers were fired and demoted, sent to the back corners of the Pentagon.

Colonel Judy Clark, the new vice commandant, was an "'80s Lady," a graduate of the first class of women. One of her jobs was to coordinate care for victims of sexual assault. Juana was thrilled at her friend's arrival, and her trust in Colonel Clark gave me hope. She started by meeting with those who had been in the now-banned survivor's group. When Colonel Clark shook my hand, she looked me firmly in the eyes. She had fair youthful skin despite her short graying hair. "It's nice to meet you, Lynn," she said, and she wrapped her second hand around the outside of mine, holding my hand in both of hers. We scooted the Counseling Center waiting room chairs to form a semicircle across from her. To follow customs and courtesies, we waited to take our seats until after she did. Colonel Clark sat on the front half of her chair, her back perfectly straight, legs crossed at her ankles, and hands flat on her lap. Clearly we had endured the same etiquette classes. I thought that Colonel Clark might begin by asking what had happened to us, but instead she spoke about her plan of action. "I'm confident we can fix this problem. But it's going to take all of us, and there's going to be a learning curve," she said. She continued on for several minutes, talking about "teamwork" and "dedication to the process." As she spoke she made eye contact with each one of us, holding our gaze for a few seconds before turning to the next, working her way around the circle one woman at a time. Gold eagles decorated Colonel Clark's shoulder boards. After twenty-seven years in the Air Force, she was only one promotion short of earning general's stars. I wondered how many times she had given similar speeches to rally her troops before a difficult engagement.

"The culture here needs to change," she said. "Alcohol is a real part of this." She repeated the phrase two or three times. I looked around the circle to Jen, Lindsey, Trish, and Reagan, plus two other women I didn't know as well. None of us had been drinking the nights we were raped. But even if we had been, that wouldn't have been the problem. The problem was largely the men who believed we shouldn't be cadets. When I considered the aftermaths of our rapes, our struggles had to do with the hatred directed at women and victims. Alcohol didn't have anything to do with my classmates calling me a whore or my neurologist refusing to treat me. But Colonel Clark didn't pause her monologue to ask my opinion, and as she was my superior, I wasn't allowed to offer it unprompted.

Despite the Agenda for Change, neither media nor Congress lost their focus. The Fowler Commission came from DC to investigate. I was able to tell them what I couldn't tell Colonel Clark. I felt heard when I described my rapist being left in a position of trust despite multiple accusations against him. They believed me when I told them about not being treated for meningitis in the wake of my rape. But when they asked me what should change, I had no idea what to advise them. What would make the one in five men who thought women were inferior shut up? What would help the prosecution of rapists? Marcus Bowman hadn't been prosecuted in my case because I hadn't given OSI a chance to investigate. I hadn't told anyone because I condemned myself for my perceived weakness. How could Congress prevent victims from blaming themselves? And how could they prevent women who *did* come forward from being retaliated against? They couldn't. They couldn't change the culture.

Meanwhile, the women who had gone on *20/20* continued their media blitz. New interviews emerged weekly. Some of the guys I shared academic classes with, the ones who didn't call them "weak," "liars," or "whores," complained that since February, people from home wanted to know what was happening and if they had ever raped anyone. All of the men at USAFA had become subject to public suspicion. Mothers of the men became furious that their sons' honor was being questioned. A few of them started a website to trash the women who had told their stories publicly. As women's advocacy groups argued on national television over issues like confidential reporting, the former cadets interviewed with *Vanity Fair* and *Rolling Stone.*

I still admired the women's courage, but was devastated by the effect their advocacy had on my life. The only thing I knew of their experiences, the half of our survivors' group who had left en masse, was that they had Hillary Clinton's personal attention and sympathy. For the rest of us stuck back at the Academy, no one cared or perhaps even knew that our lives were made exponentially harder because of the media. That the attention gave a license to all the men who hated us to call us names. That even the good guys, the ones who didn't mind women being cadets, started to despise and resent rape victims, too.

I finished the spring semester with a 3.6 GPA. Once upon a time, I would have felt defeated with an A- average, but now I was proud of it. My only problem was that my military point average was far lower. Our MPAs were calculated in large part based on an assessment given by our classmates and upperclassmen. My squadron mates had ranked me next to last, probably because most of them still despised me. Since OSI completed their investigation, the porn-sender Jesse was given six months of probation, and for two weeks the rest of the squadron wasn't allowed to leave. I should have expected that my MPA would reflect their blame. At the end of our four years, we would be ranked based on GPA, MPA, and PEA, or physical education average. My only grace was that I would be rotating squadrons to start the new academic year, and I could only hope my new squadron mates would respect me more than those in Thirty-Six; otherwise, they could score me low enough that I wouldn't earn a pilot's slot.

The day I moved out of my squadron, I packed nonessential uniforms in a trunk to store for the summer. I would be completing field-training exercises, learning how to survive in the woods and stand guard from pretend terrorists, so I didn't need my blues uniforms, parade hats, or textbooks.

Charlie and I went to Disney World that summer with another friend on a free military pass. We rode Space Mountain over and over until memories of being singled out in beat sessions became distant. Back at the Academy, on a pretend deployment somewhere to the middle of a pine forest, I practiced pulling life-size weighted dummies from a smoky building. I did push-ups in a tent with tear gas, and back on the Terrazzo, I took a summer physics class to get ahead. Finally in August I moved to Squadron Fourteen, my fresh home. The new four degrees greeted me with my name as they passed me in the hall, and if their uniforms sucked, I told them and dropped them for push-ups. After twenty-six months I had finally become an upperclassman.

The class of 2007 four degree women all had long hair they tied in buns. Even while I knew the Academy made the right choice in reversing that regulation, it irritated me that the new women didn't have to cut it as the rest of us had. I was bitter like many cadets.

My new commander met with the entire squadron that first afternoon. We all came to attention when Major Ryan walked in the squadron assembly room followed by the rest of his family. His pregnant wife carried a car seat, and three other little children clung to her legs. Major Ryan spoke with a southern accent and wore brown plastic glasses. Unlike my first two commanders, Major Ryan was not an Academy graduate. That afternoon in the squadron assembly room, Major Ryan talked about respect and goals for the squadron.

My entire sophomore class attended a briefing with General Fox, the new one-star general, in the main auditorium. His speech was also different: "Warrior Spirit means a soldier has courage, strength, and bravery. It means doing the right thing, folks. If one of your classmates is in the wrong, you need to say something. It is *not* okay to send pornography to your classmates. I can't believe I even need to say that to make it clear." I slunk into my chair, hoping the story of how I pimped my classmate over horse porn wouldn't travel back to my new squadron.

To my astonishment, the lecture from my new commanders had an effect. One other four degree from Thirty-Six had been transferred into Fourteen with me, and a few days into the academic year, he stopped me in the hallway. "Um, yeah, I was just wondering, if um," he stammered, "maybe we could start over." I didn't know what he meant, so I didn't say anything. "We were jerks unnecessarily. Could we just start fresh?" Jerks unnecessarily? Try pigs. His was the shittiest apology I had ever heard. But I could tell by his tone that he meant it.

CHAPTER 19

It is a tremendous relief when you finally
stop and face your own demons.

—Ellen Bass and Laura Davis, _The Courage to Heal:_
A Guide for Women Survivors of Child Sexual Abuse

One afternoon in October of my sophomore year, I went to the library to study, choosing a desk one floor below the cubicle where I was raped. I could have found an empty classroom in the academic building, but I realize now that I probably didn't connect the library with an anxiety-provoking trigger. Sure, I had nightmares, panic attacks, and dysfunctional sex, but those were all struggles I contained into the moments in which they occurred. I never thought about how often they came or fully understood why I had them.

My headache—that was the struggle that never ceased. I had survived my spring semester by taking narcotics, but had since run out. Every day with the relenting pain felt harder than the last. The effort to withstand it felt cumulative; I was too exhausted from one day with it to deal with it the next. For a while I told myself it would end. But by that fall of my sophomore year, I began to realize my denial. Whatever caused my headache was as tangible as the fingers on my hand. It had become a part of my body. The words of my textbook blurred. My scratchy eyes hurt to stay open. A band squeezed my head from my forehead, behind my ears, to my neck. I read each paragraph again and again, unable to understand the meaning. When I put my hand to the side of my head, my scalp was sore to the touch. The elastic holding my hair in a bun felt so tight, I wanted to rip the hair out of my head. I had longed for grown-out hair, a symbol of status and power among Academy women, but now it only caused me additional pain.

Since returning to the Academy, I had changed my major from math, my love, to behavioral sciences, the military's version of psychology. I couldn't understand math as I had before getting sick. Behavioral sciences was easier but demanded more reading. Plus, graduation required me to take multiple physics, chemistry, biology, and engineering classes. Each semester I progressed, the curriculum would only grow more challenging. This semester I had fifteen credit hours, relieved only slightly by passing a physics class over the summer, plus the other obligations required of me as a sophomore cadet: room inspections, parades, mandatory football games, training new four degrees, and working out often enough to be able to pass fitness tests. All while dealing with my fucking headache. I didn't have a choice other than to force my dry eyes to read each word. What I told myself was that my success at the Academy was the only thing left that I cared about.

It wasn't until then that I realized being completely owned by the Air Force wasn't just a four degree problem. My dearth of free will became tangible during the noon meal formation. It was cold for October and, having not eaten without vomiting since the day before, my body struggled to maintain heat, but the uniform of the day required us to dress identically, as always. That day's uniform combination: blue athletic zip-up jackets over our lightweight short-sleeve shirts with black gloves and our round flat-top parade hats. My toes and face chilled as I waited to begin marching, my core shivered. I wanted wool socks and a parka, plus a hat that covered my ears. Better yet, I wanted to be in bed with a fleece blanket. The drums began beating and our cadet commander marched us toward Mitchell Hall. I had been assigned to Squadron Fourteen by chance, but my height dictated where I stood among the block of cadets. The drums commanded my cadence, and the stride of the cadet at the end of the row determined my own. I swung my arms six inches forward and three inches behind me. I kept my toes exactly in line with the cadet at my side and my shoulders directly behind the cadet in front of me, and heaven forbid I should look at anything other than his head, even though I was an upperclassman. The Academy could dictate even when, where, and how my foot made contact with the Terrazzo—down to the exact little stone it should strike and at what instant. I hated like I never hated before that I had no choice in what room I lived and with whom and what classes I took. I couldn't even let myself fall apart for a day, lest my life would fall apart entirely.

That night my headache kept me from sleeping. My roommate, a woman from Washington who was the messiest cadet ever, was snoring. The pain seeped from my head into my neck, my shoulders, my back, my arms, my legs. I tried laying on my sides, my back, my stomach, but no matter how I positioned myself, I felt unbearably uncomfortable. I wanted to go somewhere else. Anywhere. So I went to the only place I was allowed: the bathroom. At least now I could walk there leisurely—not at attention with eyes caged—and in my sweatpants.

The fluorescent lights were punishing and the tile walls held faint urine smells, but I fell to the floor and curled into the fetal position. There in the bathroom with the walls giving me privacy, I audibly whimpered with the pain. The noises coming from my throat and echoing off the shower stalls sounded animal-like. They scared me. Before I realized what was happening, my cheeks became wet. The obligations required of me the next day—no, that same day, the morning only a few hours away—weighed on me. If my headache never ended, the responsibilities required of me that day would be equally overwhelming the next and then the next, with possibly only a few days over Christmas during which I could let myself sleep. And then what? I would graduate from the Academy, but if the Air Force discovered my continuing pain, they wouldn't give me an airplane. I would have to pretend every day for the rest of my Air Force life that I wasn't in pain. If I didn't keep it from them, I would be failing my fourteen-year-old self, who once watched the space shuttle launch and wished to make something of herself. Every push-up would be for nothing. Every piece of myself I had lost would have been in vain. But my headache. I couldn't stand another minute of my headache.

That night on the bathroom floor, I made a decision that wasn't a decision at all: I called for help. Colonel Clark, the '80s Lady who had become our vice commandant, had told survivors to call her if we needed, no matter the time. All right, Colonel Clark, I thought, I need help, and I dare you to figure out what you can do. My hip dug into the tile floor as I reached for my cell phone. I had brought it with me to the bathroom to keep track of the time. Around 1:00 a.m., I dialed Colonel Clark. "Hello?" said a sleepy voice.

"Colonel Clark?" I said, sobbing now. I choked out the words, "I can't handle my headache."

That phrase set forth a chain of events I would never be able to undo. She called Major Ryan, my new commander, who took me to the emergency room. My sixth spinal tap didn't show any signs of infection, so the doctors didn't know what to do for me other than give me an IV full of drugs. Major Ryan sat at the foot of my bed until 6:00 a.m. while I slept. For five days I stayed in the hospital in a narcotic-induced stupor. I didn't remember Major Ryan, Juana, Colonel Clark, Charlie, Erick, and a few of my professors visiting me, but they did. I was so used to being alone, I couldn't process the support of those who cared for me deeply.

When the new neurologist couldn't explain my pain, Colonel Clark sent me for a full evaluation at the Air Force's largest hospital in San Antonio. Major Ryan left behind his troop of 5 small children and squadron of 120 cadets to accompany me for the week.

The morning I was admitted into the San Antonio hospital, I puked all over the tile of an Air Force hotel bathroom. It wasn't pain that made me vomit, but fear. I was showering, with an orange bodywash scent filling the air, when a wave of panic swept over me. One of my professors had warned me that pilots who went to this Texas hospital never returned to their careers. Just as my stomach clenched, I pulled back the shower curtain to reach for the toilet, instead splashing water and bile over the plastic curtain, the floor, and the porcelain tank. The scent of the orange bodywash clung to my skin, and each time I smelled it again—as Major Ryan carried my duffle to my newest hospital room, as a nurse took four tries to start an IV, as a team of neurologists hovered around my bed—the same panic returned.

Over the next several days, a technician glued electrodes all over my scalp, Major Ryan held my socked foot during my seventh spinal tap, I ate a radioactive egg so the doctors could watch it pass through my stomach, and an MRI took yet another picture of my brain. A gynecologist, a former Academy grad, cried—he actually cried—as he read my chart, promising to test me for anything else that might be keeping me sick. A psychiatrist asked me if I had any nightmares. I lied. If I provided this psychiatrist with a shred of evidence that suggested I had PTSD, that alone could warrant my expulsion. Plus, then they wouldn't take my pain seriously. My headache would be called psychosomatic.

At the end of the week, Major Ryan walked with me to meet the head of neurology in his spacious office. The blinds were partially opened, and my eyes wandered to the low clouds outside. "Your brain shows some evidence of involvement," the neurologist said.

"What does that mean?" Major Ryan asked, concerned.

"The infection spread to her temporal lobe," the doctor replied. He handed me a piece of paper where he had documented his medical opinion. In the center of the page it said "untreated encephalitis." I knew what that word, "encephalitis," meant. Meningitis implied the infection was in the tissue and fluid around my brain, but encephalitis was one step worse: the infection had invaded the brain tissue. Later I would research encephalitis caused by herpes to discover that when it remains untreated, patients have a 70 percent mortality rate. "You're doing remarkably well, considering," the neurologist added. Considering I should be dead.

A few weeks earlier a Cadet Clinic technician had mistakenly handed me my medical chart to transport to my own appointment with a nearby Army specialist. Since government property records couldn't be shared with patients, usually they shipped them. So as soon as I had them, I went to Kinko's. As I waited for the machine to copy all two-hundred-something pages, I found the lab result from my initial spinal tap. On the day I first became ill, my spinal fluid had tested positive for herpes. That meant my neurologist knew all along what had made me sick. For nearly two years I had felt guilty for not telling Dr. Creech about my rape earlier, for lying that night in the ICU when he asked me if I was sexually active. I believed my silence was the reason it took the neurologist four months to treat me and had resulted in the chronic pain, but the neurologist had the clue he needed to help me all along. And he had chosen not to. I had an infection in the tissue of my brain for four months—needlessly. I wondered if the neurologist would have also blown off one of my male classmates.

My eyes went back to the little words in the center of the page: "untreated encephalitis." The neurologist continued: "One of the reasons you may have continual pain is because you were sick for such an extended time. Pain is the body's way of telling you something is wrong. But in your case, those nerves fired for so long they didn't realize they could turn back off after the infection dissipated." The doctor also explained that I had sustained damage to my vagus nerve, the nerve that controlled digestion. As a result, food didn't move through my system as it should, which was why I often vomited. Major Ryan asked questions to which I didn't listen. The only questions I could think of were for a different neurologist, the neurologist who didn't treat me.

I left San Antonio wearing four Fentanyl patches on my chest. Steroids made me anxious and jittery. With both drugs in my system, I felt both exhausted and unsettled, heavy with fatigue but on edge. I startled in my sleep every few seconds. I was too drugged to pack, so Major Ryan emptied my hospital room of my pajamas and toiletries. He linked his arm with mine and guided me across the airport while I closed my eyes to shield them from the bright lights.

Back at the Academy I had to pass a physical fitness test. Fentanyl patches still covered my chest, so I was groggy and sedated. The field house that morning was loud with voices. I found a bare patch of grass to drop my running jacket and pants, but instead of warming up, I sat and wrapped my arms around my legs, shielding my eyes and my ears.

I did a few pull-ups and enough push-ups, but by the run I was exhausted. The other three cadets with whom I circled the track sprinted away from me and then edged further and further from me. My brain couldn't make my legs go faster. My will couldn't make my legs go faster. I crossed the finish line and looked at my watch. I had failed the physical fitness test. For any other cadet, failing meant six months of probation before a last-chance test. But for me, it could confirm to my doctors that I was too incapacitated by pain. My case might be sent to a medical review board to evaluate whether they should discharge me. I'd have to wait to find out.

By the end of the semester, nearly a year had passed since the airing of the *20/20* episode that started the sexual assault crisis, and my friends landed their biggest interview yet: Oprah. Ongoing congressional and media attention became the new normal.

Somehow I passed all of my classes despite missing at least 30 percent of the lectures. I even kept a high A in electrical engineering, completing the course in the top 1 percent of my class. But during the second to last day of finals, Colonel Clark e-mailed me, asking me to meet her, and I knew that my academic competence wouldn't save me. When I received her e-mail I felt my heart pounding in my stomach.

When she opened her office door, she said, "Come on in, Lynn." The formality in her voice scared me. In the previous months I had eaten dinner at her house and had even spent the night. Her cats had cuddled with me one afternoon when Major Ryan gave me permission to skip a football game. Despite my fears of trusting her, surmising that she had been assigned to make the sexual assault problem disappear, she had become a refuge. She had given me hugs, praise for my strength, and plain pieces of bread when my stomach hurt. Now her voice had an edge like she was hiding something.

When I saw a group assembled around the table, I stepped backward. I assumed this meeting would be between the two of us, but there was a horde of Air Force officers waiting for me. Major Ryan sat next to the empty chair. Across from him the Cadet Clinic chief. Next to him the therapist in the Counseling Center who had helped me report the pornography to OSI the previous semester. It felt like a mob. My jaw clenched, and my shoulders were so tight they were in my ears.

"Lynn, the reason we're here," Colonel Clark started. I looked up at her, making eye contact for the first time. "Is because we've decided it's time that we did a medical review board." In my head I screamed. *Just say it! Just say you are kicking me out! For once be direct, don't be a fucking politician.*

Despite knowing what was coming, I felt dizzy and sick to my stomach. My ears rang loudly. Colonel Clark kept talking, but I couldn't hear her attempts to comfort me with words. Major Ryan said something, too. The pause in the dialogue brought me back. "Do you have any questions for us?" It was Colonel Clark speaking.

"What options do I have for medical care when I have to leave?"

"Well," Colonel Clark stammered, "we'll have to research that."

"Don't I get VA care?"

"No," said the chief of the Cadet Clinic, the only time he spoke during the whole meeting. I barely knew him and resented him being there at all. "Cadets aren't eligible for veterans' benefits." Nobody objected to his declaration.

Everyone but the chief took turns talking at me again. "You're going to be so much better off," the therapist pleaded. She looked back at me like she wanted me to agree.

I turned to Colonel Clark. "Are we finished?" As the highest ranking officer in the room, it should have been her place to end the discussion. But customs and courtesies no longer concerned me.

"Things are going to be just fine, Lynn." They were all looking at me again, still wanting, no, needing me to agree.

They didn't get it. I had no health insurance. No money. Nowhere to go. Everyone who cared for me, other than my sisters, was here at the Academy. My mother was with my rapist. And I had nothing left in the world that I cared about. The only thing I had was a two-year-old headache.

"Are we finished?" I said again. This time, I stood.

"Sure," she answered in a low voice.

I fled the room and didn't look back. Away from them, I stopped and grabbed the stair railing. My heaves for breath echoed throughout the marble staircase. My vision blurred with tears. I ran down all six flights of stairs to the very bottom and took a secluded back route to the dorms. My sobs slowed when I was back in my room; the thought of the pills in my locked desk drawer comforted me. My roommate was already gone for Christmas, so I was alone. I threw my uniform into a mass on the floor and put on thick cotton sweats. I chose one of the bottles of narcotics at random and swallowed an overflowing handful. I never intentionally thought, I'm going to kill myself, but when I swallowed them with a gulp of warm water leftover in my Nalgene, I caught myself thinking: I hope it will be enough.

While I waited for the pills to take effect, I rocked back and forth. My grief snowballed into a well of self-loathing. I hated myself for being so pitiful that I couldn't imagine a world without the Academy. I hated myself for giving in to my headache and going to the emergency room. I hated myself for letting three men destroy me. I hated myself for being so unlovable that my own mother chose my rapist over me. Lethargy swept through me. I curled into the bed and closed my eyes.

My stomach retching jolted me awake. I stumbled for the trash can across the room and clung to the plastic sides in time for my body to reject the pills. I went back to sleep, only to puke again sometime later.

I lay on the bed, eyes open, as it grew darker and darker outside. Someone knocking at the door broke the room's silence. "Lynn?" It was Major Ryan's voice. He jiggled the door handle. All I had to do to get help was unlock the door. But I couldn't. I wouldn't. If he wanted to help me, he could use his master key. I was angry even with the person who left his family to spend a week with me in the San Antonio hospital.

I didn't wake up until noon the next day. The squadron's halls were empty as I walked to the bathroom. Everyone was home for Christmas. I thought about the night before, when I refused to open the door for Major Ryan. My longing to be rescued made me feel that much more wretched. I hadn't changed at all since Roger ruined our friendship. I still wanted to be saved.

There were many people I could have called that afternoon, including Major Ryan, Colonel Clark, or my therapist. A friend of my sponsor dad who worked at the Academy. Major Tate and his family. Lindsey's sponsor family. My economics professor, who had invited me to his house. Juana. Dr. Miles, the therapist. I could have called any of the women from the old group in the counseling center, including Lindsey. Or Charlie. Or Erick, who visited my dorm room often. My sister who lived nearby, or Megan back in Missouri. Instead I sat in my room alone. I didn't think I deserved any of them.

PART V

Higher

CHAPTER 20

Forgiveness is giving up the hope that the
past could have been any different.

—Attributed to Oprah Winfrey

Colonel Clark—Judy to me now—trailed behind me through the door of my Boulder, Colorado, apartment. I was holding the gold key while she carried a hanging plant, her gift to me. In the weeks it took the Air Force to process my medical discharge, I did what I always did: I shut out my grief and rage to pull myself together. This time though, I relied on the help of those who cared for me. An Academy professor lent me money to help with the first few months of rent. He had also helped a handful of the women who went on *20/20* and *Oprah* when they had disenrolled. I chose to live in Boulder because I applied to the University of Colorado, a campus at the base of the Rocky Mountain foothills two hours north of Colorado Springs. I earned a part-time job as an intern for the district attorney's office. I went to dinner with my dad and begged him to put me on his medical insurance. "Oh, I don't know sweetie," he said. "That's pretty expensive." No kidding, I thought, that's why I'm asking. I didn't have any other chance to receive medical care otherwise. Two of my friends, including Charlie, sat at the table next to us. They offered to come and stay near me because they knew how scared I was that my dad would turn me down. Which he did. And it was the sympathy on their faces as they eavesdropped that comforted me. It took another month of cajoling, in e-mail and with phone calls, before Dad agreed to add me to his private insurance.

But in the end, he did. The impossible happened: I found a new home, health insurance, and a small amount of funds. I began a life outside the Air Force Academy.

Judy hung the plant on the curtain rod. The greenness stuck out from the drab curtains. The ground-floor apartment faced south, and the winter sun flooded through the wide living room window. The cream carpet, off-white walls, and kitchen's white tile made the rooms feel empty, but also like a canvas of opportunity. I could cover my walls with whatever I chose. I could make my bed or not. I could be as clean or as cluttered as I wanted. Even better, I had a dead bolt. I could choose who would be allowed inside my haven. My apartment two years earlier, the one I lived in while I was on leave, had only been a temporary residence, a place to stay while I waited to resume my life, but this apartment *was* my life. My new life, anyway.

I admitted to Judy that having my own place felt better than expected. She hugged me. I rested my chin on her shoulder but, as usual when someone comforted me, I couldn't feel her touch, like I was watching her hug someone else. Leaving the Academy didn't magically give me back a sense that my body was my own.

As angry as I had been at Judy for making the decision to send my case to a medical review board, it was the only choice she could have made. Regardless of whose fault it was, I wasn't physically healthy enough to be a cadet. Gaining that understanding had taken me weeks.

"Have I ever told you that when I was a cadet, I thought about leaving?" she asked. I couldn't imagine Judy, the perfect cadet, considering such a thing. Her picture even appeared on the back of *Air Force Magazine*; she was a poster child lending proof of the success of women's integration into the service academies.

"Why didn't you, then?"

"I didn't have the guts." I understood. She had been afraid of trying to establish a new life and leaving behind the prestige, just as I had been. If Judy hadn't graduated and sacrificed twenty-eight years to the military, maybe she would have married sooner and would have had the chance to have children, a loss that now saddened her. But she had become the Air Force officer of her dreams: navigator pilot, world traveler, commander. Juana had once explained to me that Judy's recent assignment to the Academy had bumped her from the pathway to becoming a general. The Department of Defense chose her to fix the sexual assault problem without concern that it meant a career dead end. That's the way it was when the government owned your life. I wondered if it was worth it for her. I wondered if the sacrifices would have been worth it to me.

I bought a shelter cat soon after moving into my new apartment. Knots covered Samantha's long fur and her eyes drooped from a respiratory infection, but the way she sought out my lap made up for the vet bills. My watch cat walked me to the door every morning before work and met me there when I returned. She sat in my lap on my thrift store futon. As I brushed her she purred and settled her face into the crux of my elbow. Samantha had been a stray, so she also knew what it meant to be lost. If my headache sent me to bed early, medicated with the stash of pain meds I kept in a shoebox, she lay right next to me through the night. My sentry.

I went into a civilian hospital twice, and to the emergency room half a dozen times that spring when the pain became so damning I thought it would obliterate me. The doctors gave me more tests, spinal taps, and drugs. Some days I only made it to work because of my bottles of Percocet, Codeine, and Vicodin. As soon as I woke up in the morning, my headache was a fiery throbbing. I had to force myself to stand. Then to walk to the bathroom. Then to dress. First khakis, then a dress shirt. Knowing I had to get into my car and face traffic and stoplights and bright sunshine and road noise made me want to crawl back into bed, but I couldn't. I had to keep my job or else I wouldn't have any money. If I took a sick day for one day of pain, what would stop me from calling in the day after? I stared at my work computer, trying to ignore the ringing phones and loud voices of my officemates.

Even on a better day, pain-wise, I was exhausted from nightmares of being trapped in a burning house with my mother or a faceless creature pinning me to my bed. I took the narcotics not just for the pain, but for this anxiety, too.

———

One morning in April my cell phone rang at 6:00 a.m. Sleepily I grabbed the phone from my makeshift nightstand and hit the little green button. "Oh, Lynn, I didn't think you'd answer it this early." It was my mother. Hearing her voice for the first time in nearly two years brought back a flood of painful memories. "I wanted to tell you that I'm here for you," she said when I didn't answer her.

Clearly news of my leaving the Academy had traveled to her. Two days earlier I had shared dinner with my cousin, who also lived in Boulder. She had probably spread the news. But I was confused why Mom was calling me. Her willingness to help me didn't make sense. "I don't even know how to reach you even if I wanted to," said my "little-girl me," the me who couldn't yet give up the dream of having a mother.

"I can give you that information, Lynn."

I tried to regroup my thoughts, to grow back into an adult, to find the words to argue against her attempt to comfort me. "I know you married him," I finally said. I didn't actually know that; I only inferred it because I knew her well enough to know that if she hadn't, she would have contacted me much sooner.

Mom didn't answer. When she spoke again, her tone had changed. "Lynn, nothing happened." She meant Thomas hadn't molested me. "Nothing happened" was exactly what I had told myself for the months during and after he abused me. We had jumped to our respective punch lines: I couldn't accept a mother who married my rapist; she couldn't accept the truth. "Then we don't have anything to talk about," I said.

"Fine, Lynn, that's your choice."

"No, Mom, it's your choice." Finally I managed a quick, spot-on retort. It was *her* choice to heal our relationship or not. All of the years I had fought with her, I had never before spoken my truth. On the day I left her, Megan spoke it for me. But not this time, this time I was strong enough to stand up for myself.

"Well then, good-bye, Lynn." My mother hung up the phone. It was the last time we would ever speak, and our conversation had lasted less than a minute.

———————

When remembering the conversation with my mother made me sadder, I told myself that what I needed were friends and distractions. I found a church, not because I thought praying to God would fix me—I had already tried that—but because after two and a half years in the military, Christian rituals comforted me. And maybe there I would meet other CU-Boulder students. And I did: a group of a dozen or so twenty-somethings. The first morning they invited me to join them in the basement afterward for coffee and donuts.

"How did you get meningitis?" one of the women asked me when I explained why I had left the Academy. I said it was a virus. I hoped my flat, abbreviated answer didn't catch their attention. "I bet that was scary for your parents." I resented the assumption and it only reminded me of my recent phone call with my mother. I didn't answer. I had hoped I could start fresh here in Boulder, but people wanted to know my past. And what could I tell them? These kids were barely out of their homes, a phone call away from their parents, their innocence and virginities presumably intact, considering their faith, but I was already a broken disappointment. I couldn't possibly explain to them what had happened to me.

I returned to the church anyway. Thankfully they accepted me, not questioning my awkward answers or unwillingness to share a shred of truth about myself. My new friends were the kinds of kids that talked about math and science continuously. They watched geeky movies, went to the zoo, bowled, and had picnics in the mountains. They were nerds, all of them, just like I had once been.

I noticed there was a guy who smiled at me more than the others. Nick always wore khaki pants and a collared shirt, a little crumpled at the back. His dimple made me smile when he did. I discovered that he loved math even more than me. He could talk about theories at length, and as long as we talked about numbers, I didn't have to answer unanswerable questions. Whenever our group went out, Nick and I gravitated toward each other. We became lost in our own conversations while everyone else talked around us. But we left our relationship at that—good friends who hung out together within a larger group.

One day in August, seven months after I left the Academy, I came home from work and found a bulky manila envelope from the Department of Veterans Affairs—my disability claim. The previous March I had applied for monthly financial compensation plus health care, despite the Cadet Clinic chief's declaration that cadets weren't eligible. I figured the worst thing that could happen was that they could deny my claim. After meeting with a series of doctors and then waiting months, the Veterans Administration (VA) notified me that the Air Force lost my medical records. They couldn't prove my claim without them. I was livid. But relieved I'd had the presence of mind to make a copy the previous fall.

I unlocked my apartment and let the door slam behind me, focusing my attention on the manila envelope. A bad-news envelope wouldn't be so thick, I hoped. On the front page, the words "totally disabled" were highlighted in the center, followed by a summary of my monthly financial compensation, which was nearly three times as much as I made at my part-time job. I would no longer have to worry about supporting myself. I would have priority medical care at VA hospitals. Plus, I would receive a check for the past seven months of back pay.

I dropped to my knees on the carpet and sobbed. Me, I-don't-flinch-even-when-upperclassmen-scream-in-my-face me, sobbed. My knees dug into the carpet, and I doubled over, holding my wet face in my hands, nearly screaming in hysterics. Samantha nuzzled her nose between my fingers to lick my salt-streaked cheeks. She had never before seen me cry.

Much later I would wonder if the full-disability award from the VA was in part due to the media attention given to rape at the Air Force Academy. I didn't know then that VA success stories weren't the norm, that most survivors weren't as lucky.

The day after I received the letter from the VA, I asked Nick to join me for dinner. It was with him I wanted to celebrate, even though Nick wouldn't know about the VA claim or why it mattered. He didn't yet know about my past. We had never before been on a date alone. We chose a brewery on Boulder's walking mall between hippie stores and street performers juggling fire. It was early on a weekday night, so the restaurant was quiet, the tables around us vacant. Nick and I chatted about which classes we would take the upcoming fall semester. He was an applied math major, a senior, and had interned the last two summers at an aerospace firm. I chose to resume a psychology major because my brain hadn't recovered enough to return to math. I still wouldn't be able to hold all the numbers and logic in my mind as I once did. I could hardly stand to think of the way I lost both my body and mind with the infection.

"There's something I want to tell you," I shared. "We're celebrating something."

"Oh yeah?" Nick asked. Normally I became irritated with people who spoke slowly, but Nick's soft voice and the way he took a minute to collect his thoughts before speaking calmed me. In fact his presence and his voice soothed me enough that I told him my whole story: that I hadn't spoken to my mother in two years, that I had been raped more than once, and that I had a sexually transmitted disease that gave me meningitis. I knew Nick might judge me, but I had already been criticized by so many people, by myself most harshly. What was adding one more person to that list in exchange for the hope that maybe, just maybe, I had a future with this man and his voice and dimple and blue eyes, which conveyed the deepest sense of genuineness.

Nick didn't turn away from my story. "I'm sorry you've been through so much," he said softly. His shock was evident on his face. I doubted anyone had ever confided in Nick even a fraction of what I just said. He was a protected twenty-one-year-old kid who had been raised in an affluent Denver neighborhood.

"You said we're celebrating something," Nick reminded me. I explained about the VA disability. "That's great," he said, but then he resumed focus on the bombs I had just dropped on him. "Are you okay now?" he asked. I said yes. I had money, a place to live, and a college that I belonged to.

Nick would later tell me about how he had become jealous of his friends, whom he saw maturing because they had to deal with tough young adult stuff like unemployment. Having always been sheltered from those types of difficulties, he prayed to God, asking for a challenge that would help him grow up. Two weeks later he met me.

On one of my last days at the district attorney's office, I had lunch with one of my coworkers. Sara was a victim advocate who had assisted with sexual assault prevention training to top Academy leadership a few months before I discharged, in the wake of the scandal. I attended the training and trusted her, and I had also shared with her pieces of my story. As we ate, I loudly and enthusiastically relayed to her the details of my disability claim, more animated than Sara had ever seen me. There was a hesitation in her reaction that I couldn't understand. Finally she leaned her elbows against the table and said, "There's going to be good days and there's going to be bad days in dealing with what happened to you." Of course I knew all about bad days. But those were behind me now. Wasn't she listening to what I was saying? "Make sure you enjoy feeling good right now," she added.

It didn't take long for Sara's prediction of future bad days to come true. For the first time since the initial sexual abuse, my day-to-day survival no longer depended on my continuing to function. I had obtained the safety trifecta: a space that was my own; a support system, including friends in Boulder, Nick, my sisters, and adults back at the Academy who still cared for me; financial stability. For the first time in my life, I had a net big enough to catch me if I fell. And that's when, in the most epic of delayed reactions, I shattered into pieces.

CHAPTER 21

There's freedom in hitting bottom. . . .
This is where restoration can begin.

—Anne Lamott, *Help, Thanks, Wow:*
The Three Essential Prayers

In November I sat on my couch while Nick made me dinner. My eyes fell closed. My head bobbed repeatedly before falling backward, startling me awake. "Lynn, you have to eat something," Nick pled. I tried to widen my eyes. In the second they stayed open, I saw the white ceramic bowl full of murky vegetable soup. A film covered the green beans and corn floating at the surface. The can of soup had sat in my pantry too long and had probably been the only remotely edible thing Nick could find for me. Nick held a spoon near my face. My eyelids dropped closed again and my head swayed backward. "Lynn, please open your eyes." I couldn't. I heard the spoon clink against the side of the bowl and Nick stand up. In my haze I wondered if he understood that the reason I couldn't stay awake was because an hour earlier, I had gone to the bathroom and quietly opened one of the orange bottles among the shoebox full and emptied a handful of chalky white pills into my mouth. Then I wondered if Nick would make me go to the ER again like he had the last time he realized I overdosed. I had woken in the ER with doctors shaking my arms. They had given me an IV drug to counteract the narcotics, then released me. Since quitting my job and starting school, I had overdosed nearly every day. Each time I felt one of the foreign emotions that constantly battered me—grief, loss, rage—I turned to the pills. I was fully practiced at dodging these emotions, but I didn't have a clue how to face them.

Nick's footsteps came closer to the couch where I sat propped up against the armrest. "I can't help you right now," he said. He stood over me but I couldn't open my eyes. "I gotta go, honey." His lips pressed against my forehead. The front door of my apartment banged shut.

I woke up the next morning still on the couch. My neck was sore, and the stagnant bowl of soup still sat on the coffee table. Remembering the slam of the front door, I became fully aware of what had happened: my boyfriend had grown tired of dealing with my issues. I didn't know if he would come back. Why would he? I wouldn't. Nick was the type of twenty-two-year-old guy who was so sweet and sincere that he believed me each time I said I hadn't taken too many pain pills. Once he figured me out, he wouldn't stay with a lying drug addict. Even though we had only been dating a few months, my chaos had already begun to take over his life. Instead of studying he often took me to doctor appointments. I knew I was about to lose Nick's grace, patience, and support, none of which I deserved anyway.

I slid off the couch and staggered to the shower to get ready for a neurology appointment. Gina, a friend from church where Nick and I had met, knocked on my door just as I finished. She was there to take me to the appointment at the Denver VA. I wasn't allowed to drive on drugs.

As we drove Gina suggested that I find a therapist. "I doubt an hour every week with some guy I don't know will help anything," I answered. And when she asked what I meant, I finally let my secrets come spilling out. I told her that the doctors I saw—in neurology, infectious disease, primary care, the ER—gave me prescription after prescription without realizing how many bottles others had given me. That I was taking way more than anyone knew. That I would have preferred to have been dead than to feel anything at all.

"I think you need to tell the doctor about the pills when we see her today," she said soberly.

Gina came with me into the neurologist's office. Since I'd seen this doctor twice before, she understood the type of continuing pain I experienced. I answered the doctor's questions in a rote way until Gina interrupted and insisted that I be honest with her. Both women waited for me to open my mouth. When I finally admitted "I've been taking too many pills," it felt like someone else speaking.

Then the doctor asked a flurry of questions: How many? What kind? From where did I get them? "From all of *you*," I answered. If I saw six doctors a month, for instance, and each doctor gave me a prescription, I had six new bottles. This easy math was lost on my doctors, these people with framed diplomas on the wall who were lauded for their intelligence.

The psychiatrist spoke to Gina next. She gave her instructions to take me back downstairs to a mental health clinic where an emergency psychologist assessed me. The psychologist urged me to spend at least one night "upstairs." My only other choice was to return to my shoebox of pills and my doting, yet fatigued, boyfriend. I nodded my acquiescence.

I sobbed as a nurse buzzed us through the locked doors of the psychiatric unit. I cried not out of the unresolved grief, but from an animalistic fear of being caged. I didn't know where I was going or when I would get to leave. I could almost watch from afar as my twenty-one-year-old body walked down the hall, covered in a smear of tears and snot. The old men in pajamas who stood in the doorways stared, their eyes wide and lips parted. I didn't look up from my blue and white running shoes as I walked by the two women with whom I'd share a room, straight to the unoccupied bed. I curled into a ball, faced the wall, and heaved with my cries.

Later that night Nick dropped off a bag he had packed for me. He would watch my cat while I was gone, too. "I'm proud of you," he said before he left me with a nurse who was still combing through my belongings, confiscating my razor and searching for anything else that I might use to hurt myself. From my cell phone, which the nurses would keep locked in a cabinet, I called my sister Megan. It was her twenty-seventh birthday, and I ruined it.

I fell asleep listening to the two other women tell me their stories. Carol, a fifty-year-old woman with a long reddish-gray ponytail, admitted to lying to different doctors to get narcotics. Linda, who had puffy splotches under her eyes and pictures of her twin seven-year-old girls plastering her side of the room, confessed the details of how she "whored" herself for eight balls. I didn't ask what an eight ball was.

Hours in the hospital turned into days without me either participating in group therapy *or* trying to get the hell out of there. Looking back I suspect I stayed because of the nurses. Nurses who shone a flashlight onto my bed every hour to make sure I was still breathing. My hospital bed was the kind with the railings that snapped into place at my side, and Nick had brought me a thick down blanket from my apartment. The down and the railing together created the tiniest of safe spaces. Even my white hospital bracelet with its miniature black letters added to my sense of ease. My name is Lynn Miller and I belong on Ward 7B where there are people to keep me safe, it said. Those simple facts were the only ones that mattered. The letters kept me from defining myself on more judgmental terms: weak, failure, victim. The relief of no longer being responsible for my own well-being kept me from asking to be released. My sense of safety was even that much greater than what I felt at home in my apartment because here, inside the locked unit, I couldn't hurt myself or make either conscious or unconscious choices about whether to live or die. I only needed to keep existing one hour at a time.

Dr. Ackley, my psychiatrist, graduated from West Point in 1959, the same year the Air Force Academy graduated its first class. He diagnosed me with severe, chronic, major depressive disorder and post-traumatic stress disorder. He offered me antidepressants and the door if I wanted it. But even then, I stayed.

"Tell me more about your mother," one of my two psychiatrists asked after I had been in the hospital for a week. Dr. Young studied under Dr. Ackley. She was fresh out of med school with far more energy and enthusiasm. She asked me about my family and I eventually confided in her, telling her story after story, starting from when I was a baby. Eventually she concluded that it was no wonder

I learned to ignore my feelings so much; no wonder school and the Academy became so important to me. Going to the Air Force Academy in a way was like running away. I thought there I wouldn't have to deal with my shitty childhood and the pain it had caused.

In the second week of my hospitalization, Dr. Young and my social worker asked me to put together my life's timeline. They said the timeline would help me face my past, but I had the impression they needed help keeping track of what happened when, and by whom. So I gathered colored pencils and sheets of paper and began listing events and traumas. I discovered by trial and error which thing happened first. For instance, I couldn't remember that when Bowman raped me it had only been one week—one week—since Civil Air Patrol kicked me out. Or that the time I played footsie with Roger in the Broadmoor was only one week after that. In a conference room with bare walls and high-backed chairs, I presented the chart to my psychiatrist, Dr. Young, and my social worker, Christina. Christina, a soft spoken blond, cried when I explained why I added the USAFA scandal to my timeline because that's when the men called me a whore and ostracized me.

Christina said there was a five-week program in Bay Pines, Florida, for veterans with PTSD from military sexual trauma. She thought it would help. "There's one problem. They don't accept patients who are dependent on narcotics."

"You mean they won't take me."

"No, I mean they won't take you while you are still taking drugs. You just need to come off of them." She outstretched a hand between us and patted the table.

I scoffed audibly. "Not a possibility." *You* deal with a constant fucking headache without drugs, I thought. I wasn't like my roommates who were going through withdrawal. I had actual, physical pain, I argued.

A few other women were admitted onto our ward as well, some also for addiction, some for PTSD or other psychiatric disorders. All of the women in the hospital during my stay had been sexually assaulted while serving our country. Many were molested as kids as well. During group therapy they shared their stories, no matter how gruesome. I respected them, despite their hard exteriors and gritty pasts. They all knew their lives needed to change, and they faced their issues head on. I admired their bravery, which I hadn't yet mustered.

One afternoon on a rare two-hour pass, I wandered the aisles of Barnes & Noble. There I found *Colorado's Fourteeners: From Hikes to Climbs*, a guide for the fifty-eight mountains in Colorado that rose above fourteen thousand feet. I traced the outline of the jagged peak on the cover, brilliantly lit up pinkish-orange from the rising sun. Whenever I saw a mountain like that one, my heart felt calm. I thought maybe someday, if my headache let me, I could climb one of these mountains. I kept the book in my hospital room. I bought a journal, too, and on a clean piece of paper I listed the reasons I wanted to become well: to climb a mountain; to have a family, maybe with Nick; to have a career in something other than the military; to help people who have been hurt like I've been. For the first time since I was fourteen, I listed things other than the Air Force Academy.

I couldn't do any of those things if I continued to take drugs. The list is what made me want to change. Becoming well needed to be a goal, something for which I needed to strive, just like I had fought to become a cadet. Being resilient didn't mean running from problems or remaining in denial about them—as I had operated for so long. Being resilient meant recognizing the trauma, finding re-sources to cope, and healing.

The next time I saw Dr. Young, I told her I was ready to come off narcotics. "We weren't sure you were going to come to that," she said, relief flooding her eyes.

Within a day, withdrawal symptoms hit me. I felt so jittery I rocked back and forth trying to calm my muscles. I spiked a fever, and the cold went straight into my bones. I normally wore thick layers to hide my skin anyway, but now I added extra blankets that I wrapped around my shoulders like shawls. I hadn't eaten much the previous eight weeks in the hospital, other than peanut butter and jelly sandwiches. Over the next ten days my abdomen shrunk, creating a hallow space below my ribs. My hips became bonier.

From the tiny store in the hospital basement, I purchased a giant poster of a hilly African landscape, drawn with white space and thick black lines. I colored in the grass in different shades of green, the tigers and giraffes in yellows and browns, and the flowers all different shades of reds, blues, and purples. I wondered if I might ever find myself in such a place, like maybe if I hiked one of the mountains in my new book. That's how I passed the time, immersing myself in a vibrant fantasy world and imagining something better for myself.

My fever dissipated after several days. I began eating peanut butter and jelly sandwiches again. Surprisingly my headache didn't worsen. If anything, it was a little better. Instead of dramatic highs and lows of intense pain followed by a drug-induced apathy, the pain leveled off so that each day was only a little worse or a little better than the day before. I felt my headache every minute, but at least it didn't become unbearable quite as often. All this time I had thought the narcotics relieved the pain, but they had propelled me onto an unstoppable pendulum.

Despite a six-month waiting list, the director of the Center for Sexual Trauma Services at the VA in Bay Pines, Florida, gave me a spot in the most immediate treatment rotation, beginning in March, two months away. The director said his program funding doubled after the scandal at the Academy, and he wanted to help those who had been there, another positive outcome of the media attention.

After two and a half months, the psychiatrists released me. I felt initially nervous to leave the haven the nurses provided, but one thing, even more than giving up drugs, had changed in the previous months: I knew it was okay to ask for help. I even knew how to form those words and let them release from my throat. In the upcoming days, weeks, months, years, there would be days during which the grief would resurface, but I would know better than to push it away. I would have to fight through it, not around it.

The morning I drove to Florida, Nick helped me pack my car. We had dated for less than a year, and already he had stood unflinchingly next to me as I faced trauma, addiction, and depression. We decided that during the five weeks I was at the Center for Sexual Trauma Services we'd give each other space. We wouldn't call or e-mail, and we'd see how we both felt when I returned.

Once the car was packed, Nick and I lingered in a long hug. Then I pulled away from him and got in the car to drive to Florida.

CHAPTER 22

What if I was never redeemed?
What if I already was?

—Cheryl Strayed, *Wild: From Lost
to Found on the Pacific Crest Trail*

On my first day at the Center for Sexual Trauma Services, I wore a hoodie zipped up to my neck, even though it was plenty warm for March in Florida. A woman with short graying hair and a blue polo shirt guided a group of us to form a circle, and I stood next to a woman named Becky among the twelve other strangers.

Two years earlier I had watched Becky on my laptop as she told her story of being raped as a cadet, first on *20/20* and then to Oprah, but Becky and I had never met. The survivors' group had formed a few months after Becky discharged, though she was good friends with many of the women in the group with me. Since then, she had spent years interviewing with the media and lobbying on Capitol Hill for true legal change in the military. The other women who had initially come forward with her had faded into the background, but Becky kept fighting. Now Becky needed to fight for herself to heal herself from PTSD. Our bond was instant.

Becky and I introduced ourselves to the other women with whom we would complete this five-week program together as a cohort, all of us nervous to speak too much or look each other in the eyes.

That evening Becky and I sat next to each other at dinner with the other women. When one of the women recognized her from appearing on *Oprah*, the others stopped eating and pummeled her with questions. In addition to being elegant and a picture-perfect version of beauty, Becky was clearly practiced at public speaking. A two-inch scar, stretching from the right corner of her lip to her jaw, was the only indication of her past trauma. The day after she had been raped, she passed out during a parade. Her face crashed into bleachers, her lip catching on a metal edge. She woke up in the Academy ICU, the same bed where I would later spend five days.

When I had watched the women on *Oprah*, I had mixed feelings about Becky and the others. I hated the chaos that erupted at the Academy because of them, I resented them for making my life harder, and I doubted true change would happen at the Academy. Yet I admired their bravery and dedication. Because of them it was a little easier to tell my own story. What I didn't know, until we started talking, was that Becky's fight in the media and on Capitol Hill wasn't always as glamorous as it seemed. Since coming forward, every time she met a new person in her life, whether it was a therapist or a potential date, they googled her and read her complete story before she had a chance to get to know them. Worse, she had been harassed and stalked repeatedly, and even received death threats, to the point where she was currently considering legally changing her name. So when the other women at the dining table regarded her as their war hero, I was glad Becky had the recognition she deserved.

Each day at Bay Pines, therapists and social workers led us in eight hours of group therapy, psycho-educational classes, and processing groups. The hardest part, for most of the women, was writing detailed accounts of our sexual assaults every Monday. The rest of the week we took turns reading them out loud to the group. "By facing the traumas, and reliving them in a safe environment," our therapist explained, "we can finally process them and leave them in the past."

Nearly all of us had been assaulted repeatedly, many as kids and also as adults in the military. Our therapist explained that perpetrators often knew how to target those who had been victimized before. I thought of Roger and how easily he took advantage of me after Thomas had already victimized me. Roger had been the only person to guess that Thomas was abusing me. Then Bowman had so easily pushed my boundaries, which had already been stretched. For instance, he insisted that I call him by his first name, even though I knew better. Bowman had been able to tell by the way I responded to him that I had already been broken. Finally I had an explanation for my repeated victimization.

It was easy for me to turn and face the blank white paper and construct emotionless sentences about being raped. I could speak about it just as easily, just as it had been in the Denver VA. When it was my turn, I read from my paper as if I was reading the *New York Times*. I didn't feel anything in my body. Unlike me, when most of the other women began writing, they sobbed. They cried again when it was time for them to read.

We sat in a circle in a small, carpeted room, and I tried to sit still in my chair as I listened to the other stories. One woman was gang raped. Another was raped by a man from her own unit while deployed in Iraq. Two of the women were raped in basic training . . . the stories went on and on. I focused my eyes on the box of Kleenex that lived on the floor in the middle of our circle when the details, the tears, and the snot dribbling from the other women's faces became too heavy to face. I didn't feel my own experience, but I felt theirs. I held their stories in my chest and in the tension in my muscles down to my toes. When I reminded myself to breathe, I inhaled the humid air heavy with secrets. I clenched together my hands and my crossed legs listening to one of the women describe how her brother, an adult in the Marines, raped her vaginally and anally from the time she was three years old. She recalled her brother hiding in her closet, dragging her against the carpet to his bedroom, and using Vaseline to penetrate her. The agony of the violation became clear on her pained face. Her head dropped, her voice becoming quieter and quieter, her words becoming simpler and simpler. She regressed into a terrorized three-year-old.

After she finished her story, she straightened her posture and dried her tears, but she still didn't look up. "It wasn't your fault," another woman said, and that's when the storyteller looked at us. I felt her relief from across the circle.

"Thank you," she answered. Even a woman who had been raped as a small, helpless child needed to hear she wasn't to blame.

I remembered Juana, the Academy victim advocate, once telling me that she didn't care what I thought I did to deserve to be sexually abused. My perpetrators were in positions of trust over me. I argued with Juana but couldn't pinpoint the source of my guilt. Was it the gun that Thomas put in my hand that made me feel so culpable? No, it was more than that. Was it because I didn't even *try* to fight Bowman off me? Was it the way I had sucked on my straw suggestively with Roger and offered a hand job to avoid being raped? No, I felt the guilt well before that. Juana said over and over that she didn't care what I did or didn't do, my flight instructor and the senior cadet were criminals. Maybe Juana had been as correct in naming my innocence as I had been in naming the innocence of this woman, who was raped as a three-year-old. Maybe that's what we all felt, that if someone else had been there during our assaults, they'd blame us as much as we blamed ourselves.

One of the women had been raped in the women's Air Force during the 1940s. She was now a petite eighty-year-old who needed a motorized scooter for mobility. Her dentures fit so poorly that she often chose to go without them. The other women called her "Grandma." Despite raising her perpetrator's baby, Grandma never told a single person about the assault. For decades she lived with her shame in silence, allowing it to fester and grow until it nearly destroyed her later marriage, her friendships, her career, and the image she saw when she looked in the mirror. In all that time, she dealt with nightmares, panic attacks, and depression. Time didn't heal her pain. Grandma only began to tell others what happened to her when she saw Becky and the others on *Oprah*.

Many of the women had held their rape as a secret for years and decades. The youngest in our cohort, other than Becky and me, was in her forties—even she had dealt with PTSD for two decades before seeking help. Grandma didn't name her perpetrator for sixty years. Becky and I didn't name ours for months. If we hadn't converted our rapists' guilt into messages about who we were as people, would we have spoken up sooner? How many more of our perpetrators would have been convicted had we felt more empowered and less shamed?

Shame—that was our most prevalent, shared reaction to our rapes. Shame was our perpetrators' weapons. The culture we lived in, particularly in the military, only reinforced the idea that we were to blame.

If I had heard stories like the ones I was hearing at Bay Pines, then I wouldn't have blamed myself. When Dr. Creech asked if I was sexually active, I would have said yes and told him everything. Perhaps the Academy would have ignored my accusation as they ignored a few of my friends, but at least then they would have had the opportunity to prosecute my rapist. There would have been a chance I could have spared Marcus Bowman's later victims.

As I stood to leave one of our groups once, Grandma put a hand on my arm. "You're lucky to be dealing with this so young," she said. Lucky? How could someone with chronic pain, who had been sexually assaulted repeatedly, who had lost everything, including her mother and career, be lucky? Eventually I saw Grandma's perspective. I was lucky because in getting meningitis I had been forced to speak the truth, to learn to advocate for myself, setting forth a chain of events infinitely more restorative than graduating from the Air Force Academy and becoming a military pilot. I wouldn't carry my burden for decades. I was here, getting help, at the age of twenty-one, at the age of possibilities.

During our last self-defense class, more than three weeks into the program, Karen, our instructor, told us, "You need to know that if someone ever attempts to rape you again, you'll be able to defend yourself." She and another staff member, Sandra, demonstrated a move in which the simulated perpetrator pinned Karen to the mat, and Karen flipped the rapist off her by twisting her hips and pushing with her forearm. I stayed in the back of the group while the other women took turns. I couldn't fathom willingly letting someone pin me to the ground and reenacting my own helplessness. Eventually I lowered myself onto the mat. Facing the tough stuff head on, not denying and running, was part of the new me I was trying to become.

My body felt heavy as I lay down on the blue mat. The upside-down heads of the other women crowded above me. Sandra positioned herself over me. She put her hands on either side of my shoulders, her knees straddling me. "Remember to breathe," she said. Sandra had been raped in the military, too.

My eyes caught a glimpse of hers. They were brown just like *his*. I felt my rapist's arm across my chest and saw his broad boxer shoulder's hovering just above me. Further down, his hand gripped his penis. My uniform pants and underwear were around my ankles. My mind began to flee just as it had in the library. I couldn't see him anymore and I couldn't feel the mat and I couldn't hear the women around me and I couldn't even feel my own skin. "Stay here." The voice came from a woman. A woman who understood me more than I could imagine. Sandra. I looked into her brown eyes again. Her eyes, not his. "Remember, he has to shift his body weight to angle himself to penetrate. That's when you make your move." I thought of how the first time Thomas touched me, I couldn't move any of my muscles except for my fingers, which clenched into fists around his shirt collars; I thought of Thomas forcing a gun in my hand, and my fear of wrapping my fingers around the ivory handle; I thought of Roger's thick forearm squeezing my chest that night in the hotel when I tried to get away; I thought of how I abandoned my body in the library instead of fighting Bowman; I thought of sitting at attention at lunch, motionless and silent, while the men branded me a whore who was too weak to be in the military. I wiggled my toes. I felt each little digit brush against my cotton socks. I felt my jeans against my legs, my fleece hoodie covering my arms, and my face's heat. I was here, in my body, being given another chance. I twisted my hips and rammed my forearms against my rapist's torso. I shoved and pushed and heaved him off of me. His back slammed against the ground with a loud whack. I was sitting now, no longer trapped. No longer pinned to the library carpet. My heart pounded, but my body felt lighter. The women who were huddled around me clapped and cheered. Sandra patted my back. I searched for Karen's kind eyes near where my feet had been. She looked straight at me, and I didn't turn away. She winked.

As I resumed my seat on the Pilates ball, my stomach clenched. I ran to the bathroom where I vomited my breakfast, egg chunks burning my throat, but I welcomed the purge, as if with it the terror of my perpetrators' violations and the shame of my own inactions spilled out of my stomach and into the toilet where a sewer would wash it away into the ocean.

On the second to last Friday before the end of the program, Karen announced that our afternoon field trip had been cancelled. Becky and I glanced at each other and knew immediately what the other was thinking; we wanted to sneak away to Key West. Becky and I had done many fun things over the weeks, including parasailing and seeing Cirque du Soleil, but Key West was at the top of our wish list. So when the therapists weren't looking, we snuck out of the hospital, giggling as we ran all the way to the car. We drove ten hours to the Keys that night, planning on returning Sunday afternoon before anyone in charge knew we were missing.

On Saturday we found an outdoor café shrouded in greenery. We strolled downtown, passing Ernest Hemingway's house and Jimmy Buffet's Margaritaville. In the afternoon we caught a boat for a three-hour snorkeling trip. Becky and I stretched out on the top deck as we sped across the water. We both wore strappy camisoles over our bikinis, exposing our bare shoulders to the spring sun. When we got back to the pier she declared that we should do something to always remember the trip, and she steered toward the tattoo parlor. I had my belly button pierced while Becky picked out a picture of a sea horse. "They're tiny," she explained, "But their skeletons make them one of the strongest fish." I held her hand while the artist drew the design on her hip.

On Easter Sunday I woke from a deep sleep, my navel throbbing. While Becky showered, I went to the mirror and pulled up my shirt. In the last month I had gained nearly ten pounds; one of the women had told me I looked a lot healthier. My abdomen had filled in. It was flat now, not hollow. My pajama pants hugged my curvy, tanned hips. My eyes drifted to the silver ring in my belly button. I hadn't felt so sexy since I was seventeen and had my first kiss. I welcomed my shower that morning, relishing the hot water and steam against my skin.

Later that day Becky and I took our time driving back to Bay Pines, stopping to dip our toes in the water. I slowed over each bridge, savoring our place among the wide blue sky and ocean.

On Monday Becky and I arrived at our first group, awake and refreshed. "Where were you kids?" someone asked as they gathered around us.

"Out," Becky said. "We wanted to keep busy."

"We didn't even see you once," one of them said.

As we stood to gather our things at the end of the session, one of the women pointed at my new pink shorts that said "Margaritaville" on the back. "That's where you were," she shouted.

"What? What do you mean?" I was so bad at lying.

But Becky saved us: "Margaritaville, that's in Key West, isn't it? Wouldn't that be like a ten-hour drive or something?" She said it without laughing, loudly enough for everyone to hear.

I wore my pink shorts again for a celebratory picnic the afternoon before our graduation. Karen grilled under the pavilion while our therapists ate chips at one of the picnic tables and some of the women splashed in the water. A few weeks earlier, a few of those same women were too afraid to go anywhere near the ocean, but now I could hear their laughter from the other side of the trees.

When I stood in line for a burger, one of the women behind me said, "Girl, those shorts really are short. Maybe you shouldn't wear them in public." I put a hand to my hip and twisted to look at my butt and exposed thighs. I had smooth, unmarred twenty-one-year-old skin and a fantastic figure. Plus, it wasn't like everything wasn't covered.

I said, "Looks cute to me."

"Whoa!" Karen yelled from the grill, turning to face me. "I think we just caught someone being comfortable in her own skin." At first I felt embarrassed at Karen's observation, but then I stopped myself. I stopped myself from a train of self-flagellation. How many times before had I experienced confidence in my body? Had I ever? I looked down again at my hips and thighs, for once comfortable in my own skin.

I live in a world where two truths coexist;
where both hell and hope lie in the palm of my hand.

—Alice Sebold, *Lucky*

On the Saturday before I turn thirty years old, I stand among a pack of ultrarunners in dim, early morning light. The tall, lean athletes are decked out in brightly colored athletic clothes, water bottles strapped to their hands and waist. They're mostly men, although plenty of women scatter the crowd, too. I'm wearing shorts and a long-sleeve top over a nylon shirt, and I'm shivering. Some of the guys next to me jump up and down to stay warm. These are some of Colorado's strongest runners, and I'm wondering what the hell I'm doing among them at the start line of a race. This is my first ultramarathon, and to finish it I'll have to travel more than fifty-two miles of rocky trail, gaining and losing nearly eight thousand feet of altitude along the way, all in less than thirteen hours. I've trained months, years, really, for this race. If I finish it, it will be a grad-uation present to myself for completing my twenties and thriving despite the way this decade of my life began.

The race director raises his megaphone from the start line. Sud-denly we're running. The course starts on a wide gravel road, and I let most of the others pass me as I ease into a slow pace. With each turnover my legs feel strong, and I want them to stay that way for as long as possible. Besides, this is a race only with myself.

Today my headache isn't very noticeable. The pain has faded to a dull throb in my forehead and temples, a dim echo of the infection

I suffered more than eleven years ago. For the first few years after leaving the Academy, I went to specialist after specialist, exhausting the resources of five different hospitals and countless practitioners in infection disease, neurology, pain management, chiropractic care, acupuncture, massage therapy, and psychiatry. Finally, six years ago, I had a series of surgeries to implant a peripheral nerve stimulator, wires that run under my scalp and neck to deliver a low-level electric charge that tingles and eases the pain. It's connected internally to a rechargeable battery under the skin on my hip. I'm fortunate that the Veterans Administration paid for the nerve stimulator. While visiting the VA hospital means reimmersing myself into a male-dominated culture, a place where men stare openly and make comments about my gender while sitting in waiting rooms, my doctors there have done their best to make me as well as they can. With the nerve stimulator I have fewer bad days. After I recovered from the series of surgeries, I began walking, then running small distances. I began hiking, too, and eventually progressed to running marathons and climbing Colorado's tallest peaks, as I had once hoped when I made the decision to stop taking narcotics. I joke to my friends that the device made me a bionic woman, that it gave me the strength to overcome the chronic headache that hasn't left me, not even for a second, since getting meningitis.

I ask my body if I can maintain this level of exertion for the next twelve-plus hours. I feel the answer in the strength of my quadriceps, the resilience in my feet, the expansion in my lungs. I've learned to listen when something hurts, to differentiate pain that demands my attention from the soreness and fatigue that can be overcome with mental perseverance. For years I was resentful at my body for becoming ill, for breaking, for ending my dreams. Running and hiking have taught me how to work *with* my body, not against it. I'm most capable when I harness my body's strength rather than demanding its compliance.

Six miles into the race, less than one-eighth of the course, I stop at an aid station. I refill my handheld water bottle and grab a fistful of potato chips and cookies—quick sources of electrolytes and sugar. After the aid station the trail heads up again, the switchback weaving through short trees. It's April and their leaves are a vibrant spring green. Runners spread out, some picking up the pace, others, like me, walking to finish our snacks. I begin running again and, for several minutes, find myself alone. I crest a small hill and the trail becomes easier, a wider swath of crushed gravel without large rocks threatening my toes. Just as I look away from my feet, an eagle soars ten feet above my head. Its broad wings are relaxed in a perfect glide that reminds me of how I feel as I fly over the trail. I stop running and turn to watch. It's only after the eagle shrinks to a speck that I realize it had a rabbit in its talons. Then I notice I identified with the eagle, not its prey.

The landscape opens to an expansive valley on the far side of the hill. Shrub-like trees speckle the hills and red cliffs hug the wide, meandering Colorado River. For several moments I stop thinking about my feet and their placement against the earth and my cadence, and I soak in the magnificence. As I run I hold both this serenity and the anguish of young adult years. My body feels the sense of admiration of this beauty, the sense of strength and exhilaration of running my first ultra, while also holding the sting I feel each time I look into the sky and see a plane's contrails, each time I drive past the spires of the Academy's chapel, each time I think about my mom.

The runner ahead of me hears the shouts before I do. We've run about thirteen miles so far, a quarter of the route, and it is only the two of us on this stretch of trail. "You must have good friends," he says, and then I notice two voices calling my name. I look up to see Nick's short dark hair and wide smile. His sister, Andrea, waves also. Since Nick and I married, she has become one of my best friends.

"You look awesome," Nick yells. As soon as I reach him, he stands and I crash into his arms, then Andrea's. I've been with Nick for nine years, the entire length of time I have been out of the military, minus the two months before I met him. What I knew about Nick then still holds true: that he respects me not despite my past but because of the resilience he sees in me, that he likes having me in his life not because he wants to save me but because he loves watching me save myself, that he will forever and always give me the space and patience I need to grow. I love him for the genuine and generous nature of his spirit. Our life together is simple and quiet, but the trauma of my past remains with us. It shows up in my mood and in the bedroom. I admire Nick for his endless patience as I continue to work through my past.

As with this race, becoming well, healing my body and mind, has taken active work and intention, not just time. It is something for which I have had to work endlessly. On some of my worst days of physical pain, I still feel quite angry to have developed meningitis. But on many days my feelings about my illness verge on an emotion closer to gratitude. Without meningitis I may never have told a single person about the rape in the Academy's library or sought help for the layer upon layer of trauma I experienced. I may never have known the sense of peace I do today.

Since graduating college I've worked in nonprofits and had the privilege of serving hundreds of other rape victims, some as young as five years old. If I hadn't developed meningitis, I never would have had the opportunity to give back to these clients.

Back on the trail, I say good-bye to Nick and Andrea and begin running again. They've given me a handful of boiled potatoes for fuel and supportive words for courage. Already this morning I've traveled a half marathon in two and a half hours; I have a little more than ten hours to go another three half marathons. The trail turns and twists to head back to the Colorado River.

Several hours and one long ascent and descent later, I circle back to the gravel road where the race began. Many of the runners will end here, completing a full marathon. I have an option to stop as well and to receive a finisher's medal for the shorter race. But once I've stepped one foot back onto the trail, I've committed to the double marathon. If I don't finish I will receive not a medal but a widely dreaded DNF—did not finish—next to my name on the results. But this race isn't about pride; it's about rediscovering my limits.

"I don't know if I can do it," I tell Nick and Andrea. We're standing a few feet from the aid station, and I'm using a fork to shove tuna and potatoes in my mouth. I swallow a bit before I finish. "But all I can do is try, right?"

Nick's sister answers my trepidation. "We'll be proud of you if you finish or not," she says. Unlike when I was a cadet, my self-worth isn't wrapped up in my external successes like this race. If I finish, I'll feel elated. If I don't, I'll come back next year to try again.

I'm a tangle of emotions as I run away from my family. I'm excited at the prospect of finishing, and terrified at the idea of being miles and miles into the desert with even fewer people on the trail. Those in front of me will finish whole hours ahead of me. Many are professional runners, sponsored by companies like the North Face.

I develop a mantra as I begin re-ascending the hill down which I just careened: *I'm strong enough; I'm strong enough; I'm strong enough.*

I walk the next two thousand feet of elevation gain. Four other runners also take the small mountain at a slow pace, staying either directly ahead or behind. We file into the aid station at mile thirty-one one at a time. The task I have in front of me hits me full force: another twenty-one miles of trail. Twenty-one miles. Even though I've run as much as sixty miles in a week, I've never run for more than forty-two in a single day. My legs feel like massive weights, my hamstrings are tight—pulling from my Achilles to my bottom, and my feet throb. But I have no legitimate reason to quit. *I'm strong enough; I'm strong enough; I'm strong enough.*

I leave the aid station third among the five of us who have packed together. I run for two minutes and stop to walk, passing then allowing others to pass.

One of the men in front of me slows, and when I catch up, he asks me where I'm from. "Boulder area," I say.

"Me, too," he answers. "Well, Denver anyway." We spend the next mile listing our favorite races and then our least favorites. Our next goals. Our favorite days in the mountains and then the worst. One of the other men joins the conversation and we chat mile after mile. I notice that when we maneuver by one another on the trail, the men nod at me or flash a quick hand in a hello in a way that communicates respect. Perhaps I love ultrarunning because I feel so much mutual reverence with other runners, including men.

Many of my mountaineering and running partners have become the brothers I wish I would've had in the military, when I needed them the most.

By mile thirty-nine the last few drops of water in my handheld bottle are as hot as the sand under my feet. It's been miles since an aid station and the afternoon sun is high and unforgiving. I feel parched, not just in my mouth but in the achiness in my joints. Each step is becoming harder. Now I'm running one minute, walking three. My chant, my reassurances that I'm strong enough, are harder to maintain. I don't know if I'm strong enough. I don't know if today's race will go as I wish.

I turn another corner and I hear their voices again. "You're getting so close!" they yell. My family is still a bend in the trail away, but their shouts carry among the cliff walls and barren rock field.

After taking food from them, I rejoin the Colorado River, and the potatoes help lift my energy. My legs ache a smidge less. When I pass mile forty-two, and I have fewer than ten to go, I'm thankful for the single digits. I run a surge, then walk, run, then walk.

I'm now feeling a tad stronger than the other runners, so I push ahead, following the footsteps of a man just ahead who is clad in all white, including a white hat that protects his neck from the sun. I remember from my run on this section of the trail this morning that in a few minutes, I will turn to the left to climb up and over one last mountain. But for now the trail stays flat and continues to meander along the river.

I don't know how many minutes it takes me to realize that I've stopped seeing the foot-tall orange flags on the left side of the trail. Just as I begin to panic that I've overshot the turn, the runner in white shuffles back toward me. "We've missed it!" he shouts. The realization is crushing. How far back is it? How many minutes have we lost? I kick myself for losing my mental focus, but then I remember the warnings of other ultrarunners that this is also part of the challenge. Missing turns happens to everyone. Ultras take as much mental energy as physical.

I follow after the guy in white for nine minutes before we see the turn we should have taken, which means this detour has probably cost me close to twenty. The other runners whom I've been running with all afternoon are already far up the hill—their red and green shirts are specks. The runner in white pulls ahead, too. He must have far more energy than I. We still have two thousand feet of elevation to climb to get up and over this last mountain, and I have no hope of running anything that doesn't give me the benefit of a downhill momentum.

Just as I am contemplating calling it quits at the next aid station, I see a guy standing next to the trail about a hundred feet above. He's waving and clapping, and he has Nick's same build—broad shoulders and muscular legs. Except it can't be him because this guy is wearing blue shorts, not cargo pants like Nick was.

"You're looking great, Lynn," the man shouts, and then I realize, it *is* Nick. He's changed into running shorts, I understand immediately, because he wants to travel these last miles with me.

"You're a liar," I joke as I reach him. I know I don't look great, but I'm still moving. For several minutes we walk side by side on the trail, holding hands.

"I have less than an hour and a half to finish," I tell Nick.

"Okay, then we'd better get going." He quickens to a jog, and I match his feet step by step. His foot plants into the ground, my foot plants into the ground. It's hard to believe the companionship I feel toward Nick right now, when only minutes earlier I felt such loneliness. But that is how my entire day has been: despair then hope, loneliness then camaraderie, feelings of weakness then strength, self-doubt then determination. In fact that is how my entire life feels: balancing between my grief and anger at my past, then my joyfulness and the peace I feel in my present life.

Nick and I are negotiating the rocky trail up the steep mountain now. Having him in front of me has given me the mental strength to keep a quicker pace despite the elevation gain. The other runners from the afternoon are far out of view, but I also now see that a few trickle behind as well. I've stopped staring at the timer on my GPS watch, and my eyes settle on the serenity of this mountain instead.

Unlike in shorter races, ultrarunners tend to finish in a trickle over many hours. When I cross the finish line, there will be a small gathering of supporters clapping and cheering just for me, celebrating my perseverance. The race director will decorate my neck with a finisher's medal. Just as with each time I've run a difficult race or stood on top of a mountain, in completing this journey I will reclaim a tiny piece of myself that I lost at the Academy. It will be a reminder that my physical pain—and the memories of the trauma that caused it—don't hold me hostage anymore. But both are still there, and I carry them with me every mile I travel.

Since I was a cadet at the Air Force Academy, I have had the privilege of hearing firsthand the stories of hundreds of other survivors of sexual violence. First in the context of my own recovery, then as an advocate and counselor, and finally as a writer. What I understand now that I didn't understand as a cadet in 2003 is that the private and public telling of what has happened to us is in many ways the path forward toward change, both in terms of individual healing and wider societal shifts. By telling our stories we educate about the dynamics of sexual violence and the culture, which often blames and silences victims. By telling our stories we can end the shame put on survivors.

Rape will stop happening in epidemic magnitudes when perpetrators are held criminally accountable. Victims cannot and should not be forced or coerced into reporting, nor should they be faulted when they do not. But victims will naturally be more inclined to report when they are less stigmatized, when they have less reason to be fearful of retraumatization or institutional retribution, and when they witness the criminal justice system working effectively for sexual offenses.

Since the women from the Air Force Academy went public in 2003, the media attention given to military sexual assault has increased dramatically, in part because of the 2012 Academy Award–nominated documentary, *The Invisible War*, and because of survivors' increasing willingness to speak publicly. Sexual assault is now recognized as a widespread problem within the military, even identified as a humanitarian crisis by the United Nations in 2015. The more attention that is given to rape, both within and outside of the military, the easier it is for survivors to share their stories. We inch closer to a culture in which survivors are no longer silenced.

Part of this cultural change requires the military to end daily harassment based on gender, gender performance, sexual orientation, and race. Harassment and sexual violence are linked; where one is tolerated, the other is, too. Cadets and service members can no longer afford to value blind loyalty to perpetrators over integrity. The voices of those who respect and value women's contributions must become louder than the minority who protest their presence. And we must make room for men to also speak of their experiences of rape.

It might be tempting to hope that at service academies where cadets rotate through every four years, it would be relatively easy to change culture in a short period of time. But one of the greatest obstacles is the insular nature of the academies, largely immune to shifts occurring in the wider world. New cadets are young, desperate to succeed, and immersed in a foreign environment where their belief systems are overhauled. Additionally, alumni continue to influence: those who graduated in my class are now midranking officers, returning to the Academy as instructors or commanders. They are sponsor families, parents of future cadets, and the leaders of our armed forces. Many of the men who raped my classmates—or lied and covered for those perpetrators—are now in positions to command units. When those of my generation perpetuate intolerance, their legacy must be disrupted.

We have to build on the momentum behind this conversation. We can do that by supporting survivors in healing, participating in the debates about proposals put forth by Congress, and continuing to better understand the complicated and nuanced factors faced by the armed forces.

FOR FURTHER UNDERSTANDING

Helen Benedict, *The Lonely Soldier: The Private War of Women Serving in Iraq* (Boston: Beacon Press, 2009).

Kirby Dick et al. *The Invisible War* (Sausalito, California: Distributed by Roco Films Educational, 2012), http://www.notinvisible.org/.

Dr. Mic Hunter, *Honor Betrayed: Sexual Abuse in America's Military* (Fort Lee, NJ: Barricade Books, 2007).

Peggy Reeves Sanday, *Fraternity Gang Rape: Sex, Brotherhood, and Privilege on Campus* (New York: New York University Press, 1990).

Diana Jean Schemo, *Skies to Conquer: A Year Inside the Air Force Academy* (Hoboken, NJ: John Wiley, 2010).

Helen Thorpe, *Soldier Girls: The Battles of Three Women at Home and at War* (New York: Scribner, 2014).

FOR SUPPORT

Protect Our Defenders, http://www.protectourdefenders.com/.

Service Women's Action Network (SWAN), http://www.servicewomen .org/.

National Center on Domestic and Sexual Violence, http://www.ncdsv.org/.

Ellen Bass and Laura Davis, *The Courage to Heal: A Guide for Women Survivors of Child Sexual Abuse, 20th Anniversary Edition* (New York: William Morrow, 2008).

Peter A. Levine, *Waking the Tiger: Healing Trauma* (Berkeley, CA: North Atlantic Books, 1997).

Glenn Schiraldi, *The Post-Traumatic Stress Disorder Sourcebook: A Guide to Healing, Recovery, and Growth*, 2nd ed. (New York: McGraw-Hill Education, 2009).

For 24/7, free, confidential support, reach out to the Rape, Abuse & Incest National Network (RAINN):

1-877-995-5247 (for military sexual trauma)
1-800-656-HOPE
http://www.rainn.org
http://www.safehelpline.org

ACKNOWLEDGMENTS

Some say memoir writing is a form of therapy. I haven't found that to be fully true, but in the writing of this book I have had the opportunity to relive my story, this time not in isolation but rather with the generous and often fierce love and sustenance of many.

The instruction and fellowship I found at Denver's Lighthouse Writers Workshop carried me through this decade-long project. I attended my first class there in 2007, and the women who squeezed around me at an oak table would support me long after those initial eight weeks. They held the space I needed to begin to share my truth. My instructor, Shari Caudron, became a long-time mentor. She once said, "Astronaut, schmastronaut . . . you're a writer!"

My classmates—Lois Hjelmstad, Anne Mahoney, Esther Starrels, and Anne Strobridge—continue to meet to share pages and inspiration ten years later. They read many, many early drafts and gave countless hours of advice and encouragement. Their belief in me, compassion, judgment-free critique, and friendship forever changed my writing and me.

I am thankful for the entire Lighthouse community, especially founders Mike Henry and Andrea Dupree, and for all of those with whom I shared workshops. Classmates and friends Cathy Bell and Laurie O'Connor read late-stage drafts; their excitement propelled me forward in the final miles of this memoir-writing marathon. Cathy's endless cheers are never far from my mind.

At the Iowa Summer Writing Festival, Lon Otto gave such generous feedback I still keep a kind quote from him taped to my computer monitor.

I am thankful for each and every friend who gave encouragement, in particular to those who read and commented on various drafts: Alissa Baumbach, Ann Beauvais, Kimberly McKay, Cameron McKay, Oritte Bendory, and Kristyn Kornfield.

Dr. Lorraine Bayard de Volo, chair of the Women and Gender Studies Department at the University of Colorado, Boulder, worked with me for a number of years on an academic essay adapted in part from this manuscript. Our effort allowed me to contextualize and theorize from my personal experience.

I am fortunate to have worked with many tireless advocates at Boulder's rape crisis center, Moving to End Sexual Assault. They motivate me to press on in the fight against sexual violence, especially Jessica Ladd-Webert, who directs the Office of Victim's Assistance at CU-Boulder, as well as Dr. Joanne Belknap, CU-Boulder professor and author.

I'm indebted to all of those who helped in my recovery journey, including the heroes I've written about here. Without them this story may have had a different ending. I also owe gratitude to the Denver VA hospital and the Bay Pines Center for Sexual Trauma Services.

In 2014 I was selected for the Medtronic Global Heroes team, a community of runners whose lives have been transformed by medical technology. My Medtronic family inspires me to overcome the challenges of having chronic pain so that I can accomplish in both my athletic and professional lives.

I knew immediately that Leigh Feldman was the perfect agent for my memoir, and accepting her offer of representation was one of my most triumphant moments. She and her assistant, Ilana Masad, are steadfast supporters.

My editor, Gayatri Patnaik, is as trustworthy as she is dedicated. She did a tremendous amount of work to prepare my manuscript for publication, and her acumen was invaluable. I'm fortunate to have had my memoir in her care.

I am immensely proud to be published by Beacon Press and am appreciative of the support of the entire Beacon team, including Helene Atwan, Tom Hallock, Alyssa Hassan, Pam MacColl, and Caitlin Meyer.

My sisters have graciously allowed me to share this story, even though it is in part theirs as well. I'm similarly thankful to the other women from the Air Force Academy.

Sometimes what a memoirist needs most is actual therapy; I couldn't have written this memoir without the refuge that is my therapist's office.

Nicholas Hall helped to restore my faith in love and trust. The foundation that is our marriage made it possible for me to endure the challenging process of writing and publishing this memoir.

Lastly I would like to acknowledge that the telling of my story of sexual violence is a privilege paid for by the survivors, advocates, and writers who have come before in this movement.